CU00806448

KIRKHAM

THROUGH THE MISTS
OF
TIME

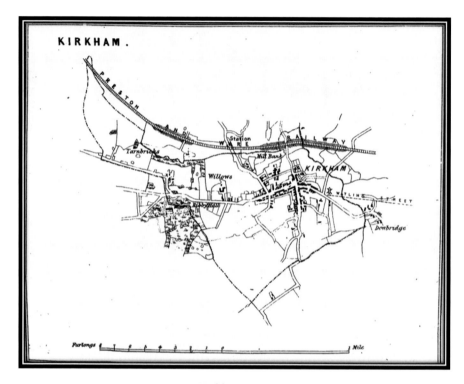

Kirkham 1851

I would like to thank my wife Samantha, for her invaluable help
during the three years it took to produce this book.

Copyright © Michael Townsend, 2018
Published by Michael Townsend

British Library Cataloguing-in-Publication data
A catalogue record for this book is available from the British Library

ISBN 978-1-9164748-0-2

Typeset by Scotforth Books
Printed and bound by Jellyfish Solutions

Contents

Who remembers these three sisters, Leila, Gertrude, and Sarah Bligh?

Illustrations

Photographs marked DDS and DDX are courtesy of Lancashire Archives and can be viewed and copies made at the Lancashire Archives Preston. The files are DDS/ACC8299/6 and DDX752ACC11189.

The Photographs marked RRC are courtesy of Red Rose Collections are can be viewed online at www.redrosecollections@lancashire.gov.uk.

Flax and Cotton

In 1600 A.D., there were two places of note on the Fylde: Poulton le Fylde, which was growing around the ports on the River Wyre, and Kirkham, growing around its Market Square. Kirkham had four streets formed in a cross; Freckleton Street, Poulton Street, Preston Street and Church Street. The Lords of the Manor, up until the dissolution of the monasteries, were the Abbots of Vale Royal. Afterwards, it was the Dean and Charter of Christ Church Oxford who conveyed it to the Cliftons of Lytham. The Vicar and the Thirty Sworn Men, along with the two bailiffs, looked after the town's daily business. In 1630, the population of Kirkham was 600, but this was about to change dramatically. Over the next 300 years the town would evolve to the challenges it encountered, but always surviving and remaining an independent place.

Between January 1631 and June 1631, 44 deaths occurred in the fifteen townships that made up the parish of Kirkham, an average of seven a month. On 14 July 1631, the wife of Thomas Watson of Kirkham was buried in St Michael's graveyard ... the plague was in town. From that day until Martinmas (11 November), 304 people died, 194 in August and September alone. The following lists from the Kirkham Parish register show how the death rate in July began to grow as the plague took hold.

w. Rich. Kirkham of Berkes [WB]	24 Dec.
Jhn. Grimbaldson, TR	28 ..
Hen. Shoerock, F	9 Jan.
Rich. Benson, R	17 ..
w. Arthur Sharples	17 ..
Jenet Tomasson, EC	17 ..
Jhn. Whytsyde, N	24 ..
w. Wm. Cooke, BR	27 ..
Jas. s. Jhn. Nixon of Ockenhead	28 ..
Robt. Smaley, WA	30 ..
Rich. Hull, S	7 Feb.
d. Jas. Threlfall, T	10 ..
w. Tho. Browne, WA	11 ..
w. Rich. Flecher, WA	16 ..
w. Jas. Tompson, S	22 ..
Mary Browne d. Tho., K	5 Mar.
Rich. Townend, P	6 ..
Robt. Browne, F	8 ..
Anne France, K	14 ..
Rich. Hulle, T	24 ..

1631

w. Robt. Hornbie, R	14 Apr.
w. Jhn. Hull, T	16 ..
Mylles Thornton, G	17 ..
Alice Hulle, T	20 ..
Jhn. Rabie, T	22 ..
Wm. Fisher, S	29 ..
Robt. Hornbie, R	6 May
Tho. Gibbone, K	12 ..
w. Jhn. Crooke, BR	12 ..
Jhn. s. Rich. Eccleston, CO	14 ..
w. Geo. Buller, S	17 ..
Tho. Hankinson, S	22 ..
Jhn. Kirkham s. Wm. Kirkham, G	23 ..
Wm. Kirkham, G	2 June
w. Rich. Goose, G	3 ..
Jas. s. Tho. Kirkham, G	4 ..
Mrs. Morley, BR	10 ..
Mary d. Tho. Eccleston, S	11 ..
w. Jhn. Swarbrecke, R	12 ..
Tho. Eccleston s. Rich., CO	13 ..
Jhn. Thornton s. Myles, CO	16 ..
Alice Goosse, G	17 ..
one child of Jas. Wildings, P	23 ..
one child of Tho. Abraham, WA	24 ..

Margt. Bower, F	25 June
w. Robt. Short, L	27 ..
The first that dyed in Kirkham of the sickness was the wife of Tho. Watson.	
Rich. Burskowe, K	2 July
w. Rich. Eccleston, CO	7 ..
Jas. Griffine, K	7 ..
Tho. Pateson s. Edw., S	9 ..
w. Tho. Watson, K	14 ..
Tho. Watson, K	17 ..
Jhn. Bryninge, S	23 ..
one child of Tho. Bannister and w., K	25 ..
w. Jhn. Bryninge	25 ..
w. Hen. Singleton	26 ..
Wm. Bryning, K	26 ..
Jhn. Singleton, K	26 ..
Hen. Wilkins s. Samuel Wilkins	27 ..
Jane Roulinson	29 ..
Tho. Roulinson and one other child of	
Jhn. Roulinson, K	30 ..
Alice Barker	3 Aug.
Isabell Fearnshead	4 ..
Jenet Fearnshead	6 ..
Ann Topping	6 ..
w. Jhn. Rowlinson	6 ..
w. Wm. Hall, TR	6 ..
Walter Bradshaw	6 ..
Geo. Singleton	7 ..
Wm. Parker	8 ..
Tho. Banister	9 ..
Izabell Santer	9 ..
Jhn. Lithom	10 ..
Rich. Thisleton	10 ..
Wm. Ryley	12 ..
Jhn. Sowerbutts	16 ..
w. Wm. Ryley	16 ..
w. Jas. Browne	16 ..
w. Jhn. Johnson & chyld, CO	16 ..
w. Jhn. Fisher	16 ..
Jhn. Johnson	18 ..
1 chyld of Tho. Davis	18 ..
2 children & w. Geo. Browne	18 ..
Margt. Hankinson	18 ..
w. Jhn. Fearnshead	18 ..
Hen. Parker	18 ..
Benj. Greenacres	18 ..
Jayne Edwardson	18 ..

---

1 chyld of Jhn. Rowlinson	18 Aug.
Tho. Pker	18 ..
Wm. Pker	18 ..
Ann Woods	18 ..
Rich. Woods	18 ..
Rd. Fearnshead	18 ..
Edmond Edwardson	18 ..
Wm. Griffin	18 ..
Ann Griffin	18 ..
Jhn. Wilson	18 ..
Wm. Smyth	18 ..
Margery Schowlcroft	18 ..
Wm. Browne	18 ..
Tho. Thornton	19 ..
Grace Hodgson	19 ..
Rich. Pateson	19 ..
Wm. Pateson	19 ..
w. Wm. Browne	19 ..
Parnell Parker	19 ..
Rich. Fearnshead	19 ..
w. Geo. Crookey	19 ..
Jhn. Griffin	19 ..
Peeter France	19 ..
w. Wm. Bonney	19 ..
Tho. Bayne	20 ..
w. Wm. Pateson	20 ..
Ro. Rowlinson	20 ..
w. Jhn. Claton	20 ..
w. Rich. Crook	20 ..
w. Jas. Davie	20 ..
Eliz. Smyth	20 ..
Tho. Griffin & w.	21 ..
w. Wm. Hall	21 ..
Jhn. Corles	21 ..
Jhn. Aspinall	21 ..
w. Rowland Aspinall	22 ..
Tho. Hall & w., TR	22 ..
2 children of Jhn. Cardwell, W	22 ..
1 of Wm. Hornbie's	22 ..
Hen. Hodges & w. & 2 children	22 ..
Mr. Henry Clifton	26 ..
Wm. Southart	26 ..
w. Wm. Swarbreck	26 ..
Tho. Hall	27 ..
Mary Parker	27 ..
w. Jhn. Lithom	27 ..
w. Geo. Edwardson	27 ..

Eliz. Smyth	28 Aug.
Hen. Barker	28 ..
Wm. Woodcock	28 ..
Tho. Southart	29 ..
Robt. Bonny	29 ..
Elin Parker	29 ..
Parnell Parker	29 ..
Rich. Parker	30 ..
Jenet Fearnshead	30 ..
Jas. Fearnshead	30 ..
Robt. Fearnshead	30 ..
Jhn. Pateson	31 ..
Eliz. Woods	31 ..
Jhn. Wilson & w & 1 chyld	31 ..
Parnell Parker	1 Sept.
Rich. Sowerbutts	1 ..
Margt. Bonny	1 ..
Ann Woodcock	1 ..
Margt. Farhurst	2 ..
w. Jhn. Sowerbutts	2 ..
Margret Burscoe	2 ..
Hen. Schowlcroft	2 ..
Lawr. Wilding	3 ..
Jas. Parker	3 ..
Saetie Parker	3 ..
Jhn. Browne	3 ..
Robt. Wildinge	3 ..
Cuth. Robinson	4 ..
Raphe Woods	4 ..
w. Law. Barnes	4 ..
Jas. Tomlinson	5 ..
w. Wm. Southart	5 ..
Mary Farhurst	6 ..
Margret Parker	6 ..
w. Wm. Walshman	6 ..
Wm. Tomlinson	6 ..
Wm. Barker	6 ..
Jas. Smyth	6 ..
Rich. Barnes	6 ..
Jhn. Smyth	6 ..
Elin Smyth	6 ..
Chris. Jacson	6 ..
Tho. Hall	6 ..
Rich. Cardwell	6 ..
Jhn. Wildinge	7 ..
Jas. Farhurst	7 ..
Anne France	8 ..

168	KIRKHAM PARISH REGISTER	1631		1631	BURIALS	169
Jhn. France		8 Sept.		Jhn. Griffin		29 Sept
Wm. Swarbreck		9 "		Ann Clarkson		29 "
Jas. France		9 "		Jhn. Bonny		29 "
Jhn. Tomlinson		9 "		Eliz. Werton		29 "
Rich. Wilding		10 "		Elin Barker		30 "
w. Jhn. Griffin		10 "		2 children of Lawr. Milner's		30 "
Eliz. Hornbie		10 "		Jhn. Wilding		3 Oct.
Law. Bradkirk		10 "		One child of Tho. Milner's		3 "
Robt. Hornbie & 1 chyld		12 "		Robt. Wholey		6 "
1 chyld of Robt. Hornbie		12 "		Wm. Porter		7 "
Rich. Whytsyd		12 "		Eliz. Bonny		7 "
Wm. Ryley		13 "		Jas. Bonny		7 "
Wm. Kerbie		13 "		Jenet Claton		8 "
w. Robt. Greaves		14 "		w. Wm. Porter		10 "
Tho. Hardman		16 "		Jhn. Swarbreck		12 "
Wm. Milner		16 "		3 children of Tho. Hall		13 "
Jhn. Bonny		16 "		w. Wm. Hall		13 "
w. Jhn. Bonny		17 "		Geo. Hardman		13 "
Jhn. Boulton		17 "		Ann Croft		13 "
Robt. Bonny		19 "		Jhn. Armsteed		13 "
Hen. Hankinson		19 "		Ann Singleton		13 "
Wm. Wholey		20 "		Marie Smyth		13 "
Tho. Benson		20 "		Wm. Hardman		16 "
w. Wm. Tomlinson		20 "		w. Jhn. Grimbouldson		16 "
Margery Tomlinson		20 "		Lawr. Milner		16 "
Tho. Singleton		21 "		Jhn. Milner		16 "
w. Jas. Lea		21 "		w. Wm. Marser		17 "
Hen. Boulton		21 "		Tho. Hardman		17 "
Jhn. Harrison		21 "		Hen. Porter		17 "
2 children of ww. Whaleys		22 "		Rich. Grimbouldson		17 "
Rich. Crook & w.		22 "		Rich. Browninge		20 "
His mother & 3 children		23 "		Tho. Milner		22 "
w. Tho. Benson & 3 children		24 "		Jhn. Milner		24 "
w. Wm. Wholey & chold		24 "		Wm. Milner		24 "
w. Tho. Milner		24 "		2 children of Rowland Kerbie's		27 "
Eliz. Smyth		24 "		Tho. Walthew		28 "
Agnes Smyth		24 "		Marie Woodcocke		29 "
Ellin Wilding		24 "		Alice Milner		3 Nov.
Jhn. Claton		24 "		Siselie Milner		3 "
Hen. Claton		25 "		Mr. Browne		14 "
Ebz. Claton		25 "		Wm. Newsam		20 "
Jhn. Harrison		26 "		Wm. Brownynge & 1 chyld		22 "
Ellin Greaves		27 "		w. Wm. Brownynge & 3 children		26 "
Geo. Greaves		27 "		Chris. Johnson & w.		26 "
Wm. Kitchin		28 "		w. Tho. Hall		26 "
w. Cuth. Robinson		29 "		w. Tho. Hankinson		27 "
Wm. Clarkson		29 "		Jhn. Cowlbron		27 "

After the plague cleared and the civil war ended, Kirkham settled into a period of growth which saw it become the centre of the Fylde's agricultural development. The Fylde consisted of 20,000 acres of moss, but with land drainage by the area's two main land owners, Lord Derby and Lord Clifton, the Fylde became the garden of Lancashire. The foods grown were beans, oats, wheat and potatoes. Windmills sprung up all over the Fylde, and small farms were built. The rural population outside of Kirkham stayed small, but every April men would arrive from Ireland to work on the farms, leaving again in September.

Fylde have been greatly facilitated by the presence of large quantities of marl, which, mixed with the lower portion of the peat, produces a soil of great fertility.

9. The population of the Fylde is very scanty, and the greater proportion of the work on farms is done by Irish labourers who arrive in large numbers early in April and return to their native country about the end of September. Their ordinary wages are 2s. a day, finding their own food, with the exception of butter-milk, which is supplied to them gratuitously at the rate of a quart per day. At harvest time they have an additional 1s. a day. Wheaten bread is their only substantial food. They sleep in barns and outhouses upon straw, with a sack for a pillow. Their object being to save money, many carry back to their country from 10l. to 12l. of the wages of the half-year. They are most efficient labourers, and a more industrious, honest, cheerful, easily managed, and well-conducted class of men is nowhere to be found.†

10. This periodical immigration of Irish labour has become a necessity in the Fylde and is an essential

Report from The Commissioners for Agriculture 1868

The labourers from Ireland generally returned to the same farmstead each year. Both farmers and labourers were equally pleased to see each other.

This influx each year caused problems for Kirkham, but without it, the cultivation of the Fylde would have been impossible.

In 1694, the population of Kirkham was 405. In 1790, this had reached 1,448. The town had 322 homes, the most densely populated area being Preston Street. This street had 363 people living in 94 homes. Even though the Fylde had become the garden of Lancashire, there was no work in the countryside. The only people who could live beyond Kirkham were the farmers and the seasonal workers. Most people left the countryside for the town. The people coming to Kirkham were working in the flax industry.

In the mid-eighteenth century, merchants started moving to Kirkham. The ones of note were Cornelius Langton, Thomas Hankinson, Hugh Hornby, William Shepherd and John Birley. These men were working with 'flax', a strong, coarse fibre. They set up spinning mills and weaving shops in Kirkham and the town became a centre for sail cloth manufacturing. There were also smaller concerns producing sacking, rope and twine. Langton, Shepherd and Birley worked together, mainly at the Flaxfield Factory, but they also sent spun flax to the hand weavers living on Preston Street and Freckleton Street. Hugh Hornby married Thomas Hankinson's daughter, who later inherited her father's business concerns.

At the turn of the nineteenth century the Birley family was working independently, with a large factory Flaxfield for weaving, bleaching and spinning flax, a heckling shop opposite the St Michael's church gate, and a small factory behind Croft House, on Preston Street.

The Hornby family had three factories, one on Moor Street, one on Freckleton Street and one at the bottom of Back Lane, 'Marsden Street'. Their warehouse was on Poulton Street. They also had cottages on Old Row, Hornby Court and Back Lane.

Kirkham was still a market town though, with trades, shops and inns in 1829 as follows.

Butchers: Robert Dewhurst, Thomas Hoole, Richard Rawcliffe, Thos Singleton, Wm Yates.

Coopers: Thomas Ireland, James Porter.

Corn Millers and Flour Dealers: Richard Barnes, Cath & Ann Billington, Thos Parkinson, Thomas Singleton.

Farriers: Stephen Hargreaves, John Rogerson.

Fire & Office Agents: Guardian, T Crossfield, Norwich Union, Robert Forsyth, Royal Exchange, Richard Hodgson.

Grocers and Tea Dealers: Wm Billington, Wm Brown, James Cook, John Preston, Wm Rossall, Wm Tomlinson, John Whalley, John Whiteside.

Hair Dressers & Perfumers: Edward Dobson, Joseph Dobson.

Inns: Black Horse, Edward Parker, Kings Arms, Wm Brewer.

Ironmongers, Richard Rossall, Wm Tomlinson.

Joiners and Cabinet Makers: James Sharples, Richard Whalley, John Whalley.

Linen and Woollen Drapers: Brash, Jenkinson & Crossfield, Thos Catterall, Thos Hall, Samuel Rossall, Ellen Udall, Hardman & Whalley.

Liquor Dealers: Carter & Cummings, Robert Forsyth, Thos Hodgson.

Millner's and Dress Makers: Jane Carter, Elizabeth Hodgkinson, Jane Leach, Elizabeth Snape, Nancy Shorrock.

Plumbers, Painters and Glaziers: Henry Dobson, Robert Hall, James Winstanley.

Shop Keepers and Dealers in Sundries: James Spencer, Wm Westhead, John Whalley.

Straw Hat Makers: Ann & Mary Moon.

Surgeons: Wm Knipe, George Parkinson.

Tailors: Wm Aspinall, Thos Kirby, George Warbrick.

Taverns and Inns: Black Bull, Jas Hulme, Bowling Green, Wm Moon, New Bull, Geo Westhead, Post House, Jas Hardman, Royal Oak, Luke Brown, Swan, Henry Lawrence, Wheat Sheaf, R Dewhurst.

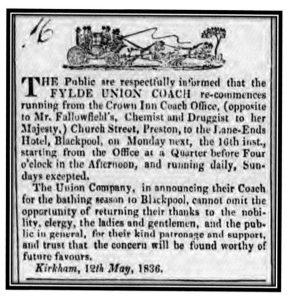

THE Public are respectfully informed that the FYLDE UNION COACH re-commences running from the Crown Inn Coach Office, (opposite to Mr. Fallowfield's, Chemist and Druggist to her Majesty,) Church Street, Preston, to the Lane-Ends Hotel, Blackpool, on Monday next, the 16th inst., starting from the Office at a Quarter before Four o'clock in the Afternoon, and running daily, Sundays excepted.

The Union Company, in announcing their Coach for the bathing season to Blackpool, cannot omit the opportunity of returning their thanks to the nobility, clergy, the ladies and gentlemen, and the public in general, for their kind patronage and support, and trust that the concern will be found worthy of future favours.

Kirkham, 12th May, 1836.

Miscellaneous:

Tallow Chandler, Richard Hardman.

Nail Maker, Wm Hartcliffe.

Mill Wright, John Hayes.

Auctioneer, Peter Lawrence.

Watch Maker, John Leech.

Livery & Stable Keeper, Wm Noblett.

Pawnbrokers, Rawcliffe and Whiteside.

Confectioners, Ellen Riley.

Tinman and Brazer, Tim Roberts.

Saddler, William Turner.

Stamp Distributer, J Wallworth.

Hatter, William Yates.

There was also the Kirkham Savings Bank (open Mondays at eleven o'clock), and Joseph Hornby was the treasurer. Post arrived from Preston at the Post

Office Inn at 7 a.m. and was dispatched at 3:30 p.m.; the Post Master was Joseph Hardman.

Before the railways arrived in Kirkham, people used the Fylde Union Coaches to travel. The union coach met the Waterwitch coaches at Preston. Here you could catch a Waterwitch to Bolton, and then travel further afield by train. There was a Waterwitch to Liverpool, and the ports. For Lancaster and Kendal, you could catch the Waterwitch Packet Boat, from Preston which travelled along the canal. Imports and manufactured goods were exported from the Wyre ports, Skippool and Wardleys.

By 1830 the Hornbys had withdrawn from the flax trade. John Birley had started to produce fine linen and began working with cotton. Thomas Patterson and George Butler were the new names for linen and cotton. William Segar & Sons were producing sacking in Birley's old factory on Preston Street.

In 1807, the first steam engine appeared at Birley's Mill, a 32-horse power engine from Boulton and Watt; as the site expanded they were to have three engines in total. The other mills to get engines were the mills on Marsden Street and Freckleton Street. The engine at the mill on Marsden Street was 12 horse power. Later, when Phoenix Mill was built, the engine used was 20 horse power. Wesham Mills' original engine was 70 hp, while Brook Mill was using a 320 hp engine when it closed. The last mill to be built was Progress Mill, with a 500 hp engine. The biggest engine was at Sunnybank, with a 600 hp engine.

The hand weavers lasted well into the second half of the nineteenth century. In 1821, there were about 2,000 hand weavers in Kirkham, but by 1851 this had reduced to 500. The work with hand looms was more intensive, but the pay was better. The original hand weavers worked in their cottages but by the end of the mid-nineteenth century weaving shops started to appear in Kirkham. The journeymen were usually employed in these shops, using Dandy Looms. One was Bran Hall, next door to the gas works and there was one on the Wrangway, a two-storey building, behind the old loom on Station Road.

> **FREEHOLD PROPERTY IN KIRKHAM.**
> TO BE SOLD BY AUCTION, by Mr. L. BROWN, at
> the house of Mrs. Lawrenson, the Bull Inn, Poulton-
> street, Kirkham, in the county of Lancaster, on Friday,
> 2nd day of May, 1856, at six o'clock in the evening,
> subject to conditions then and there to be produced,
> ALL those SIX COTTAGES, Weaving Shop,
> Shippon, and Gardens thereunto belonging, situate
> at Bran-hall, near to the Gas Works, in Kirkham afore-
> said, in the occupation of John Greenall and his under
> tenants.
>
> For further particulars apply to Mr. ROBERT LUND, of
> Blackpool; or to Mr. HENRY WARD, of Treals; or to the
> AUCTIONEER, Black Horse Inn, in Kirkham.
>
> ———
>
> A SINGLE MAN wanted as Ostler.—Apply to the
> AUCTIONEER, Black Horse Inn, Kirkham.
> Kirkham, 18th April, 1856.

The machinery could easily get jammed with these small engines, as happened on 7 September 1863, at Flaxfield; only it was sabotage. John Lennon wanted time off work to help his mother with shearing the sheep. He asked his friend, Robert Sharples to show him how to jam the machinery and cause a break down. They waited until the workers went home for breakfast; which was between 8 a.m. and 8:45 a.m. Robert placed a bolt between two sets of wheels and then took it out. John then replaced it between the wheels.

At 8:38 a.m., Edward Oatway, engine tender for no. 3 engine, which powered no. 10 room, started the engine, but it would not turn. He reversed it with steam, but it still wouldn't move, he then tried to move it with a bar. When this didn't work he sent for the engineer, Millwright John Whiteside. The engineer found the bolt between the wheels.

The lads had been witnessed, standing by the frame by James McKnight, a 'jobber'. He said, 'He saw them standing by the frame, which he was surprised to see, was stopped, but didn't witness anything else.' John Sharples a 'Doffer', said at Kirkham Court, 'He was there when Robert Sharples, asked his brother how to put the bolt in, and watched him place it between the wheels.' Both, John Lennon and Robert Sharples were committed to Preston sessions for trial.

At the Michaelmas Quarter Sessions, they both received two months' prison sentence for misdemeanour.

In 1831, John Birley died and his sons Thomas and William took over Flaxfield Mill.

Of the old mills belonging to the Hornby family, the one on Moor Street was demolished and the new workhouse built on the site. The one on Freckleton Street was taken over by William Houghton and Thomas Singleton took over the Back-Lane Mill.

Both buildings were tow weaving and spinning mills. Tow is a by-product of the flax industry. When flax is processed it leaves a coarse broken fibre, which was used to stuff upholstery. These short fibres could also be spun and then woven into a cloth. The cloth was hard wearing and used for work clothing or to make sacks.

THE Valuable FLAX and TOW MILL, situate in Back Lane, within Kirkham, in the County of Lancaster, lately in the Occupation of Thos. Singleton; with the Engine and Boiler House, Work Shop, Weaving House, Barn, 13 Cottages, and Outbuildings thereto adjoining; together with a STEAM ENGINE, estimated to be of 12 Horse Power, Boiler, Main-geering and Fixtures thereto belonging. And also, all those Two Closes of LAND, in Kirkham aforesaid, commonly called the Great Yarn Croft, and the Little Yarn Croft, containing together 1A. 2R. 10P. of Land.

There is upon the Land a spacious Lodge, with an excellent supply of Water; and in the Mill, Calender, Roving and Spinning Frames, Carding Engines, nearly new, and other useful Articles and Apparatus connected with the Trade of a Flax and Tow Spinner, which the purchaser will be required to take at a Valuation, to be made by two indifferent persons. The Machinery is in excellent order, and may be commenced working immediately.

As the Premises are near the line of Railway from Preston to the Wyre Harbour, they are well worthy the attention of Persons intending to commence the business of Flax and Tow Spinners.

Thomas Singleton sold his mill in February 1839

William Houghton was declared bankrupt in September 1838 and sold the Freckleton Street Mill. He bought the Back-Lane factory and was back in business producing linen, sacking and sail cloth.

When he sold the Freckleton Street Mill he kept some of the mill cottages at Hornby Court and Freckleton Street. William Houghton was reported by the town's surveyor in 1857, because seven of his houses on Back Lane were without privies. In 1915, his future relations were still being sanctioned over the state of the homes:

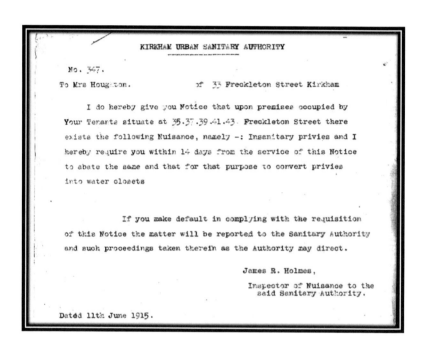

KIRKHAM URBAN SANITARY AUTHORITY

No. 347.

To Mrs Houghton.   of 33 Freckleton Street Kirkham

I do hereby give you Notice that upon premises occupied by Your Tenants situate at 35.37.39.41.43. Freckleton Street there exists the following Nuisance, namely -: Insanitary privies and I hereby require you within 14 days from the service of this Notice to abate the same and that for that purpose to convert privies into water closets

If you make default in complying with the requisition of this Notice the matter will be reported to the Sanitary Authority and such proceedings taken therein as the Authority may direct.

James R. Holmes,

Inspector of Nuisance to the said Sanitary Authority.

Dated 11th June 1915.

Mrs Houghton received two letters, the second of which was badly typed. She ignored the council as in November 1915, her solicitors Finch, Johnson and Co. of Preston, had advised her that they could only ask her to make the premises sanitary. The solicitors also advised Mrs Houghton that the council could not compel her to convert the privies into WCs, but possibly they could be repaired and be made sanitary.

```
                    KIRKHAM URBAN SANITARY AUTHORITY
                    ----------------------

    No. 346.

    To Mrs Houghton       of   33. Freckleton Street, Kirkham

          I do hereby give you notice that upon premises being occupied
       by your Tenants situate  at 1...3 4 Houghton Court and 12.14.20.22
       Marsden Street there exists the following nuisance, namely -:
       Insanitary privies and badly paved yards and I hereby require you
       within 14 days from the service of this notice to abate the same
       and that for that purpose Convert privies into Water Closets and flag
       Back-yards.


          If you make default in complying with the requisition of this
       Notice the matter will be reported to the Sanitary Authority, and
       such proceedings taken therein as the Authority may direct.

                              James R. Holmes.

                              Inspector of Nuisances to the said
                                     Authority.
          Dated 11th June 1915.
```

William was a shareholder of the Kirkham Gas Company. He owned the 'Anchor' public house which was to become the 'Ship Inn' on Freckleton Street. Inn Keeper James Jolly was witness to Mr Houghton's will on 5 May 1860. After his death in November 1875, Houghton Court and Mellor Terrace were built on the site of his mill.

In 1841, the railways arrived, and William and Thomas Birley went their separate ways. William focused his attention on the mills in Preston, and Thomas stayed in Kirkham running Flaxfield Mill with his sons.

John Birley was fundamental to the flax industry in Kirkham. The man who was to become instrumental to the cotton industry was Roger Charnock Richards. This new man of cotton was liberal in politics and a non-conformist. He was to challenge the Conservative, Church of England men of Kirkham.

◆◆◆

R. C. Richards arrived in Kirkham in the late 1830s from Walkerfold, Clitheroe after serving his apprentice as a chemist and druggist. He lived on his family's farm in Wesham and started importing 'Peruvian Guano' from Peru. This was a fertiliser created from the excrement of seabirds or bats.

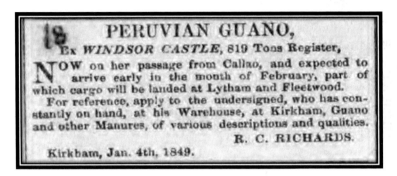

Richard went into partnership with James Whalley and they bought the Freckleton Street Mill, which they converted to cotton production. Richards was also selling insurance for *The Guardian* and was a coal merchant. In 1850, R. C. Richards began to expand cotton production into Wesham, which at the time was a rural place with only a few houses, an inn and some farms. He formed a partnership with William H. Bowdler and erected Phoenix Mill, a cotton weaving shed. He formed another partnership with Richard Holden, and they built Wesham Mills, a cotton spinning mill. The other smaller concerns in Kirkham working in the small sheds were Robert Hatton, rope maker and Richard Dugdale, sacking and sailcloth.

LAUNCH.—On Monday last considerable numbers of people assembled on the side of the Ribble, at Freckleton, to witness the launching of the "John's," a vessel built by Mr. Mayor, of Freckleton, for Messrs. John Birley and Sons, Merchants, of Kirkham. She is about 150 tons burthen, and is expected shortly to try her sailing powers in a voyage to Riga, in the Baltic. About 12 o'clock the stoppers were removed, and, as if frightened from her resting place, by the loud hurrahs and roar of cannon, she glided rapidly down the incline and was soon safely afloat.

The year 1850 also saw John Birley and Sons' new ship being launched at Freckleton, for the Baltic Trade.

The cavernous weaving shed of Phoenix Mill, waiting for Parkinson's Biscuits to move in.

These new mills were state of the art at the time, with steam engines, large cavernous rooms without dividing walls and decent homes for the mill workers, with pubs and shops nearby.

After steam engines were introduced the problem of water supply emerged. Mill lodges were built and mills with large roofs like Phoenix had all the drain pipes emptying into the lodge. This dirty water was sprayed into the sheds when steaming. The factory act of 1901 stopped the use of recycled water; from that point on they had to use a clean water supply for the steaming. Wesham Mills and Brook Mill could fill their lodges with water from the Wrangway Brook.

Flaxfield was in a worse position because it had three steam engines and small roofs. To solve this, a lodge was built in the middle of the factory, which could be supplied with water from four reservoirs. Two were behind the factory and two were on Barnfield, where the water could flow downhill and fill the lodge. John Helme, who had worked for John Birley for 67 years, retired from his job as Keeper of the Lodge when he was 89 years old. He died 10 months later in October 1848, aged 90. All this was irrelevant after 1864, when the town established a water supply. On sunny days these reservoirs were used for bathing.

On a hot Sunday in July 1876, Richard Conway was bathing in the reservoir behind John Birley's, when he saw 16-year-old John Thomas Bowman standing on the bank. At about 3 o'clock he heard a shout that he had fallen in and was drowning. Richard swam to the spot and dived down but could not find him. The police found his body after an hour's search.

———◆◆◆———

Sadly, people used the mill lodges to commit suicide. On Monday 21 May 1878, Ann Singleton, aged 33, was found drowned in the lodge of Richards Brother's mill on Freckleton Street. At 9:30 p.m., she was sitting with her husband at 27 New Row, when she left the room. Her husband John thought she was going to bed and followed her up an hour later. When he got upstairs she was not there. After searching the house and premises, and not finding her, he sat up waiting until 3 a.m. He went back out, and after standing on some steps, he thought he could see something in Messers Richard's lodge. He called his son who thought it was his mother. The police were called and PC Thomas Oversby found her body floating face down in the water at 4 a.m. Mrs Singleton had been ill for three years and during the week had seemed 'much put out of the way.' At the inquest in the police station the jury returned the verdict, 'Found Drowned.'

REARING OF A MILL.—On Thursday, the 7th instant, the new mill of Messrs. Richards, Holden, &c., near the Kirkham railway station, was reared. During the day we observed several flags waving in the wind, one of which had a motto inserted on it, "Success to the Wesham Mills, Westhampton." We understand the latter is the name by which the town is to be distinguished. On the roof tier being hoisted to its proper place, Mr. Richards, one of the firm, fastened it with a nail, and also addressed the workmen and friends in an approprite manner on a temporary platform erected on the roof, and treated each to a glass of the "cratur." We understand the mill is intended for cotton spinning, and calculated to contain about 130,000 spindles, and will furnish employment for upwards of 150 hands. In the evening the workmen and friends, numbering upwards of one hundred, assembled at the house of Mr. Joseph Appleyard, the Railway Hotel, and were each regaled with an ample meal of real old English fare, roast beef and plum pudding, together with a copious supply of "John Barleycorn." The tables were presided over by Messrs. Richards, Holden, Bowden, Brynyng, and Shaw; it is needless to state that ample justice was done to the good things provided. The company was afterwards enlivened by drinking healths, and joining in singing the old chorus so well known as "Jolly good Fellows," after which the company separated, highly gratified with the evening's entertainment.

Preston Chronicle **1852**

In the mid-nineteenth century, if you were Church of England, you would more than likely work at Brook Mill or Flaxfield Mill. Independents would mostly work at Phoenix or Wesham Mills. During the church rate auctions, the gates of Wesham Mills were locked because large numbers of the workers were anti-church rates. However they could not keep the Phoenix Mill workers in when the cart went past, carrying the belongings of Mr Catterall. The police and the carter had to suffer the abuse as they passed by. The girls from Flaxfield Mill were encouraged to disrupt the meetings on the Market Square.

In May 1856, John Greenall, who employed 60 hand weavers, sold Bran Hall. John Birley and sons bought it and used it as a warehouse.

> **FREEHOLD PROPERTY IN KIRKHAM.**
> TO BE SOLD BY AUCTION, by Mr. L. BROWN, at the house of Mrs. Lawrenson, the Bull Inn, Poulton-street, Kirkham, in the county of Lancaster, on Friday, 2nd day of May, 1856, at six o'clock in the evening, subject to conditions then and there to be produced, ALL those SIX COTTAGES, Weaving Shop, Shippon, and Gardens thereunto belonging, situate at Bran-hall, near to the Gas Works, in Kirkham aforesaid, in the occupation of John Greenall and his under tenants.

By 1860, R. C. Richards had withdrawn from the cotton industry and was spending time on his true passion – farming. In 1862, the cotton famine struck. Kirkham was badly affected but not as bad as some other Lancashire towns. Throughout the famine, Flaxfield Mill continued running at full time, still employing 600 people.

In 1865, William Harrison built Brook Mill, a spinning mill. In 1875, the next mill was built, Fylde Mill on Orders Lane. This was a Co-operative Mill, which was designed to allow working class men to buy shares in it and have a say in how it was run. Fylde Mill's condition to be a director was that you had fifty shares, which were sold at five pounds. No working-class man had that amount saved. There were nine directors, who were William Harrison (Brook Mill), Robert Catterall (seed dealer), John Ward (ironmonger), William Segar Hodgson (first chairman), Edward

Bryning (cloth agent), Robert Cross and Cuthbert Gardner (both building contractors), John Hardman (grocer) and Thomas Ogden (mill manager).

Industrial action was rare in Kirkham and Wesham, but 1890 saw 10 months of unrest. The Factory Act of 1878 was created to regulate the working hours in cotton mills and factories; mainly for women and children. This still meant 12-hour days, which included a half-hour breakfast, a one-hour dinner break and half day on Saturday. Unions were now representing workers, and a Kirkham or Wesham weaver would join the Preston and District Power-Loom, Weavers, Winders and Warpers Association. All this was there to improve the life of the cotton workers, but not at Phoenix Mill.

In 1890, at Messrs Walkers, Moss and Co., the work force was told that anybody who joined a union would have to leave the mill. Life at the mill for the weavers was becoming intolerable. The main complaint was 'over steaming', which is when steam from the boilers was sprayed into the weaving sheds to create humidity to prevent the cotton threads from snapping. The tacklers turned on the jets in the morning and any weaver found touching the jets was fined 1 shilling. If it happened a second time they would be sacked. The weavers hated steaming because of the health implications of working in damp conditions. The water used in the boilers was recycled and steaming spread contagious diseases. The workers at Wesham thought it caused pneumonia and sciatica.

The second was 'Fetching Up', or unofficial overtime: the engines should have been started at 6:15 a.m. but they were started at 6:05 a.m, the engines stopped at 8:05 a.m for breakfast and restarted at 8:20 a.m, 15 minutes instead of 30 minutes. Dinner was only for 40 minutes and the engines were run until 6:10 p.m, ten minutes over.

The third was the speed the looms ran. The weavers had to earn 12*s.* 3*d.*, per each pair of looms, which was increased to 12*s.* 6*d.* and then 13*s.* This meant 200 picks a minute, where the average speed in other mills was 180 picks. Anybody not up to this speed was asked to leave.

The fourth was pay. The unions had tried to standardise the different pay in the different mills in one town. They made lists of the different size looms, or different fabrics, and what a weaver should be paid. The 'lists of sorts' were named after the different towns they were compiled, 'Burnley Lists', 'Blackburn Lists' etc. The Phoenix Mill weavers wanted to be paid by the 'Cuerden Mill List' at Bamber Bridge.

The fifth was excess 'Driving', when the 'Overlookers' fined the weavers to keep discipline and to make them work faster. On Friday 2 May the 600 workers of the mill walked out without union support, and went on strike.

On the Saturday, a mass meeting was held by the railway station, addressed by Luke Park, secretary of the Preston Weavers' Association. He said he could not lead them, because they were not in the union. However, by the end of the meeting most had agreed to join it. He told them to decide what they wanted to achieve and to approach the manager with their grievances. A deputation of twenty weavers was sent to speak with the mill manager Mr Rawcliffe.

On the matter of steam, the manager was willing to stay within the limits of the new act of parliament and had obtained indicators (hydrometers). He denied he had called up weavers before him, because they had only earned 25s. 6d. per pair of looms a fortnight. The deputation pointed out that two weavers had been 'called up' for only earning 25s. 9d. and 25s. 10d. The deputation wanted to know why the Cuerden weavers, who were part of the same firm as Phoenix, were paid more. Mr Rawcliffe said, 'The firm pays the Burnley list because they were working Burnley goods.' He refused to reduce the speed of the looms. He told the deputation that, 'Mr Moss had told him that he had received a big order and the work, could be carried out at Cuerden.' He continued, 'The looms only made money running at 13s. so he was saving money by having the mill standing.' Another delegation was sent later in the day, but they were turned away. The mill was closed, and the machines were being overhauled. Both sides dug in. At the end of the day, 400 weavers had joined the union.

On Tuesday 3 June another mass meeting was held by Luke Park, although he advised the strikers he would not meet Mr Moss until all operatives had joined the union. He told the strikers, 'Mr Moss would only pay the Burnley list, until the new universal list was produced, and then change the levels of pay to that.' He advised then to ask all the Kirkham weavers to put a voluntary tax of 3d. a week to help the strikers. They then voted to continue with the strike.

On Tuesday 10 June a notice was placed on the mill gates.

> Having been informed on most reliable authority that a great proportion of our workpeople are very wishful to resume work on our terms, namely the Burnley List, and the new list at once when settled, we now wish the public to know that we have decided to open our doors at eight o'clock on Thursday morning and if there is not sufficient quantity of weavers comes up to run both sheds we will start one shed, as to give those weavers an opportunity who wish for work. –Pro Walker, Moss and CO, R Rawcliffe manager.

The strikers gathered at the top of Whitworth Street well before eight o'clock. There were five police officers and superintendent Stafford, stationed on the street to keep order. Both police and strikers waited to see what happened next.

Nothing happened until 10 a.m., when a dozen weavers returned to work along with some tenders. By 11 a.m., 40 weavers had returned to work, one engine was started, and 140 looms were running. Some of the strike breakers tried to leave early, but were met by the hostile crowd, bolstered by the Kirkham mill workers. They were jeered and called 'Knobsticks' and 'Cowards'. Ten strike breakers from Wrea Green were allowed to return home along the railway track, escorted by a policeman, to avoid the crowds. The following morning the Wrea Green 'Knobsticks' (strike breakers), escorted by a policeman, were jeered crossing the fields, by some of the Wesham weavers. Fewer people returned to work than the day before, but still some looms were running. Some of the tenders who had resumed work were stopped by their parents from going in on Friday. None of the overlookers, cutlookers, winders, warpers or twisters returned to work.

By 21 June, all the mill workers had joined the union and Mr Park took up the negotiations on behalf of the strikers. He could also appeal to other branches of the union for relief funds. The Burnley and Preston branches had given £5 each to help the hard-pressed workers, who had now been on strike for seven weeks.

On Monday 7 July Mr Park, Mr J Rawlinson and Mr Moss met in the Mitre Hotel Manchester. It was agreed to address all complaints that the strikers had about the excess steaming, driving, meal breaks and fetching up. Mr Moss agreed to give all their weavers their looms back, the arrears of wages would be paid; when mill workers went on strike, any wages owed for that week would not be paid. The Burnley list would be used until the new uniform list was produced. Mr Park could enter the mill with Mr Rawlinson and measure the looms for producing the list of sorts.

A meeting was held in the Co-op on Thursday morning on 10 July. The strikers voted to return to work on the agreed terms. That afternoon, Phoenix Mill was running at full strength.

Some of the weavers were not satisfied with the settlement and a meeting was arranged on 20 July in the Co-op hall. Luke Park went through the settlement in detail. The firm had produced a list of 86 sorts, paid at the rate of the Burnley list. There was a reduction in pay on some sorts, but overall it was a 2 per cent gain. The broad looms had a 4 percent gain, 70 sorts had a 1 ⅝ per cent gain.

The trouble was, the work they were now involved with didn't show a gain. Mr Park said, 'They were better paid with the Burnley list, then under the universal list as it now stood.' He continued, 'The sorts did not always remain the same, but would change in time and the weavers would reap considerable advantage.' He added, 'Whatever they had gained or lost in their late struggle, they had gained respect, and they could now have any complaints they had to make, inquired into by their officials without the weavers troubling themselves.'

There were a few outstanding issues mentioned at the end of the meeting. The tenders were being paid 5 shillings a week, compared to Preston tenders who received 5s. 6d. The second was the winders wanted to know, if there was a 'Winders List' and should they be paid for the carrying of twist.

The following month Mr Park was back in Kirkham. The weavers at Fylde Manufacturing Co. thought they were being under paid. It was questionable whether it was low wages or bad material, as weavers were paid by the weight of the cloth. A meeting on 4 August was held in the Co-op hall, chaired by Mr Park. At the end of the meeting it was resolved to put the matter in the hands of the officials. He asked the weavers not to take matters into their own hands but be guided by the union. A deputation was formed and on Mr Park's guidance went to meet the mill manager.

In November, Mr Parks went to the mill to measure the looms and was refused entry, the manager told him the deputation said they were satisfied with their pay. A meeting was held at the Co-op hall, where this was denied. At the meeting Mr Park read out a list of what the weavers were paid and what they should be paid.

Number of picks	Weaver paid	List Price
Thirty-one	3 *s.* 2 ½ *d.*	3 *s.* 8 ⅜ *d.*
Thirty-three	3 *s.* 6 *d.*	4 *s.* 4 ⅛ *d.*
Thirty-five	3 *s.* 8 ½ *d.*	4 *s.* 4 ⅛ *d.*

A weaver then asked about the oil money (for oiling the looms). Mr Park said, 'They have no right to stop any money out of your wages for oiling, it is illegal, and if they [the weavers] would move a resolution that it be done away with, he would promise that the association would see that it was.' At this time the weavers paid the man who oiled the looms ¼ pence per loom.

━━◆◆◆━━

Mr Park was refused entry into the mill because in 1879, the board passed a resolution not to allow any union official to enter the mill. In the afternoon of 12 December, the weavers refused to work until Mr Park could examine the list price under which they worked. At a meeting on Wednesday at the Bowling Green Inn, the strikers were told that the board agreed to hold a meeting to rescind the 1879 resolution. The weavers agreed to return to work on Thursday morning. Most of the weavers' concerns had been addressed and things settled until 7 February 1891.

On that day, two weavers were 'Bated' for mixing the wefts, having used 44*s.* counts instead of 46*s.* One weaver was fined 1*s.* the other 1*s.* 6*d.* A deputation met the mill manager who said the fines would stand. The engine was stopped, and the weavers went on strike. Mr Park went to the mill and was informed they'd joined the Masters' Association and the matter was for Mr Park and Mr Tattersall, secretary of the Masters' Association, to sort out.

The Masters' Association took a hard line. They would not let any weaver back until they forfeited 1 shilling per loom and one of the fined weavers had been sacked. On Wednesday 18 February this was reduced to 7½*d.* per loom, to which Mr Park could not agree. The company stopped negotiating. The weavers could return on Thursday morning at breakfast time and forfeit 8½*d.* per loom or stay on strike. On Thursday morning 40 weavers went back to work. More started arriving and by 10 o'clock all the looms were running.

When Flaxfield Mill closed in 1895, it was the end of an era. This saw the end of the large Irish contingent living in Kirkham. Most of the Irish workers went home and with the mechanisation of agriculture the yearly influx had reduced in number.

In 1907 a new mill, Bankfield, was built. This was a room and power mill, where different firms could rent space and run looms with the motive power provided. Companies could be more flexible during fluctuations in the cotton market. Also, if a firm went out of business, the effect was not felt as badly as an entire mill closing.

This mill saw the third major strike in Kirkham, which also turned out to be the longest.

On Wednesday 15 June 1910, 183 weavers at the Kirkham and Wesham Room and Power Co. gave seven days' notice to cease work. The weavers' concerns on the union price lists were not addressed, and the weavers belonging to the four tenants at the mill walked out.

Springfield Manufacturing Company was the first to settle the dispute with its weavers. On 1 August 1910, 70 of their weavers returned to work. The difference with this strike was that the weavers worked for different firms. By 1 November 1910, there were only 70 weavers still on strike. Luke Park was back in Kirkham, holding a meeting in the National School where they passed a resolution that all Kirkham weavers, pay loom money to the strikers. The remaining striking weavers were replaced with 'Black Leg Labour.' The strike lasted until March 1911, when it was agreed to re-employ the remaining striking weavers, as vacancies occurred.

Luke Park was a Kirkham lad born in 1840. He went to the Willows School and later to the Catholic school on Fox Street, Preston. He started work as a handloom weaver, weaving checks and shirts in a house before starting at Whitworth's and Barrett's Phoenix Mill. He moved to Preston and became

Chairman of the Preston Power Loom Weavers Association in October 1875. This was a failing organisation until he took over and he transformed it into a successful union which used the system of mutual bargaining. He was on the board of the Northern Weavers Amalgamation on the formation of the body in 1884. He died on Tuesday 27 September 1921, aged 81.

The mills were a dangerous place to work, with many accidents occurring over the years.

In November 1872, the 15-year-old son of blacksmith John Ward had his arm crushed in the machinery at Richards and Parkers Mill, Wesham. Dr Walker had to administer chloroform and amputate his hand from above the wrist.

Mrs Iddon was working in the cardroom at John Birley's in June 1893. At 06:40 a.m. two drums became loose in the no. 2 spinning room and the engine was stopped. She used this stoppage to clean her machine by putting her arm through the pulley. At this moment the engine was restarted, smashing the woman's arm in two places. Dr William Wright Shaw set the fractured limb.

In October 1893, W. H. Willacy was working as a spinner at Wesham Mills. He was fastening some wire to a machine when it broke and penetrated his eye. The same week Jane Stanhope lost her middle finger weaving at Phoenix Mill.

It wasn't just the moving machinery; the boilers and engines were also dangerous.

An alarming accident occurred at Messrs. Carrington and Dewhurst's mill, shortly after six o'clock this morning. When the hands arrived it was found that the engine would not start, and while the fireman and P. Willacy and A. Dixon, overlookers, and J. Dixon were trying to discover the defect a valve burst, and severely scalded these four men. Dr. W. W. Shaw was at once called, and found them to be seriously injured. The mill is closed.

December 1901 at Freckleton Street Mill

John Birley's mill also had its own gas plant. On Friday 24 November 1893 at 2 a.m. there was a gas explosion at the mill. Night watchman William Muncaster heard a bubbling noise, which came from the purifying house; one of the purifyers was short of water. He started to fill the purifyer with water, when there was an explosion, which blew the roof of the building off. Muncaster was thrown across the room and was badly burnt. He managed to leave the room and get help. The police, Mr Woods the foreman and gas man J. Threlfall came to his aid. William was taken to the watchhouse were his injuries were dressed. They thought that when he opened the door to the gas plant, a gas light on the wall in the ajoining room ignited the gas.

William Fisher, a 'creeler', was killed at Brook Mill in November 1896. He was travelling in the lift with two others. When the lift didn't stop at no. 4 spinning room, he tried to jump, but slipped and fell. He died from his injuries in Preston Royal Infirmary.

At one time, when travelling up Station Road, there were mill cottages on the right, then Milbanke Estate. On the left was open countryside as far as the eye could see. Travellers followed the wall of Milbanke House, down towards a bridge which crossed over the Wrangway Brook. The other side of this bridge was Wesham. When the railways were built in 1840, the border between Kirkham and Wesham was blurred slightly. Later, when the bridge over the railway tracks were built and the old Wrangway bridge was taken down, the border disappeared, but it still is the Wrangway Brook.

Looking at old maps of the area, it seems that Phoenix Mill is in Wesham and the spinning mills are in Kirkham but this is not the case. Both spinning mills were in Wesham, hence why Selby Mill was originally called Wesham Mills. There was a time at the start of the twentieth century that part of the Wesham and Kirkham councils planned to amalgamate. Kirkham wanted this because heavy traffic came into Kirkham, over the railway bridge turning right down to the spinning mills and to the goods yard. Kirkham had to maintain the roads, but all the business rates went to Wesham. Wesham didn't want to join with Kirkham, and it never happened.

The main mills were:

Bankfield Mill/ Sunny Bank, Weaving Cotton, 1907–2002

Brook Mill, Cotton Spinning, 1864–1936

Flaxfield Mill, Flax Spinning and Weaving, Cotton Waste Reprocessing, 1754–1967

Freckleton Street Mill, Flax and Cotton Weaving, 1790–1908

Fylde Mill, Cotton Weaving, 1875–1930

Phoenix Mill, Cotton Weaving, 1852–1930

Progress Mill, Cotton Weaving, 1914–1971

Selby Mill, Cotton Spinning, 1852–1935

William Birley Remembers

In June 1887, the *Preston Chronicle* published a series of articles where people reminisced about old Lancashire. The articles were called 'Lancashire Reminisces', and were very popular at the time. William Birley was among those interviewed. Although he spent most of his adult life in Preston, some of his accounts of the past involved old Kirkham. He said,

Well, one of the biggest differences in the cotton trade today, with say 60 years ago is the hours. People then worked six in the morning until seven at night, with about an hour and a half for meals. Now it's six in the morning, until five or six at night. This change happened not all at once, but over several years, at four distinct points in time. The operatives worked until four on Saturday afternoons, which is two to three hours less than today. There is no doubt that manual labour has decreased to an enormous degree, consequent on the immense improvements in machinery, and the mode of preparation is as different as possible. When I went to business self-acting mules had not been adopted to any great extent. Hand mules were principally used, the first firm to adopt the 'self-actor' being Messers Birley and Co. of Manchester; relations of mine.

In the old days, he continued, Cloth was conveyed from the mill to the market or to the buyer, either along the road by huge wagons, or where possible, by canal. I well remember that the flax used at the mills at Kirkham, with which I was connected until about the year 1841 came from Russia, and was conveyed by sailing vessels to Wardley's, from which point it was carted to Kirkham. Cotton, too, had to be brought from Liverpool either by road or canal as far as Burscough, and the rest of the way by cart. The structure of mills has changed wonderfully. I fancy that production in mills are three times as much in the number of the pounds, as was the case fifty to sixty years ago, consequent in the improvements of machinery. The earnings of the people are very much greater, and in the throstle spinning and cardrooms … I think I shall be speaking within the mark … have more than doubled. A change, too, has been the method of payment. In the old times the operatives worked by day, now nearly all work is done by piece. Fifty years ago, a grown woman was receiving about one shilling per day or thereabouts, but now they usually get from 2*s.* to 3*s.*, or more, per day, especially in the weaving department. In around 1840, power looms were little used, those in operation being similar to the handlooms, with a speed of 96 picks, as against 200 or 220 picks in the present day.

As to the dress of the period, Farmers and farm servants generally appeared in knee breeches and leggings, and the women wore bedgowns. I should think that the position of a domestic servant, particularly a woman servant, has improved more than that of any other of the labouring classes. Their wages are quite double what they were when I commenced housekeeping in 1846, and almost everything they purchase is 50 to 60 per cent less in price.

———◆◆◆———

Starting with Churches, My early recollections of the churches are that the pews were much different from those of the present day. They were old-fashioned square pews, with free seats for the labouring population, who used to go into them and take the same seat in a tacit understanding that regular attendance at church, established a prospective right to a particular position, so long as they chose to occupy it. With some few exceptions, I think the habits of the population of the country, at any rate, are wonderfully improved. The flax dressers who at that time got very high wages compared with other operatives, would not work on the first two days of the week and the same course was followed by the weavers. But during the last three days of the week they worked almost morning, noon, and night.

There was a great deal more drinking then than now, and … it was only with the greatest difficulty that men-servants were kept sober. Teetotalers were ridiculed by all classes; the general principle being 'Fill what you like, and drink what you fill.' If a man were drinking wine he had to empty his glass and turn it upside down on the table, before the bottle came round again to him. Since then the manners of the male sex have greatly improved. I wish I could say the same of the female in every case. The first 10 or 15 years after I came to the mill [Swainson and Birley, Preston] I am sure that a woman would have been ashamed to be seen going into a public-house, but now they brazen it out. The 'vaults' are the most abominable thing on the face of the earth. In the Kirkham division, we won't license a place with a vault attached to it.

As to the demeaner of the people in the Fylde, … they were always most respectful, so much so that on one occasion the late Bishop of Manchester was struck with it, and asked the Reverend Brown, who proceeded Canon Mason at Kirkham, if it was usual for all passers-by to raise their caps, to which he replied in the affirmative. At that time, what is now called a dress coat was worn as a morning coat, and the gentry wore large ruffles on their shirts, and powdered their hair.

Great improvements had been made in the condition of the roads: The roads in the township of Clifton, have been paved since the late Reverend Moore, came here in 1820; they were mere sand roads, but were now paved with boulders. For travelling there was what was called at that time the 'Fylde Union' coach; but the letters were carried for about 20 years, without missing a single day, by a man called 'Tite' (short for Titus, I suppose), who rode from Preston to Poulton and back, with saddle bags in front. He would start from Preston, call at Kirkham, and then on to Poulton.

As to the amusements of the people, travelling players would make periodical visits to the neighbourhood, as well as morris dancers, jugglers, tumblers, and such like; a barn would be fitted up as a theatre. There was the towns Club Day almost as it exists at the present time. Carriages were very scarce then, only being kept by the landed gentry – the Hornbys, the Birleys, and a few other prominent residents in the Fylde. But farmers kept their shandries, in which they either drove to church or else had to walk. There was, and is yet, in Kirkham a public 'hearse' house, with hearse and harness complete, so that any person had only to take a horse, and he was allowed to use the hearse for a funeral free. Generally however the coffin was carried by friends of the deceased and was covered with a white pall. After the funeral the customary thing was to ajourn to some public-house and have dinner; and since I went to live at Clifton, I have attended more than one of these dinners, the custom still prevailing to some little extent.

—◆—

Mr Birley was asked what he thought of the position of the farmers: I think the monetary position of the farmers is very much worse now than then. These were Yeomens then, many of them with their own estates, and many of them living upon the Clifton and other estates for a very small sum of money, who then had several members of the family inserted in the lease. It is possible, though not likely, that there may be one or two of these still in the parish of Kirkham. In consequence of this practice, the land was very badly cultivated indeed; but a good many of the principle farmers at that time died fairly well. Some of them, fathers and sons, lived in the same township for 100 or 150 years or more.

As to the service in the churches, It is much more cheerful now than in the old times. From my earlier recollections, however, they have had an organ in Kirkham Parish Church, and when I was at school at Singleton the sacred music was furnished by a bass fiddle, a flute, a bassoon, and a clarinet; and the clerk invariably in those days, gave out the first one or two lines of the hymn. I recollect going out by steamer from Fleetwood to Scotland during my honeymoon, and whilst in Scotland I went to a Presbyterian place of worship, where I was much struck with the fact that, when the prayers were read, the congregation stood up, and sat down during the singing of the hymns. But I believe that custum is exploded now, and that even the most rigid Presbyterians and Calvinists in Scotland, are beginning to think that an organ is not an improper instrument, to 'assist' at church services.

Dinner … was then served amongst the gentry at a much earlier hour than at present, people generally sitting down on no account later than 4 o'clock. Manners and customs all round have very much improved. When you go to dinner now, you sit down about seven or half-past, and twenty minutes after the dinner is over, the gentlemen join the ladies, instead of as formely, sitting over the wine for about two hours, and only just leaving it in time to see the ladies depart. In spite, however of the great many improvements at the present time, there are many pleasant recollections of the old days.

William Birley was 76 years old when he gave this interview.

At the start of the twentieth century, until the start of the First World War, the cotton industry was doing well in Kirkham and Wesham. The older mills installed new looms, and the old steam engines were replaced. Two new weaving sheds were built; although Freckleton Street Mill was lost to fire. The war put a stop to all this expansion and heralded the slow death of the Lancashire cotton industry.

The effect of the war was almost immediate, and by August 1914 there were only 50 people working in the mills. All were closed apart from a few weavers working at Bankfield. By October 1914, the mills were starting to work intermittently. By 1915 things were back to normal and this year saw Flaxfield Mill, re-open after being silent for 20 years, and started re-processing cotton waste. In September 1916, new lighting regulations saw the mills running from 6:30 a.m. until 6 p.m., to save on gas lighting, which in turn saved coal.

The cotton industry was suffering on all fronts, the shortage and the cost of coal, problems importing and exporting goods and recruiting staff. However, to encourage men who were fit to join the army, mills like Progress Mill refused to take men eligible for service. After the war, Progress Mill workers were behind a movement where weavers could refuse to work under an Overlooker who had been a conscientious objector.

> WANTED, YARN WAREHOUSEMAN, ineligible for service.—Apply, Whittle and Turner, Ltd., Progress Mill, Kirkham.

After the war, the cotton industry coughed and spluttered back into life. In 1920, the Kirkham and Wesham mills were at their peak. There were approximately 3,520 looms running in Kirkham and Wesham, employing about 2,000 people. The two spinning mills employed a further 360 people, with about 100 working at Flaxfield.

The Kirkham Medical Officer, Dr Court, wrote in his annual report in 1920 that the majority of mill workers suffered from anaemic and dyspeptic ailments, due to the atmosphere in the mills, and to a wrong dietary, especially the latter. Kirkham had an advantage over the large east-Lancashire towns, with its rural surroundings, giving it a more healthy atmosphere. The proximity of the coastal resorts also helped with the clean air environment.

With the amount of work in Kirkham and Wesham, and the health benefits associated with the area, people moved from east Lancashire to the Fylde coastal towns and commuted to Kirkham by train to work in the mills.

On 3 November 1924, Miss N. Herbert, a weaver, caught the 17:38 train from Kirkham with six other girls. Fifteen minutes later, three of them were dead. The Liverpool to Blackpool express had just passed Moss Side station, when one of the wheels on the engine broke. The train stayed upright until it met a set of points, which led into the new gas works being built (where the council tip is now). The train at this point jumped off the rails, crashing onto its side, demolishing Warton signal box. Two carriages toppled over, the third caught fire, the rear one was undamaged. By luck, the fire started sometime after the crash and Lytham fire brigade was on site to put the fire out.

The driver was killed, but the fireman survived. The Warton signalman, William Hornby, aged 19, who lived at 19 Station Road, Kirkham, also survived. He was knocked unconscious and didn't remember the crash, he stated that he was walking across a field, when somebody told him there'd been a crash and help was needed. In total 15 people were killed and 44 injured; most of the dead were weavers, including:

Emma Pickup aged 48, her sister Margaret Pickup aged 56, William Walsh aged 33, Mary Morrison aged 44, Ethel Cox aged 32, whose sister Florence survived, Miss Ida Greenwood aged 21, and her sister Miss Annie Greenwood aged 29, and Thomas Hartley who wasn't a weaver but worked in a mill.

The other were: Commander C. H. Creame, William Crook the engine driver aged 67, Ernest Tonge, advertising contractor aged 46, Leslie Dawson, Ernest Pickup, goods clerk, and Henry Oldham.

Commander Creame worked for the White Star Line and was on the train because he'd been to the head office in Liverpool after running his ship *S.S. Bardic* aground in thick fog off Lizard Point. Despite having both legs nearly severed, he told rescuers to help the other passengers before himself and never once complained. Mr Tarbruck of Clifton Street was on the train and helped Mr Creame, and thought he was the bravest man he'd ever met. Commander Creame died later in hospital. The *S.S. Bardic*, which had run aground on 30 August, was refloated a month later and towed into Falmouth.

Life goes on, and the work went on, until the annual week holiday. Workers didn't get holiday pay, so saved up money over the year, which the mills paid in time for the July trip, to the Isle of Man. Here the holiday maker could walk up and down the promenade with one half of the population of Kirkham and Wesham. The other half would be promenading up and down in Llandudno.

> Kirkham's annual holidays commence next week, and the various saving clubs at the mills and workshops have this week paid out their funds, which total £5,994. It is expected that there will be a big exodus from the town, with Llandudno and Douglas as the favourite resorts. The disbursements have been: Messrs. Whittle and Turner, £2,100; Selby Mill, £1,040; Sunny Bank Weaving Co., £680; Fylde Manufacturing Co., £700; T. Moss and Sons, Kirkham, £966; Redmayne and Isherwood, £100; Aero Mill, £300; and Horns Mill, £108.

This article shows the payments for the year of 1925. The people of Kirkham needed to enjoy these holidays because the town was about to be thrust into a depression not seen since the cotton famine. During the First World War, Japan and India started to produce their own cotton. Approaching the end of this decade, India started to export cheap cotton to Britain. Despite pleas from the cotton industry the government refused to put tariffs on imports.

By 1930 the cotton industry had collapsed in Kirkham and by the end of 1932 the unemployment rate had reached 49 per cent; the third highest percentage in the country.

Both Fylde Mill and Phoenix Mill closed for good in 1930. The two spinning mills stopped production and the other weaving sheds reduced to short time. By 1932 the council was trying to create work with building projects, one of which was on the recreation ground, but the largest was the building of the Kirkham by-pass and widening the Blackpool main road at Tarnbricks.

In 1930, the weight of traffic passing through Kirkham on a daily basis was 12,977 tons. This consisted of 3,349 cars and 1,557 HGVs and buses. The new by-pass was to begin at Ribby Woods and re-join the old road at Church Farm. The road was 1¾ miles long and cost £91,845. The surface was made with ten different types of material, so the Department of Transport could test which was best used for road building.

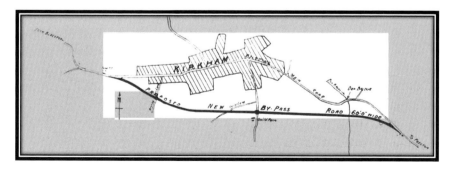

County surveyor's plan from 1930

The by-pass was opened by Mr L. Hore-Belishaw, the Transport Minister on 4 December 1934.

Councillor Eddie Sergeant was tasked with encouraging new firms to Kirkham and at this stage was having some success. Selby Mill re-opened in 1933 and Brook Mill was back in business. Part of the Fylde mill was converted into a cheese factory, and in 1934 a rope and twine plant started operating in the remaining part of the building. In 1933, 800 people were unemployed in Kirkham, which by 1934 had reduced to 300, an unemployment rate of 12 per cent. Those in employment numbered 2,400.

Despite the council's efforts the unemployment rates stayed high until the next war. Selby Mill closed permanently to spinning in 1935. In 1936, Brook Mill also ended its career as a spinning mill when it closed its doors. In 1937 a new company set up a soap manufacturing plant in the building creating 40 jobs, however this year the unemployment rate climbed to 14 per cent. The Second World War kept Progress Mill going, producing material for parachutes. Bass Smeaton Ltd was making army webbing at the start of the war in Selby Mill and Brook Mill. Later on during the war, they moved into Phoenix Mill.

After the dusts of war had settled, spinning cotton was a thing of the past, but the weaving went on. There were just two firms left, Whittle and Turner at Progress Mill, and Sunnybank Weaving Company at Sunnybank Mill. Flaxfield Mill, which was still re-processing cotton, was the first to go in 1967. Progress Mill closed in 1971, but part of the work was sent to Sunnybank. Sunnybank was now alone, weaving a cloth for mattresses. Thirty years after Progress Mill closed, Sunnybank followed suit. Being too small a concern to warrant further investment it closed, and the clacking of looms became an echo of the past.

Spinning And Weaving

Between May and October ships would land bales of flax from the Baltic to be processed by the Kirkham mills. The flax plant is about four feet in length and the flax fibre runs the entire length of the plant.

The first process in flax production was called 'retting', where the flax plant was soaked in water to split the linen fibres from the woody fibres of the stalks. The second part, 'dressing the flax', was called scutching or heckling, and usually took place in a building called a Scutching Shed or Heckling Shop. The flax passed through a braking engine where it was beaten by iron bars to remove the seeds and wood. Then it was combed with a carding engine, the flax passing between two large revolving barrels, with hundreds of fine pins. These cleaned the flax even more and the three carding engines used, gradually becoming finer, to leave fine fibres all running in one direction (just how a person would comb their long hair). The short fibres called 'tow' were used locally to produce sacking; the long fibres for linen.

A L L that well-built MILL or FACTORY, situate in Freckleton-street, in Kirkham aforesaid, with the Heckling Shop and Calender House thereto adjoining, and other the Apurtenances, late in the possession of Mr. William Houghton. The Factory (exclusive of the Heckling Shop and Calender House) is about 30 yards long and 8 yards wide, is two stories high, and contains one Breaking Engine, three Carding Engines, Rowing and Drawing Frames, four spinning Frames, and other Machinery calculated for the spinning of Tow from 2 to 20 Leas to the pound. Part of a new Engine and two new Boilers are upon the premises, and in the course of fitting up. An eligible opportunity is here offered of commencing the Flax and Tow Spinning and Manufacturing Business at a very moderate expence.

This advert from the *Preston Chronicle* in 1838, selling the Freckleton Street mill, shows the equipment used

The flax was now ready to be spun. The lengths of flax were formed into a continuous ribbon, called a 'slither', in a machine called a 'spread board'. The slithers passed through drawing frames to stretch the slither to make it longer, stronger and finer. The roving frames reduced the threads again, twisting the single threads together to form a compound thread. The flax was wound onto a reel 90 inches in diameter to create a 'lea' of flax which was 300 yards long. In cotton spinning it was called a 'hank' and was 840 yards long.

Winding room, Phoenix Mill

Before the weaving process became mechanised, the spun flax was delivered to hand weavers who lived in cottages mainly on Preston Street and Freckleton Street. After 1809, when the first steam engines had arrived in Kirkham the spinning process became mechanised, but the weaving was still done by hand. There was no way the hand weavers in their cottages could keep up with the increased production, so weaving shops were built, or old buildings were converted into weaving shops. All this changed when the weaving process became mechanised some years later.

In the cotton mills the hanks of cotton were sent to the winding rooms to be wound onto the bobbins. The smaller bobbins for the 'weft' fitted into the shuttles, which were beaten left and right through the gap in the warp called a 'shed'. The large bobbins were used to create the 'warp' during the warping process, and these threads ran from the back to the front of the loom.

During the warping process, the larger bobbins were placed into a frame, the amount depending on how many threads were needed. The threads were drawn through a winding machine, then through a reed to keep the threads evenly spaced onto a warper's beam. The threads were then sized and wound onto a weaver's beam. Sizing or slashing soaked the threads in a starch like substance to help prevent breakages.

The threads were now threaded through the heddles with a small hook, ready for mounting onto the looms. The heddles went up and down creating

Sizing or slashing
room at Progress Mill
1915

Weaving room
Progress 1915

Progress Mill
warehouse

the shed where the shuttle could pass through. During plain weaving two heddles were needed, each one alternating to give a pattern of under one and over one. Edward Whalley worked at Fylde Mill when they changed from plains to twills. Twills needed four heddles to give a pattern of over two and under two or over one and under three.

The cloth shown in the warehouse at Progress Mill is called 'Loom State Cloth'.

Cotton doesn't seem to have been dyed in Kirkham, but in the early nineteenth century flax was being dyed and treated at Freckleton Street Mill, the 'finishing process'.

Next was pre-shrinking and scalding: the cloth passed through vats of caustic soda, then through rollers which squeezed out the remaining caustic soda before being scalded. During scalding the cloth travelled on rollers through numerous baths of hot water to clean the cloth and remove the last of the caustic soda.

It was now ready for bleaching and dying in the bowk house. The cloth was soaked in vats of bleach, before the excess was squeezed out. The cloth was washed again before passing through vats of dye.

The last stage was drying in the calender house, calendering and folding. The cloth was dried by passing between rows of steam heated metal rollers. The last part was 'ironing' or 'calendering', where the cloth passed under pressure through metal rollers, and then was folded, ready to be sold.

Bankfield Mill

The foundation stone for Bankfield Mill was laid on Saturday 30 March 1907, by Mrs Sara Hale of Mowbreck Hall. Bankfield was a Room and Power Mill, built by the Kirkham and Wesham Room and Power Company. The company rented out space for different firms, and provided the power for one thousand looms, with its 600 hp cross compound engine built in

Preston by J. Fosters. The mill began production in 1908 and employed 300 people. The firms using the building in 1915 and 1938 are listed below.

1915	1938
Kirkham Manufacturing Co., 212 looms.	Geo Stanfield and Co.
J. T. Horne, 90 looms.	Kirkham Manufacturing Co.
H. R. Penny, 116 looms.	Sunnybank Weaving Co.
Springfield Manufacturing Co. Ltd, 246 looms.	Jacquard Weaving Co.
G. Stanfield and Sons, 100 looms.	
Cryer Bros, 114 looms.	

When Progress Mill closed, some of the looms were moved to Sunnybank. The large building to the left of the chimney was called Bankfield Sheds. Weaving stopped in the sheds in the 1930s.

It was used as a store by the military during the Second World War. After the war, it was split into industrial units. Sunnybank Weaving Company continued to weave in the smaller building on the right, which was now called Sunnybank Mill.

Sunnybank Mill, 1972

Brook Mill

Brook Mill, a five-storey cotton spinning mill consisting of 30,000 mule spindles and employing 150 people, was built in 1864 by William Harrison. The brick building had a large roof cistern for water, an internal hoist, yarn warehouse, stables, waste warehouse and a gatekeeper's house. The large lodge could keep itself supplied with water, when needed from the Wrangway Brook, and the mill had its own five-ton weighing machine. The machinery was powered by two steam engines, creating a combined force of 320 hp. Inside the boiler house were two boilers, one 30 ft long and the other 28 ft long.

In 1888, after being in debt for 10 years, William was bankrupt, and the mill was taken over by his sons, trading as Messrs T., R., E. Harrisons. They ceased trading in 1892, and the mill was bought by James Butler and Co. He ran the mill until it stopped spinning in 1936. After that, it was used by Fylde Industries as a soap manufacturing plant and as mixed industrial units; army webbing was made there at the start of the war.

Empty again during the Second World War, the Blackpool Artillery was barracked there and later the mill formed part of the accommodation of Brookwood POW Camp. After the war Preston farmers used it as a warehouse, until it was demolished in the 1960s.

Flaxfield Mill

Flaxfield Mill was built in 1754 by John Langton and William Shepherd, later John Birley joined, and they formed a company called Shepherd, Langton and Birley. In 1804 John Birley son of the previous John Birley, bought out his partners and ran the mill as John Birley and Sons producing sail cloth, sacking and linen.

The factory had several mills three to four storeys high on a six-acre site. Also associated with it were 52 cottages, a poor apprentice house and a shop. Flaxfield also had its own fire brigade and fire engine. It was the first mill in Kirkham to install a steam engine, by the mid-nineteenth century it employed over 1,600 people. Most of these were immigrant workers from Ireland, who lived in one of the 52 tiny cottages along Mill Street and Wrangway (Station Road). During this period Kirkham suffered serious overcrowding and insanitary conditions. All but one of these mill cottages remain, no. 1 Mill Street.

The mill's boom time was during the Napoleonic Wars, supplying sail cloth to the Royal Navy, but by the late 1800s, steam ships were replacing sailing ships and trade declined. The mill was very inefficient and required three engines amongst its sprawling buildings. Early in 1895 two thirds of the mill were silent, and with only 400 employees remaining, the mill closed.

The workers received two weeks' pay, and most left for Lisburn in Ireland where new similar mills were being opened. This was the only time the mill had ceased working (apart from breakdowns); unlike most weaving companies it operated continuously throughout its working life.

Flaxfield Mill 1920

Workers reprocessing cotton 1920

The Mill was bought by Messrs Redmayne and Isherwood of Blackburn in 1915 and reopened reprocessing cotton waste. One part was badly damaged by fire in 1962 and in 1967 the other part storing cotton waste was destroyed by fire. The building was sold in 1972 and demolished to make way for housing.

Freckleton Street Mill

Freckleton Street Mill was developed by Joseph Hornby in the 1790s. A flax mill, it incorporated new buildings and converted old cottages. When Hornby left the sailcloth business, the mill was taken over by William Houghton, who converted it for flax and tow spinning. Mr Houghton put the factory up for sale in October 1838.

R. C. Richards took over the building and changed it from flax to cotton. It now consisted of two spinning sheds, a weaving shop, a bowk house (for bleaching) and two rows of workers' cottages named Old and New Row.

Mr Richards' nephews took over in 1860, running it under the name Richard Brothers. It closed in 1863 during the cotton famine, but re-opened in 1865. The new owners were Messrs Hardman and Co., who ran 164 looms. The mill was put up for sale again in April 1867. Carrington, Woods and Co. became the new owners.

⬥

When John Woods retired from the firm in 1895, it changed its name to Carrington and Dewhurst. The mill changed hands two more times, to William Scholes in 1904 and George Ward and Turner 1907.

In March 1908 the mill burnt down. The engine, boiler, part of the warehouse and the external walls survived. Some people wanted the mill rebuilt, but this was never going to happen. The building wasn't practical for a modern weaving mill. Weaving mills are generally single-storey buildings and weavers tended not to like working at Freckleton Street Mill, because the beams had to be carried upstairs. The surviving looms were sent to the new mill being built called Bankfield. The Kirkham Steam Laundry was built on the site.

One Kirkham Weaver who didn't like working at Freckleton Street Mill was Edward Whalley, who also experienced the Cotton Famine first hand.

EDWARD WHALLEY AND THE COTTON FAMINE

We don't really know what life was like for a Victorian mill worker in Kirkham. We know they worked long hours, from six in the morning to six at night, Monday to Friday and a half day on Saturday. They entered the mills doing part-time work as children, and went full time at the age of twelve. Poverty was always around the corner, as the mills could just close or go on to short time working at little or no notice.

Edward Whalley was a former weaver who lived with his widowed daughter, Jane Ann Boaler, on Freckleton Street. He was 85 years old, slightly deaf and blind in one eye (after being scratched by a bramble in a Lytham Park). Edward was the father of fourteen children, of which seven had died. He was widowed in 1900, when his wife Prudence died. His age made him a rarity and he was interviewed by the *Preston Herald* on 18 December 1915. This interview gives us some insight into a Kirkham weaver's life.

He left school at eleven to work in Birley's Mill for two shillings a week. Later, he was sent to Preston to learn weaving with his brother; where the Birleys had cotton mills. He returned to Kirkham as a 'tackler' for a year, before returning to weaving at Mr Barret's Phoenix Mill. Whilst there, he returned to tackling and his daughter Lily took over his four looms.

He later took up a position at Freckleton Street Mill, at the time being run by John Woods. He stayed there for three years, but didn't like it, as you had to carry the beams upstairs. He decided to go for a better paid job because of his responsibilities. He gained a position as an overlooker at the Fylde Manufacturing Company's Mill, on Orders Lane. He stayed there for twenty years and mentions that when the looms changed from 'plains' to 'twills', the work was done in their spare time without pay.

He thought people in 1915, had life easier, with better wages and food. He was brought up on water porridge, oat cakes and when they were lucky, a bit of white bread and apple pie, sweetened with treacle. In his opinion, people were healthier and looked after their money better.

Edward goes on to talk about 'The Cotton Panic', also known as 'The Cotton Famine'. He left Kirkham with Mr Harry Woods and the 'Kirkham Subscription Band'. They travelled around the main towns of Lancashire and Yorkshire, to raise money to send home. He sent seven shillings a week home and was in Halifax when he heard news that the Kirkham Cotton mills were restarting. That morning the band played until they all had enough money to pay the train fare and left. Edward and Mr Woods decided to walk back, however. It took them fourteen hours to get to Preston, where they stayed overnight, and carried on to Kirkham in the morning. They would have been quicker but the two trotters Mr Woods bought had affected him so much.

Edward was friends with Dr Thomas Shaw and Dr Benson, and he also knew the mill owners, Mr Catterall, Mr Bowdler and the Birleys. In 1915, however, he claimed that he didn't know half of Kirkham.

The Cotton Famine was a disaster for Lancashire, when over 250,000 people lost their jobs and faced starvation. It started to hit in October 1861, during the American Civil War. The boom years for the Lancashire cotton trade were in the years 1859 and 1860. By 1861, the merchants in China and India were looking at warehouses full to the roof with cloth and nobody to sell it to. When the American Civil War started in April, there was enough raw cotton to last six months. The North Americans started to blockade the southern ports and the supply of raw cotton from America dried up. The price of produced cotton collapsed, and the price of raw cotton went through the roof. By October 1861, the Lancashire Mills started closing or running at 'short time'.

By December 1861, thousands of people in Preston alone were applying for Poor Relief. People started leaving Lancashire for Yorkshire, to work with the 'woollens' and some began to emigrate. The Lancashire Famine Relief Fund was set up and people all over the country started to donate money and goods. This was then filtered through to smaller town relief committees, who distributed it to the needy.

By November 1861, three mills, Phoenix, Selby and Freckleton Street were on short time. Luckily, John Birley and Son's flax mill was still running as normal, so this reduced the effects of the famine. At the start of 1862, the three mills stopped production. Around 500 operatives were made redundant at Phoenix Mill, 180 at Selby and a few weeks later 100 at Freckleton Street. The workhouse could not cope with these numbers and the welfare clubs were not equipped to provide this level of support. Kirkham was a few months behind Preston, and when the famine struck, plans for soup kitchens and support were already in place.

THE KIRKHAM RELIEF COMMITTEE thankfully acknowledge the following donations, viz. :—

	£	s.	d.
Amount previously advertised	424	3	8
Mr. William Singleton, Kirkham	1	0	0
Miss Annie Lawrenson	0	10	0
Mrs. Birley	20	0	0
Earl of Crawford and Balcarres	50	0	0
Miss Fisher, Kirkham	2	0	0
Mr. James Duckett, Kirkham	2	0	0
Mr. James Brash	1	0	0
W. Leyland Woods, Esq., Chichester	5	0	0
Rev. Richard Doyle, Willows	1	0	0
Collection in Frindsbury Parish Church, Kent, per Rev. James Formby, vicar	50	0	0
Stephen Roberts, Esq., Maiden Bradley, near Frome, per Rev. G. R. Brown	6	0	0
Collection at Kingston Deverill, per Rev. G. R. Brown	9	1	4
Miss Langton, Bath, for bedding	10	0	0
Mrs. Parsons, Bath, for bedding	10	0	0
Mrs. T. L. Birley, Kirkham, for bedding	10	0	0

R. C. Richards, one load of meal.
Messrs. Pearson, Knowles, and Co., 40 tons of coals.

ERRATUM.—In the list previously advertised, Messrs. Hardman, £2 2s., should have been the Misses Hardman, £2 2s.

W. HULLEY, } Secs.
O. BARRETT, }

Kirkham, December 15th, 1862.

The accounts from the relief funds, were published in local papers

All the leading Kirkham families were involved in the relief fund in some form or other, as this advertisement for a charity ball shows. The small imports of cotton began in late 1863, but Manchester, took most of this. It wasn't until August 1864 that raw cotton imports resumed normality. The famine finally ended in 1865.

Going Back to the Mills...

Fylde Mill

FYLDE MANUFACTURING.—The object of this company is to carry on the business of cotton manufacturing at Kirkham, in Lancashire. It was registered on the 5th inst., with a capital of 30,000*l.*, in 5*l.* shares, the following being the first subscribers :—

	Shares.
* William Harrison, Kirkham, cotton-spinner	100
* Edward Bryning, Kirkham, cloth agent	50
* Robert Catterall, Kirkham, seed merchant	50
* John Ward, Kirkham, ironmonger	100
* William Segar Hodgson, Kirkham	100
* Robert Cross, Kirkham, building contractor	100
* Cuthbert Gardner, Kirkham, building contractor	50
Thomas Ogden, Kirkham, cotton-mill manager	50
* John Hardman, Kirkham, grocer	50

The number of directors to be nine. Qualification, fifty shares. The subscribers are to be the first. General meeting to determine remuneration.

Fylde Mill was a cotton weaving mill built in 1875, on Orders Lane, by Fylde Manufacturing Co. The mill was a co-operative and was known locally as the Co-op mill. William Segar Hodgson was the first Chairman and the mill began production in December 1877. Terraced houses were built for the workers; the streets being named after the mill and shareholders.

It had nearly 600 looms and was powered by a 265 hp steam engine. The mill closed in 1931 but reopened in 1934 as a rope and twine works.

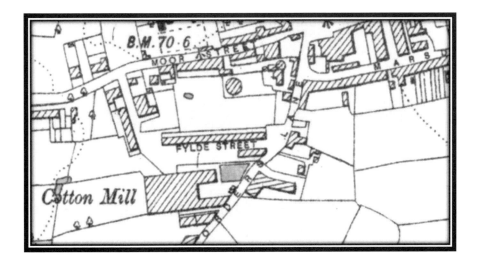

Fylde Mill 1895

Windmill Land Dairies, owned by Pye James of Winford Creameries, started producing milk and cheese in the building. The rope and twine works closed after a few years, but the dairy kept going until the building was demolished in the 1970s. The telephone exchange and houses were built on the site.

Phoenix Mill

Phoenix Mill was a large cotton mill built in Wesham in 1852, by Roger Charnock Richards and W. H. Bowlder. They sold the mill in 1857 to Messrs Whalley and Hardman.

TO BE SOLD BY AUCTION, (without reserve), by Mr. LUKE BROWN, at the Railway Hotel, Kirkham, on Monday, the 29th day of June inst., at half-past four o'clock in the afternoon prompt,

ALL that newly-erected WEAVING SHED, situate at Westhampton, near the Kirkham Railway Station, together with the warehouse, counting-house, gasometer, engine and boiler belonging thereto, and the use of the siding from the railway to the same premises. There are 232 looms in the shed, 184 Todd's patent, and 48 Harrison's, all new; and there is room for 120 more. The shafting, tape, winding frames, and warping mills, are sufficient to supply the shed when filled with looms. Engine, 20 horse power. The area of the land is 3,464 square yards, and the purchaser will have the option of purchasing an additional quantity on the same terms as the original purchase. The premises are subject to a rent of £20 per annum for the use of the siding. The mill is now at work, and immediate possession may be had. The sale will take place punctually at the time advertised.

For further particulars apply to Messrs. RICHARDS & BOWDLER, Kirkham; or to Messrs. HAYDOCK & CATTLEY, solicitors, Preston.

Preston, June 18th, 1857.

Whalley and Hardman failed after a few years, and the mill was taken over by Whitworth and Barrett. It changed hands again. Walker and Greenwood ran the mill until Thomas Moss joined in 1881, when it became Walkers, Moss and Co. They built an extra weaving room and installed a new engine. The mill now had over 1,100 looms and employed 600 people.

From 1898 until 1930, when the mill stopped weaving, it was run by Thomas Moss and Sons, known locally as 'Mosses'. The building stood empty until 1957. That year, Parkinson's Biscuits moved there from Preston, after their factory on Watery Lane burnt down. It became Fox's Biscuits in 1966, as it is today.

Phoenix Mill with its own private railway sidings

Progress Mill

Whittle and Turner's mill, Progress Mill was built in 1914, on land in Orders Lane, belonging to Kirkham Grammar School. It was the last cotton mill to be built in Kirkham. Whittle and Turner had been running looms in Bankfield Mill before this. The building had nearly 1,000 looms and was powered by a 500 hp, Single Cylinder Tandem Compound Engine. It made fine cotton. Unlike the other mills in Kirkham, it produced cotton continuously through the depression of the 'thirties and only stopped weaving in the early seventies.

On 3 June 1954, Mr Percy Gornall had just taken a reading from the boiler. When he left the room, the boiler blew up. The blast blew him into the yard

Progress Mill's
half-timer in 1915

Weavers, Progress
Mill 1915

outside, and a 70 ft flame leapt out of the 120 ft chimney stack. He was unhurt, but the 300 workers were sent home, until the boiler was fixed, five days later.

When the Mill closed in 1971, some of the looms were taken to Sunnybank Mill. The building was then split into separate industrial units.

Selby Mill

Wesham Mill was built by Richards, Holden and Co., and consisted of a six-storey cotton and flax spinning mill, with other smaller additional buildings. The mill began production on 7 October 1852 and employed over 180 people. It had 69,000 mule spindles and was powered by a small 70 hp engine.

One of the additional buildings was a scutching shed, which caught fire in April 1856. This was before Kirkham Fire Brigade was reformed. Birleys'

Selby Mill left next to Brook Mill

fire engine was sent out and used water from the lodge to put the fire out. The fire was so fierce that the building could not be saved. Luckily the wind direction saved the main mill from catching fire. Ten sacks of unmanufactured flax and a large quantity of flax seeds were destroyed, to a cost of £1,000. The cause was an overheating shaft in the scutching room.

After Mr Holden retired, James Parker joined the firm, now trading as Richards, Parker and Co. When Mr Parker died, W. H. Bowdler joined. Once again, the name changed, now to Richard Bowdler and Co. until 1895 when it became The Wesham Mill Co. In 1924, Selby Mill Ltd took over the building became known as Selby Mill. The mill closed in 1930, but re-opened three years later, re-creating another 150 jobs.

The reopening was short lived. By the outbreak of the Second World War, the mill was being used as a warehouse by Preston District Farmers' Society. It burnt down in 1944, killing the night watchman.

Although it was not a textile mill, Bone Mill is still worth a mention...

Bone Mill

On the site of the square block of houses, formed by Marquis, Smith, Best and Dyer Streets, stood a mill called Bone Mill. Bone Mills were used to render down bones from local slaughter houses, to use as fertilizer. This was done by first boiling the bones, to make them brittle, and to remove the fat. The fat was skimmed off to be used as grease for carts and coaches. The bones were chopped up by hand, then mill-stoned into powder.

The mill was owned by the Fleetwood Brothers and was called the Fylde Bone Works. In 1877, it was taken over by Henry Edward Hargreaves and called Fylde Bone and Manure Works. It closed at the end of the nineteenth century.

On 23 January 1900, E. G. Hothersall opened a farmer's auction market in the building. It could hold 150 cattle or 1,000 sheep and saved farmers

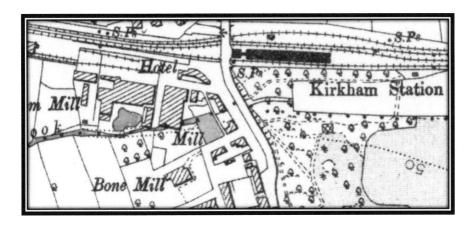

Bone Mill behind Selby and Brook Mill

having to travel to the Preston auctions. In 1937, the building was demolished, and houses built on the site.

Phoenix Mill, SunnyBank Mill and Progress Mill buildings still survive. Brook Mill, Flaxfield Mill and Fylde Mill were all demolished. Selby Mill and Freckleton Mill were destroyed by fire.

Freckleton Street Mill Fire

Freckleton Street Mill caught fire at around 8:30 p.m. on Monday 23 March 1908. Two passing boys saw the fire in a former cottage used as a taping room, which was next door to the engine room. The town brigade was called, and the firemen arrived at the town's yard ten minutes later, where the fire engine was kept. It only consisted of three men, who worked for the council. The previous firemen had all been forced to resign after the club day disaster in 1907. No horses could be found, so they pushed the engine with the help of some volunteers, the half mile up the hill, to the mill.

When they arrived, the fire was spreading into the building facing Freckleton Street. They only got two jets going because despite offers of help, they'd forgotten the stand pipes. Next door to the taper room lived Mr William Dixon, his wife and six children. William was employed as a tapesizer at the mill.

As the fire spread, the well-meaning crowd, helped him remove his furniture and belongings by throwing it out of the windows. They caused so much damage to his belongings he said, 'what was worth many pounds, was now only worth two pence.' To make matters worse, somebody also stole six pounds he kept in a box in the kitchen.

He initially thought all his children had been rescued, but when his cottage set on fire, he realised that his three-year-old was still in bed. He dashed in, and brought her out unharmed. By 10 o'clock his cottage had burnt down.

Preston Brigade was called but refused to come out. The weaving shed facing Old Row was now on fire and later collapsed. Blackpool Brigade was called and also refused to come out.

Freckleton Street in those days, was only 18 ft wide. The people in the opposite cottages emptied their homes and escaped through their back yards. Mr Henry Shaw of 81 Freckleton Street had to carry his ill mother-in-law out of the cottage.

**Freckleton Street Mill
after the fire**

The fire was spreading.

Lytham Brigade agreed to come out and turned up at 11 o'clock with a full complement of men. The fire could now be held back as the warehouse on Marsden Street was emptied. Bundles of cotton, spare parts for looms, and office books were thrown out of the windows. Mr E. Nickson, a local vet of Moor Street, was passing as this was in progress. He was struck on the head and knocked out. He was taken to the Joiner's Arms. Dr Shaw was called, the vet had concussion.

The fire was out by six in the morning. The front block on Freckleton Street had totally collapsed and the rest of the mill was a burnt-out shell. The cost of the fire was over £10,000. The mill with 200 looms and 100 staff was never rebuilt. The looms and staff were relocated to the new mill being built at Sunnybank.

By the time of the next mill fire in 1941, the Kirkham Fire Brigade had been modernised for the war effort.

Selby Mill Fire

Selby Mill was a six-storey cotton spinning mill on Richard Street, Kirkham. It set on fire in the early hours of Saturday 30 September 1944. Night watchman Robert Armistead, aged 43, of 3, Porter Street Wesham, died in the fire. Another watchman on duty with him, Malcolm Camp, aged 20, of 5, Whitworth Street, escaped.

Although they were night watchman, they carried out other work within the mill. After having a break at 1:30 a.m. they resumed work on the fourth floor of the mill but did not see anything unusual. About 5 a.m., Robert saw smoke and shouted to Malcolm to get a fire extinguisher, whilst he went to call the fire brigade. Malcolm looked out of the fire escape window and could see smoke billowing up from below. He saw the fire brigade arriving. Malcolm called to Robert to get out and ran down the fire escape. He told the brigade there was a man still inside.

The brigade had already been informed about the fire by Wesham Post Master Joseph Whiteside. Winifred Halsall of Victoria Road was on duty at the telephone exchange, and saw a permanent glow on the mill line indicator, which meant that the line was dead. Five minutes later she received a call from J. Whiteside.

Five brigades were engaged, Blackpool, St Anne's, Kirkham, Preston, Wesham and the Military Service Units. Altogether twelve pumps and two turntables were used. Section Leader F. W. Hunt of the fire brigade said, 'It would have been hopeless to enter the building.' Brook Mill next door had also caught fire, but was successfully extinguished. Robert's body was not found until Monday 9 October, after an eight-day search. A few charred remains were found but no personal possessions. The mill was destroyed apart from one corner. Sadly, he left a wife and six children, aged between 3 and 19. He was laid to rest in the graveyard at Christ Church, Wesham.

The inquest was held on Tuesday 10 October, the Coroner Mr Ashton said, 'Mr Armistead could have escaped but lost his life doing his duty.' The fire was a mystery and the verdict was death by misadventure.

Preston and District Farmers' Trading Society Ltd, who used the mill as a warehouse, placed an advert, thanking The National Fire Service, United States Army, The Royal Army Service Corp and The Royal Airforce for their support, but omitted any thanks to the civil defence reserve, who later placed this advert in the paper:

'While the civil defence reserve does not look for recognition when on rescue work, I feel that you would like to know, that unit 7 of the civil defense reserve column 10, were working on the Selby Mill fire at Kirkham, from Saturday night September 30th till Sunday October the 8th, when the remains were found by this unit under my command. Yours, Y. B. Noyes.'

It took until the Second World War to create a decent fire brigade, a process that was started in the early 1860s...

Kirkham Fire Brigade

In the early 1860s, the Local Board of Health turned its attention to the Town's Fire Brigade. Until this point, although the town had its own fire engine, there was no fire brigade and Kirkham relied on John Birley's fire engine and crew.

A fire brigade committee was set up, which included Thomas Langton Birley, R. Lund and John Catterall. The old engine was repurchased from Messrs Radcliffe and Whiteside (pawn brokers), to sell it and raise money towards a new fire engine. A manual engine was bought for £60 – a new design from Roses of Manchester. This new engine could spray the water over 30 yards. They also built a new fire station on Station Road, in the corner of the Work House Gardens, for £121. Whilst this was being built, the new engine was stored in the stables at Mr Lawrence's Black Bull Inn. The Brigade consisted of ten part-time firemen and the fire engine was exercised once a month. Things were further improved when Fylde Water Works positioned fire hydrants around the town.

By 1873, the engine was becoming neglected, so a new hose was bought along with new ladders, six leather buckets and two axes. The wheels were also repaired. In 1878, the local board wanted to increase the brigade to fourteen men, but the fire committee kept it at ten. The ten men were all provided with silver helmets, belts and jackets. Captain Roberts was ordered to return his brass helmet, and wear a silver helmet like his men.

Old Fire Station

The building on the left was the surveyor's office. The Fire Station was the building on the right. The downstairs window was the original entrance to the Fire Engine House. Upstairs was an office and the land behind the building was the Town's Yard.

Wanted.—The following letter was read from Mr. George Butler, the superintendent of the Kirkham fire brigade: —" To the chairman of the Fire Engine Committe.—I have to report, as I have been told many a time, that the present fire engine is good for nothing, and it does not give satisfaction to many of the ratepayers. I think if the Board could get a steam fire engine it would be a saving of the rates. The expense of working the engine that we have is 15s per hour, and it will only just land water to the top of Weaham Mill, whereas you can get a steam fire engine that will throw four jets over the highest mill that we have in the district, and a far larger quantity of water, at a cost of 1s 6d per hour. The engine we have is nothing like what we should have considering the mills that are at work. I hope you will give this letter your best consideration, because the loss of a mill would be a serious loss to the town, and we should not be prepared to meet a mill fire with the present engine."—A member stated that they could secure a one cylinder steam fire engine for about £350. It would weigh about a ton, and only require one horse. They would be able to raise a good sum by selling their present manual engine, which cost over £100, and was still a good one notwithstanding what Mr. Butler had stated.—It was resolved to refer the matter to the Fire Brigade Committee, who would ascertain the cost of a suitable engine, and also the approximate cost of maintaining the same, and report to the next monthly meeting.—The Board then went into committee for the pur-

Kirkham could unfortunately not afford a full-time brigade and relied on volunteers, which then created additional difficulties. Firstly, was the time it took to get to the fire station after the bell was rung. Secondly, the difficulty of finding two horses to pull the engine. In most cases, the firemen man-handled the engine to the fire. George Butler was superintendent for many years, and complained in 1890 to the Kirkham board about the out-of-date manual engine. He was proved right in 1908, when Freckleton Street Mill caught fire. The Brigade had been encouraged to resign after the 'Club Day Disaster'. Only three council workers manned the engine with some volunteers; the mill was destroyed.

In 1908, a new steam fire engine was bought for £311. A completely new brigade was recruited. These new firemen arranged various displays at different locations within the town.

> **Fire Engine Practice**
> The Kirkham Fire Brigade held a practice on Saturday afternoon at the cotton factories in Wesham. The engine was backed to the Wesham Mill Company's lodge, whence a water supply was obtained. Four jets were applied, and a large volume of water was sent over the factories. A large number of Wesham inhabitants watched the excellent performance of Kirkham's new engine.

At one of these displays at the Market Square, in front of a large crowd, the sparks from the engine set fire to a nearby thatched roof, much to the firemen's embarrassment.

The Kirkham brigade was ridiculed in the press and was portrayed as a 'Dad's Army' type outfit, but they were capable of great strengths of endurance.

In January 1909, just after Mr Duckworth had renovated the stables, coach house and harness room at Ribby Hall, it caught fire. The fire was noticed at 5 a.m. by William Gardner, who was on his way to work at Moss Side. He informed the groom, who lived at Ribby Cottages. A servant cycled to Kirkham to fetch the fire brigade. Whilst waiting for the fire engine, the groom, servants and game keeper, rescued the frightened horses.

When the servant arrived at the town yard, where the engine was kept, he raised the alarm by ringing the bell. The firemen were all on the spot within a few minutes. A fireman was tasked to find two horses, but none could be found. The men, with a few volunteers, decided to push the two-ton-engine one mile up hill to Ribby Hall. The engine had to be dragged a further 200 yards across a field, to a pond, to get a decent water supply. The firemen were unable to save the building but worked on the fire until 11 o'clock. There were only the walls left standing; two carts, all the hay and chopping machines were lost. The cost of the fire was estimated to be £500.00. Luckily, two horses had been found to transport the engine back to Kirkham.

At a meeting in 1910 the council decided to build a new fire station on the corner of Moor Street and Orders Lane, on the site of the old charity school. The station was to have a fireman's cottage, stables for the horses and an office for the town surveyor.

After the new fire station was built, Wesham paid £10 a year to Kirkham Council for fire cover. In 1912, the council raised this to £30 which Wesham refused to pay. They relied on cover from Singleton until they set up their own brigade. In August 1912, Wesham received its two second-hand engines, purchased from Southport Brigade who were now using motorised engines.

One of the engines was a 450 gallons steamer, which used compressed air to raise the steam more quickly. It could have three jets going, blasted through ¾ inch nozzles, reaching over 100 feet.

The other engine was a chemical engine. This worked by adding bicarbonate of soda to the water in the tank. When this was combined with sulphuric acid, a chemical reaction forced the water from the tank through the hose. The chemical engine was sent first to hold the fire until the steamer arrived.

The steam engine cost £175 and the chemical engine £68, both were stored in a building on Derby Road, until a new fire station opened in 1914.

In 1939 the Auxiliary Fire Service was formed, and Kirkham and Wesham Brigades received second hand self-propelled engines from Blackpool Fire Brigade. These were old 1920s Leyland trucks. Town brigades were strengthened for the war, with full time fire fighters. In 1940, Blackpool moved an engine to Wesham fire station to use as an outpost for the duration of the war. In 1954, Kirkham and Wesham Fire Brigades were amalgamated and the fire station in Kirkham was closed. The engine house entrance on Moor Street was bricked up and a window fitted, so the room could be used as an office.

Q. What do you get in a town like Kirkham with lots of hills, crowd lined streets, and a 1-ton fire engine (without brakes), and somebody says, 'Wouldn't it be good, if the fire engine led the Club Day parade...'?

Kirkham Club Day 1907

On 1 July 1907, Kirkham Fire Engine took part in the Club Day Parade. It was an ancient manual engine which weighed 20 cwt (1 ton), had no brakes and used slippers to help it down hills. A public subscription was raised to pay for horses and the decorating of the engine, the surplus going to the men. Superintendent Octavius Fleetwood was in charge and rode on the engine with six firemen. The two horses were supplied by Mr Dickinson. The horse in the shafts were driven by Henry Threlfall of 12 Clegg St and the front horse in the chains by a man called Woods.

The engine stopped at the top of Preston Street at around 11:45 a.m., a slipper was put under the wheels to hold the engine, but the engine rolled over it, pushing the two horses downhill. They tried it a second time and failed again. The horses began to panic and bolt, the firemen dropped down off the engine all except for Fleetwood. They managed to release the front horse and the remaining horse galloped down Preston Street with the engine and veered into the crowd standing at the Fishstones.

Two people were killed. Francis Hudson aged 4, of 3 Whitworth St, Wesham died from head injuries. James Edward Balshall aged 34, of Poulton St, died later in the afternoon, from terrible head injuries which resulted in a ruptured brain.

Also injured was Henry Hudson, the father of Francis, with broken legs and a fractured skull. John Swann of Albert St sustained internal injuries and suffered shock. Esther Thompson of New Row had a broken collar bone and internal injuries. William Cope had an injured right hip. James Newsome of Poulton St broke both ankles and had shock. James was injured whilst trying to stop the horse.

Esther and James were taken to the workhouse infirmary on Moor St, and all injured parties recovered in time for the inquest.

At the inquest, James Gardener of 10 Church St (who witnessed the accident whilst standing opposite the Fishstones, at the corner of Freckleton Street), said he saw the engine being pulled down the hill by one of the horses and another running in front of it, leaving the procession behind them at the top of the hill. The engine then veered into the crowd at the Fishstones. He went over to help, and carried the injured child to Dr Shaw's Surgery, who pronounced him dead.

Another witness, Ralph Hall of Freckleton, was standing on the Fishstones, two yards behind the deceased man. He called a warning to a bus driver to get out of the way, then almost immediately after that, the engine struck. Something protruding from the engine struck Mr Balshall in the head knocking him down, the rear part of the engine then passed over him.

Susannah Hudson was standing with her family when the engine struck, knocking down several people including her husband and son.

Thomas Hull was recommended for saving 28 Sunday School children from Wesham Parish Church, who were travelling up Preston St, towards the runaway engine in a waggonette. On seeing the engine, he turned it around and galloped back down the hill, the engine swerved behind them into the crowd.

This accident happened partly because the slippers failed. When a heavy Victorian cart went down a steep hill, the driver put the hand brake part way on, so that the horses had to drag the cart downhill, and the cart didn't run away. The Kirkham Fire Engine, which was at the time 49 years old, didn't have brakes but used slippers. A slipper is a metal shoe attached to the cart by a chain. The shoe was put on the floor in front of one wheel, and the cart was moved forward onto it. When the chain went taught, the slipper stayed under the wheel. The slipper was dragged along the cobbles and the friction kept the cart under control. At the bottom of the hill the cart reversed, and the slipper was picked up with a hook because the slippers got very hot. It was then clipped back onto the cart.

Both drivers said the slipper failed because the chain was too long and that Octavius Fleetwood, a Blacksmith of Moor Street, had fitted it. The drivers borrowed the slipper off a showman's van, at the recreation ground on Mr Dickinson's orders. Octavius denied fitting it at the inquest, and a fireman named Fuller was called to give evidence. Fireman Fuller said he 'distinctly saw Fleetwood attach the slipper.'

Superintendent Fleetwood still denied attaching it, but said that he had taken it off. The Judge John Parker was not impressed, but let the conflicting statements go. He then asked Octavius how many times had he been out with the engine in the two years he had been in charge? The answer was – once to a fire and twice in a procession. The verdict was accidental death, and it was recommended that the engine had a brake fitted, or used more powerful horses before it went out again.

Octavius Fleetwood carried the blame for the 'Club Day Disaster' as the national press called it. It wasn't out of malice, but a mistake that led to the disaster, however he still carried a heavy burden. As a blacksmith, he would have been well known in Kirkham, and would have known the dead and injured and come across their families after the event.

How he was treated is now lost in time, but we know that the town rallied around the victims. The council set up a fund for people to donate money, and the Kirkham Pavilion Theatre put on benefit nights for each of the victims.

The first show at Mrs Newell's Theatre was 'Shall We Forgive Her' and raised £13 0s. 3d. for Mrs Swan; Lilla Newell's Traveling Theatre was visiting Kirkham for six months.

Two people came out of the disaster as heroes, Thomas Hull and James Newsome.

KIRKHAM CLUB DAY DISASTER.

A COMMITTEE has been APPOINTED and a PUBLIC SUBSCRIPTION LIST OPENED on behalf of the Sufferers in the above distressing Accident.

Chairman of Committee: Rev. W. T. MITTON, the Rectory, Kirkham.

Hon. Treasurer: F. S. PLANT, Esq., Lancaster Banking Co., Kirkham.

Hon. Secretary: Councillor JOHN HALL, 40 Poulton-street, Kirkham.

Contributions are earnestly invited, and will be gratefully acknowledged by the Secretary.

Donations Received:—

	£	s.	d.
W. W. Ashley, Esq., M.P.	10	0	0
Bishop of Burnley	1	0	0
The Rector	0	10	0
E. F. Peat, Esq.	0	10	0
Mr. W. Greenhalgh	0	10	0
Kirkham Football Club	0	15	1½

Mr Thomas Hull was credited with saving 30 lives when he steered his waggonette out of the way of the runaway engine. On Saturday 20 July 1907, Mrs Hale put on a garden party at Mowbreck Hall in his honour, for the 28 children and two adults in the waggonette who were;

Alice Falmundson, Georgina Bossie, Lillie Swan, Evelyn Kent, Nellia Marquis, Edith Christopine, Rossie Warburton, Sylvia Stirzaker, Anne Crane, Alice Catterall, Ella Aiken, Gladys Willacy, Emma Lupton, Edith

Barker, Maggie Bell, Mary Butler, Buby Taylor, Florry Ratcliffe, Ambrose Warburton, James Harris, John Catterall, Waiter Kirby, William Kirby, Joe Hudson, James Ball, Tom Christopher, George Rossall, Richard Benson, Headmistress Miss Powell and her assistant on the day, Miss Edmundson.

After a speech by Rev. S. R. Barnes, Mr Hull was given a silver plaque by James Harrison of Rawlinson Street, and Sylvia Stirzaker gave Mrs Hale a basket of flowers. Bessie Warburton thanked Mr and Mrs Hale, to round off the occasion.

James Newsome, a carter, tried to stop the runaway horse by grabbing hold of the horse's harness. He managed to get hold of the reins, but they snapped, and he fell under the engine. For this act of bravery, he was given an award by Colonel Moorsom, Chief Constable of Lancashire. The award was a certificate of the Society of St John of Jerusalem, signed by the Prince of Wales.

The fire engine was the responsibility of the Town Council formed in 1895, prior to this it was under the Local Board of Health's control...

Local Board of Health

Local Boards of Health were set up in response to Cholera outbreaks by the Government's Public Health Act of 1848. These boards were given powers to control sewers, clean streets, regulate environmental risks, and provide a proper supply of water.

There were two ways to create a board, one was a petition by ten percent of inhabitants, or if the death rate exceeded 23 in 1,000. Kirkham was the latter, and William Lee, an inspector from the general board, was sent to Kirkham.

He was escorted around Kirkham in January 1851 by Edmund Birley, Rev. Parsons, Thomas Langton Birley, Charles Birley, R. C. Richards,

Adam Wright, Richard Moore, John Whitside, John Barnes, William Parkinson, James Rogerson, Henry Fisher, Andrew Halliday, and Police Inspector Francis Crean.

SEWERS AND DRAINS

There were no sewers in Kirkham, but an open stream called the 'Skipbourne' flowed along Orders Lane, across Townend, and along the back of Mill Street. It crossed halfway along Mill Street, and then flowed behind Flaxfield Mill, and eventually into the Wrangway Brook. Into this stream went all the sewage and waste from the homes along its route. The gas works and Flaxfield Mill also polluted the stream with their waste. The Wrangway Brook was also stagnant and full of animal and human waste. These brooks eventually flowed into Carr Brook, before emptying into Dow Brook.

There was also an open drain down the middle of Church Street, paved with pebbles. The waste from Preston, Freckleton, and Poulton Streets flowed along this. Within eight yards of the church gate, the drain went underground into a culvert. The culvert emptied into a tank in a meadow near the church, which was constantly overflowing. The Vicar, Reverend Parsons said:

> "One of the things I have particularly to point out is the offensive state of the Close, for want of proper drainage. During the two years I have been here there has not been so much epidemic disease in the cottages spoken of, but I understand there was shortly before. There has been an attempt to cure the stench from the outlet of the drain at the bottom of Church-street, but it was exceedingly offensive, and a family in a cottage near to it was frequently sick. Altogether I hope that the Public Health Act will greatly improve the town; it is much needed, and the necessity has been felt by all the respectable inhabitants."

The houses distant from these streams used cess pits for waste, or just threw the night soil into the streets. The worst places for human waste were the overcrowded lodging houses. Some residents, in the old thatched houses on Moor Lane just used the rear of the house as a toilet. The houses on Hornby

Square used a pit surrounded by a wall, which had collapsed. A woman living there said:

> "It is enough to poison us all. We have to watch the children, like a cat watching a mouse, to keep them from being drowned in it. One fell in about seven months since, and was nearly drowned."

On Moor Lane, New Drop and Hornby Square there were 39 houses, 199 residents and only 4 privies. Along with the human waste, the slaughter houses also tipped their waste into the street. This mixed with the liquid from heaps of manure piled up around the town.

Roads

The roads in Kirkham were a good width and were paved with rough stones from the workhouse. There were hardly any footpaths, and the township was responsible for five miles of roads. Mill Street was used by the public, but maintained by John Birley and Sons. There were three bridges, one over the Wrangway Brook on Station Road, and a wooden bridge on Carr Lane. There was also a bridge on Mill Street crossing over a stream. There used to be a bridge at Townend, but this was taken down when a culvert was built. The culvert was 25 yards long, made of bricks and covered with stone slabs. The piece of land between this stream and the Swan Inn was known locally as 'The Causeway'. The streets were lit by 28 gas lamps, which were used from October to May.

Water Supply

There were three water pumps in Kirkham, one in the Market Place, another on Preston Street, and one on Poulton Street. The water was hard, and in general of poor quality. There was also a pump on Carr Lane, but this was 150 yards outside of the town boundary. 27 large homes had their own pumps, and 48 homes had private wells. This meant that 331 houses relied on the three water pumps. 53 families on Freckleton Street had to carry their water an average of 250 yards.

Mr John Winstanly, a plumber said, 'The average person must travel 100 yards to the pump and back, and the water was carried in a four-gallon tin pail.' He kept the three pumps in repair for 15 shillings a year.

FIRE

Richard Moore, a solicitor, said that most of the houses had insurance. In the town 10 per cent of the houses were thatched and paid more for insurance than the slate ones. There were two fire engines, one belonging to the town and one owned by John Birley and sons. The town one was bought by subscription, and was maintained voluntarily by Mr Birley who said:

> "There is no fire brigade. If any fire should occur we should at once send our own men with the engines. There has been no serious fire in the town for ten years. At that time our drying-house was burnt down. The damage was nearly 1,000*l*. Water would have to be obtained from the pumps and the brooks in case of fire."

HOUSES

Kirkham suffered from chronic overcrowding, mainly due to a large immigrant population from Ireland. The population in 1801 was 1,561, in 1831 it was 2,469 and by 1841 it was 2,903. There were 565 houses in 1831, but by 1850 this had reduced to 547. This meant that an extra 433 people lived in a town which had reduced its housing stock by 18 homes.

The Inspector visited some of the overcrowded lodging houses in Kirkham at night. One was on Poulton Street, a thatched house made of mud and stud, which was about to fall down. John Malley was the tenant, and in the living room lodged four males and three females, all in one bed. Under the stairs lived a man and a woman. In a room upstairs, there was one bed with three women, a bed with one man, a woman and a young girl. Another bed shared by a woman and her 16-year-old brother. In this room was also a fourth bed with two men and a shakedown with a man and a woman on it. The inspector said, 'The room was six feet high and the window two feet square; the stench was unbearable.' The lodgers paid *2d.* per night which made £1 4s. and 6d. a week, John Malley paid £12 12s. a year rent for this two-room house. Malley also rented the house next door:

> The same person is tenant of an adjoining house. In the lower room there was in one bed a chimney-sweep and his boy, both unwashed. In a shake-down, seven persons, consisting of four girls, a boy, a man, and a woman. In the room upstairs there were in one bed a man and woman ; in another, a man, woman, and two boys ; in a third, two women and a girl ; in one shake-down, a woman and two children ; and in another, a man and two boys. The dimensions of this house are similar to those of the other, and the atmosphere was quite pestilential.

Inspector Crean of the County Constabulary said:

> "There are nine regular lodging-houses in the town, and several others that take in lodgers occasionally. Four out of the nine will only have one low room, and one bed-room each. *Three have no privies at all.* Six have no back doors. None of them a separate privy. They are chiefly low built, thatched, dilapidated old buildings. I frequently go into their rooms at night. About twelve months since I found fifteen persons in one room, about fourteen feet by twelve, by six feet high. I saw four beds, and they were not all occupied, for the lodgers had not all gone to bed. Some of them were playing cards upon one of the beds ; males and females indiscriminately in the room. As far as my experience goes the males and females all herd together in all the lodging-houses like brute beasts. The stench in these places is very bad. I have gone into them both as inspector of nuisances and also as a peace officer. There is not a doubt that persons resort to them who are in the habit of breaking the laws. They are generally vagrants."

HEALTH

The inhabitants of Kirkham mainly suffered from influenza, bronchitis, pneumonia and rheumatism. Among the Irish community it was low typhus fever, but Dr Gradwell put this down to the poor accommodation they lived in. There was a scarlet fever outbreak in 1843, with over 300 cases and many deaths. In 1849, there were 12 cases of cholera with two deaths. Measles was prevalent, the children who seemed to recover often dying of pneumonia.

Dr Thomas Shaw thought that most of the deaths in Kirkham from disease was preventable, the substandard lodging houses and the want of proper privies being the main causes. The death rate for Kirkham was 25.95 per 1,000, above the rate of 23 per 1,000 set by the government. The people of Kirkham also had a low level of survival.

In Kirkham, there was a large number of Irish immigrant workers, and these could be split into two groups. The first group worked in Birley's Mill and lived in the mills cottages. Amongst these, was a large number of young women. The cottages were small but had drains and the privies were a good distance from the house.

The second group were mainly men who travelled around looking for work, mostly on farms, 'harvest men'. The Workhouse also attracted vagrants and destitute people to Kirkham. This is the group Dr Shaw thought spread Typhus, because the disesase spread inside a lodging house, but never to other houses. He said:

" I cannot call to mind an instance of the fever spreading to houses WHERE THERE WAS NO VISIBLE CAUSE OF FEVER IN THE VICINITY."

The table below shows the survival rates in Kirkham:

Figures from 1841	Under 1 year	Under 5 years	Under 15years	Under 20 years
Fylde per cent	20.3	32.9	40.7	45.1
Kirkham per cent	*21.6*	*39.1*	*44.6*	*55.4*
Kirkham 5-year average	*23.3*	*42.1*	*49.0*	*53.5*

Fylde figures also include Garstang and Clithroe

These figures illustrate that just under half of Kirkham never reached the age of 20. The average age of death in Kirkham was 27 years and 10 months – compared with 33 years and 9 months for the rest of the Fylde.

LAND DRAINAGE

The two main drains were the Wrangway Brook and Carr Brook. These two, along with Spen Brook, flowed into Dow Brook, which itself flowed eventually, into the River Ribble. The Sewage from Kirkham was in the future to follow this route to a sewage works at Freckleton. In 1850, a quarter of farm land was drained according to Land Agent and Farmer Henry Fisher. The old drains were dug as a trench, and peat in the form of a wedge was placed inside. These he said, 'Have been known to last 50 years but now pipes and tiles are taking over.'

The farmers were spreading three types of fertiliser on the land: Peruvian guano, £11 11*s.* a ton; three c.w.t covered one acre. Crushed bones £6 10*s.* a ton; nine c.w.t covered one acre. Farmyard manure 20 tons per acre. The town manure or human waste was only good to dress meadows but because it was full of ash and refuse it was valueless. This meant that if the residents wanted to empty the cesspits, or the town to empty the sewage tank in the Church Croft, there was nowhere to spread it.

TRADE AND MANUFACTURING

In 1851, there were two mills in Kirkham, John Birley employing 350 females and 200 males. The other mill was Richards and Whally (Freckleton Street Mill) employing 110, two thirds were female. There were also several small factories making sail cloth, sacking, and cotton with hand looms employing 100. The town was full of a large number of agricultural workers, and trades associated with any town similar to Kirkham. The Inspector was also shown around John Birley and Sons' mill by Thomas Langton.

Mr. Birley afterwards kindly conducted me over his establishment. In the preparing-room there was a dust from the flax, making the air cloudy, and I think the inhalation of this might in time produce an injurious effect upon those employed. There are ample means of ventilation on both sides of this, and all the other rooms, by swivel sashes; but at the time of my visit they were only opened on one side, and Mr. Birley said that if the other windows were opened the men would complain of being cold. In the hackling-room there was a similar dust, for want of the men availing themselves of thorough ventilation. I found the spinning-rooms very hot, from the circumstance that each thread has to pass through hot water; but the occupants of these rooms have also the power of better ventilation. Mr. Birley informed me that the reelers earn about 10*s*. 6*d*. weekly; spinners, 5*s*. to 7*s*. 6*d*.; men sorters, 17*s*.; and boys 4*s*. 6*d*. to 6*s*. There are from seventy to eighty short-time hands.

William Lee concluded that:

My inspection of the mills and of the town convinced me that the high rate of mortality in Kirkham is not to any material extent the result of the trade occupations of the people. Even if the health of the mill workers is slightly affected by want of ventilation, the remedy is simple, and within their own control.

When Mr William Lee compiled his report, he worked out what it would cost the town in its present state. The extra payments to sick clubs, the time spent walking back and forth to the water pumps, fire insurance, the cost of funerals, the list goes on. So, unlike today, when we would work out what it would cost to set up a board, he worked out what it would cost not to set up a board. He came up with the figure of one thousand pounds per year. Kirkham duly got its board of Health on 10 January 1852. The first chairman was Thomas Langton Birley and on the board were Edmund Birley, Thomas Shaw, Roger Charnock Richards, Adam Wright, Charles Brown and Richard Moore.

THE GENERAL BOARD OF HEALTH.
At the Court at Windsor, the 10th day of January inst., Her Majesty, having taken into consideration the report directed to be made by the General Board of Health with respect to the township of Kirkham, in the county of Lancaster, hath ordered and directed that from and after the above date the Public Health Act, with the exception of the section numbered 50 therein, shall be in force throughout the entire township of Kirkham aforesaid, and that at the first election of the local board T. L. Birley, Esq., shall perform the duties of chairman thereof, and in case of his inability or refusal to perform such duties, Richard Moore, Esq., jun., shall perform them.

The board could now set rates and borrow money in order to start improving the town. A Surveyor, a Clerk, Treasurer and Officer of Health were employed, and work began, starting with the sewers.

Sewers

In 1853 the board borrowed £1,115 to build sewers and carry the sewage directly into Carr Brook. Glazed pipes connected the houses to main drains 15 inches in diameter which ran downhill into Carr Brook, and all new houses had to be connected to the sewers.

In 1862, J. W. Loxham complained about the stench coming from Carr Brook and a delegation was sent to Carlisle to look at a system of deodorizing the sewage. The system was taken up in which carbolic acid was added to the sewage. The deodorizing began in September and by December 20,000 gallons of waste had been treated using two gallons of deodorizing fluid every 24 hours.

Complaints continued, and a tank system for sewage costing £628 was adopted in 1868. A new pipe was laid leading into the sewage tank at the bottom of Dow Bridge. This failed, and the sewer outlet was extended an extra mile before emptying into Dow Brook.

By the 1880s, the sewers in Kirkham were leaking through the pipe joints and because the pipes were oval they were constantly blocking up. In 1886, a new plan was proposed which included Wesham's sewage.

The sewage from Wesham was to join the start of the Kirkham sewers, at the Wrangway Bridge, where the surrounding houses were connected. From here, the sewer was to follow the course of the old pipe, eventually emptying into Freckleton Brook 400 yards below the Freckleton Corn Mill. The 15-inch pipe from Wesham, was to join the 12-inch one at Kirkham and flow through an 18-inch pipe to Carr Lane. From here a 21-inch pipe carried the sewage to Freckleton. The other three sewers leading from Kirkham Town Centre, joined the sewer as they intersected it. Drains were built which emptied into the sewer to help wash the waste along the pipes. A weir was also built near the Wrangway Bridge to help with this.

The sewers were built with man hole covers and air vents. These were laid it straight lines between the angles. This was so a light could be shown at one end and a person at the other end could see if the pipe was blocked or not. The scheme costs £3,500 and in effect moved the problem to the River Ribble, which was already being polluted by Preston's Sewage.

In 1892, a sewage treatment works was built in Freckleton. This finally solved the problem of the Kirkham sewerage, nearly 40 years after the board had started on it.

Roads

In the first few years, Carr Lane's wooden bridge was replaced with a brick bridge. Later on, the bridge over the Wrangway Brook was widened. A cinder path was laid up to the train station. Thomas Moxham began laying pavements, Church Street and Preston Street were the first to be flagged in 1863 with 2 ft square flags. The wider pavements used a mix of flags along with small stones from the workhouse to create footpaths. The roads were built with stones from the workhouse and all new streets had to be 36 feet wide.

All doors were to be numbered, odd one side and even the other, starting from the Market Square. Wrangway was renamed as Station Road, Back Lane renamed to Marsden Street. Moor Lane became Moor Street and Old Earth Row became Orders Lane, which was said to be a play on words. All other streets were to be named with street signs which had lettering three and a half inches long. The market place was to be given its ancient name 'The Square'.

The pavements in the town were flagged or laid with stones. However, the ones leading out of the town centre like Station Road were laid with cinders. The cinders worked, but when it was windy the cinders blew about and blocked the drains. They started using a form of asphalt, made from gas tar, ashes, sand, and lime: which was laid 2-inch deep and rolled flat.

WATER SUPPLY

In 1854, a new water pump was installed on Freckleton Street to save residents from the long walk they had to make. The problem of a clean water supply was too large for an individual local board; Lytham had tried it but to no avail. A company was set up, Fylde Waterworks Company and in 1864, water pipes were laid in Kirkham connecting the houses to a clean water supply.

FIRE

For the first few years after the board was set up, the town relied on Birley's Mill Fire Brigade. In 1858, a fire brigade committee was set up to create a town brigade. The old engine was sold and a new one bought by subscription for £60. The engine arrived in 1863 and was stored in the stables at the New Bull Inn until a fire station was built. The fire station was built on Station Road in 1865 and a brigade of 10 men was formed. They were paid each time the engine was exercised, once every month.

Another improvement in 1864, was when the Fylde Water Board laid their water pipes, they also positioned fire hydrants around the town. In March 1865, the Blackpool Volunteer Brigade came to Kirkham with their fire engine 'The Water Witch', pulled by four grey horses for a display. They galloped up to Carr Hill House and sprayed the house with water for half an hour, before trotting down to Church Street. Here they sprayed Mr Moore's House (Ash Tree House) which was the tallest in Kirkham, the jet reaching twice the height of the house.

After, they went to Town End and the Kirkham engine was brought out. Here both engines were connected side by side to the Hydrant outside the Swan Inn. Both engines went to work, and the Kirkham engine was said to be able to spray the water the furthest. After the display the firemen all went to the Gun Tavern for beers.

HOUSES

A committee was set up in 1853 to investigate the state of the Lodging houses and the surveyor was tasked to inspect them. The committee also ordered all householders to empty cess pits and privies, clean the backyards, clean and white wash their homes.

In 1857, the surveyor reported three lodging houses overcrowded: Terrance McGann's with 12 lodgers, Patrick Maley's with 16 lodgers and Mrs Moore's on Wrangway, who had five lodgers in the pantry with no bedding or bed, and seven upstairs.

The surveyor also reported Mr Lawrence's Back Lane, whose nine houses had only two privies with no drain for a bog, and William Houghton, who owned seven houses on Back Lane, all without privies.

All new buildings had to be approved by the board before being built and the next thirty years saw the main Victorian development in Kirkham. New homes were built on Marsden Street, Poulton Street, and Clegg Street by builders like Matthew Clegg, John Catteral and Richard Billington. Twelve cottages were built on Mill Street and two on Barnfield by Birleys and Co.

The run-down houses on Moor Street were pulled down and William Benson and Thomas Marquis built new homes. Houses started to be built around Orders Lane, in connection with Fylde Mill and the run-down houses on Poulton Street were demolished and replaced with the Co-op building. New houses on Station Road and Freckleton Street were built. On Birley Street, houses and a drill hall for the LAV were built. Pubs, shops and a police station were built. As all new buildings were connected to the sewers with proper toilets, drains and a fresh water supply, life began to improve. When Flaxfield Mill closed, hundreds left to go back to Ireland, and the overcrowding was further eased. By 1890, the medical officer reported that the town's housing stock was more than sufficient.

Health

There were two doctors practising in Kirkham in 1852, Dr Thomas Shaw and Dr Gradwell. By 1888, there were five doctors with practices:

Thomas Cardwell, 22 Poulton Street.

Charles Court, Moor Villa, Moor Street.

Thomas Shaw, Harvey House, Preston Street.

William Wright Shaw, Ash Tree House, Church Street.

E. Atherton Thompson, Preston Street.

The patient went to the doctor's house, where he held surgeries, and they paid with money from the friendly societies, which most people joined. In 1852 there was no hospital to move infectious people to. Later a small-pox hospital was built on Orders Lane, so that small-pox patients could be treated separately from other infectious patients. Other infections were treated at the workhouse.

In 1890, the population was 4,074 and that year there were 137 births, of which 72 boys and 65 girls. The birth rate was 33.6 in 1,000, double the death rate. That year there were seven cases of zymotic diseases, which only led to one death. There were five cases of typhoid, one of scarlet fever and one of erysipelas. 1890 saw 75 deaths, giving a death rate of 18.4 in 1,000, well below the 1852 level.

By 1893, the smallpox hospital was empty and was becoming an area of high crime and so the building was pulled down. Shortly after, the workhouse refused to take in any more infected people, because they could just about cope with their own patients. This left Kirkham without an isolation ward and plans were made with other town boards to remedy this. Mr Birley let the board convert two cottages at Bran Hall, Orders Lane into a temporary hospital.

In 1902, a new infections hospital was built at Moss Side and in 1907, the joint Fylde, Preston, and Garstang Smallpox Hospital opened in Elswick. By the time it opened, small pox had been virtually eradicated and in 1914 the hospital became a TB sanitarium. This sanitarium, for 70, adults was on the proviso that patients would leave within seven days if a smallpox outbreak was to occur.

DRAINS

The main drain, running along Orders Lane and Mill Street, was bricked over with 80,000 bricks from Treales Kiln on Carr Lane. A scavenger was employed to clean the drains and Mr Leyland Birley of Milbanke was told to remove his dam on the Wrangway Brook, which he built to water his horses. The gas works and Birley's Mill were also told to stop polluting these brooks. The open drains, like the one on Church Street were incorporated into the sewers system. Gullies were laid with pavements to allow the water to run away, eventually into the sewers. More farm land was drained, using clay pipes, which also emptied into the sewers to help wash the sewage along the pipes.

The Local board of Health lasted until 1894, although it changed its name to the Local Board. Times were changing, and people weren't happy with these boards. They were mainly made up of the upper classes and were Conservative in thinking. 1894 saw the start of the Kirkham Urban District Council, which was elected. Whatever the politics, the Board completed what it set out to do and cleaned up the town.

Before the Local Board of Health, the Thirty Men looked after the town…

The Thirty Men

Before the Local board of Health was set up, Kirkham was run by The Thirty Men, who along with the Vicar and Bailiffs looked after the religious and general business of the town. The townships included were: Kirkham, Freckleton, Newton, Clifton (Treales, Wharles, and Roseacre), Warton, Bryning with Killamergh, Ribby with Wray, Westby with Plumpton,

Weeton, Singleton, Greenhalgh with Thistleton, Larbeck with Eccleston, Wesham with Mellor, and Hambleton.

Two men were elected from each of the 15 townships, which gave rise to the name 'The Thirty Men'. The group met in the church vestry, apart from when they fell out with Vicar Fleetwood, who locked them out of the church in 1636.

Edward Fleetwood was the vicar at Kirkham from 1629 until 1650. He was an ardent Puritan, who was trying to impose the new religion on an isolated community. Many of the leading families in the Parish of Kirkham were still adhering to the old Catholic faith. The Thirty Men were less concerned with the 160 recusants in the area than the Vicar. In 1636, Edward Fleetwood produced a five-point plan to try and impose his will on the Thirty Men.

1. They shall not lay gualds themselves, without the consent of the vicar.

2. That the vicar, shall have a negative voice in all the proceedings, and that they shall determine nothing, without the consent of the vicar.

3. They shall not put, or elect any new thirty men, without the vicar's consent.

4. They shall not meet in the church upon any business, what so ever unless they acquaint the vicar.

5. If there be any turbulent or factious person, that the rest of the company shall join the vicar and turn him out.

After they refused to agree to his terms, the Vicar locked them out of the church. The Thirty Men started to meet in the graveyard. They appealed to the Bishop, with a petition signed by 392 parishioners. The Bishop John Cestriensis, thought Fleetwood was a silly, wilful man who was prone to tantrums. The Bishop had no joy with the vicar and appealed to the archbishop of York. The case went to the consistory court of Chester.

In the meantime, the vicar continued to rant against Popery, the Quakers at Freckleton, and the disrespectful parishioners. The Thirty Men, however, were allowed into the church on 5 November 1638, to lay taxes. They were again locked out until the court in Chester found against Vicar Fleetwood. They were re-admitted on Easter Tuesday 1639.

There was another explanation for Fleetwood's arrogance. He was involved in the case of the Kirkham Monster, which ended up coming to the notice of the government in London, as a sign of God's Will.

The wife of William Haughton of Prick Marsh, Kirkham, a well-known Catholic family, was once heard saying that, 'Puritans and Independents all deserved to be hanged,' and that, 'I pray God, rather that I shall be a roundhead or bear a round head, I may bring forth a child without a head.' On 20 June 1643, Mrs Haughton gave birth to a still-born child, which was headless.

The midwife, Mrs Gattaker, informed Fleetwood, who had the grave opened. He said, 'The child was indeed headless. The eyes were where the paps usually are, nose upon the chest, mouth above the navel.'

Colonel John Moore heard about the 'monster' and asked Vicar Fleetwood and Mrs Gattaker to sign a testament, which was sent to London. The authorities there had a pamphlet printed and distributed, as proof of God's approval of the Puritan cause.

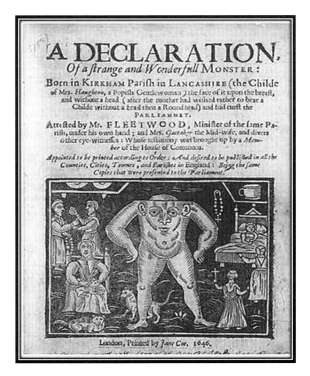

'A declaration of a strange and Wonderfull Monster'

The following figures were from the year 1825:

Joseph Hornby was paying 20*s*. to the Bailiffs each year for the use of a piece of land called 'Iron Latch'; the rent never went up even after 180 years.

The Bailiffs held the following pieces of land:

'Poor Field' or 'Town Old Earth', an acre, 2 roods, 12 perches. This land was purchased by Mrs Clegg, (widow of Rev Richard Clegg) and Mrs Phoebe Sale, who both paid £20 each. Humphrey Threlfall rented this land for £7.

'Bailiffs Field', 3 roods and 37 perches, purchased by Thomas Brock for £50 in 1755. William Fisher rented this land for £4 5*s*.

'Moor Croft', 1 rood and 4 perches, bought by Margret Clayton in 1768. Joseph Hornby exchanged this land for 'Bryning Lane Croft' in 1801, which was 1 rood and 1 perch in size. Thomas Latham used this plot as a garden for a rent of £4 a year.

Joseph Hornby lived next to 'Moor Croft' until he built Ribby Hall. He obtained this land and built one of his weaving shops on it. The house and factory were demolished when the Moor Street Workhouse was built.

The Bailiffs also rented out their pew in St Michael's Church for 30*s*. The last income was from the interest of 4 per cent on the £40 held in the Kirkham Savings Bank.

The income was spent on maintaining the town's, gas lamps, streets, roads and the Fishstones. The remaining money was spent purchasing meat, which was distributed amongst the poor of Kirkham. It was distributed the day before Christmas Eve, known locally as 'Flesh Day'. In 1823, 194 people received this gift.

The role of the Bailiffs diminished with time, as the Local Boards of Health took over maintaining the town. In 1864, the Bailiffs gave the Local Board £50 for maintaining the roads. This was probably the money from the Savings Bank. When the County Police was formed, this took most of the remaining responsibilities from the Bailiffs. The old Kirkham fairs had stopped and by 1851, the weekly Tuesday market was obsolete.

The last two Bailiffs were Thomas Gardiner and John Rigby. The role was now ceremonial, just like the 'Lord of the Manor', yet 'Flesh Day' was still going.

A BOON TO THE POOR OF KIRKHAM.—On Christmas Eve the bailiffs of Kirkham, Messrs. T. Gardner and J. Rigby, distributed upwards of half a ton of beef amongst the poor people in Kirkham, thus enabling a considerable number of families to partake of a joint on Christmas Day.

Preston Herald 1890

The other Kirkham Charities in the 1825 'Report of the Commissioners' were as follows.

Bread Money

In September 1741, Mrs Mary Nightingale left £20, the interest to be spent on loaves for the poor. In 1825, the total fund was £97 in the hands of Messrs Birley, who paid interest at 4.5 per cent. The Vicar also donated £2 12s. per annum into the Bread Money Fund. The bread was distributed on Sundays and Holidays.

	£.	s.	d.
Out of these funds, amounting to 6l. 19s. 3d. per annum, there is given away by the churchwardens, on each of 33 holidays, 7d. in penny loaves, to seven poor people, amounting to - - - - - - -	-	19	3
On each Sunday loaves to the amount of 2s. 1½d. which are given amongst eight or ten poor people; and if any is left, which sometimes happens, it is sent to the houses of needy persons in the town; annual amount -	5	10	6
The remainder is also distributed in bread, but not on any particular day -	-	9	6
£.	6	19	3

Clegg's Charity

In 1670, Reverend Richard Clegg left £12, the interest to be paid to a preacher, for a sermon every Easter Tuesday. A shilling's worth of bread was also to be donated amongst the poor, who came to church that day. The interest was worth 10 shillings in 1825; it was again held by Messrs Birley.

Elizabeth Brown's Charity

In December 1739, Elizabeth Brown bequeathed £40, the interest to be distributed at Michaelmas amongst the poor and needy widows of Kirkham. In 1807, the trust was in the hands of Cornelius Langton and Betty Langton. After Cornelius died, Captain Langton held the funds paying interest at 5 per cent. In 1825, Mrs Langton was distributing the money in sums of no less than 1 shilling. Prior to this it had been given out in sixpences.

Harrison's Charity

In the Returns made to Parliament in 1786, it is stated, that Mr. *William Harrison*, of Kirkham, by will, dated 7th January 1767, gave 140*l*. two-thirds of the income to be distributed in Common Prayer Books, Bibles, and other religious tracts, to poor people living in the town of Kirkham ; and one-third in like manner in the township of Little Eccleston with Larbreck.

This money is in the hands of Messrs. John Birley and son, who have allowed five per cent for it till lately, but the interest is now lowered to four and a half per cent. The interest is laid out in the purchase of books, some of which are sent for distribution to Little Eccleston, and the rest are divided amongst the trustees, each of whom gives away his portion amongst the poor of the township of Kirkham. The books given away, are Bibles, Testaments, Prayer Books, Catechisms, Wilson on the Sacrament, and such others as are furnished by the society for promoting Christian Knowledge, of whom all the purchases are made.

Mrs Bradkirk's Gift

Mrs. *Mary Bradkirk*, about the year 1816, requested her relation, **Zachary** Langton, esq. of Bedford-row, London, to purchase in their joint names, the two several sums of 120*l*. and 200*l*. in the navy five per cents, for the purposes hereafter mentioned. This was accordingly done, and soon afterwards she appointed certain persons as trustees, and the stock was transferred into their names.

The £120 stock was transferred into the names Zachary Langton, Joseph Hornby, Thomas Langton and Thomas Birley. The dividends of £100 were to be shared equally between five poor persons of Kirkham. When one of the persons died, they were to be replaced. The dividends of the £20 stock to be paid to the Parish Clerk, Joseph Brewer, until his death and thereafter to the Parish Sexton.

The £200 stock was transferred into the names Zachary Langton, Joseph Hornby, Thomas Langton and William Birley. The dividends were to be shared equally between five poor persons of Bryning with Kellamergh and five poor persons of Ribby with Wrea. The recipients had to be members of the Church of England and attend church at Kirkham, or Wrea Green Chapel, unless prevented by illness or infirmity.

All these charities were taken over by Kirkham UDC in 1895. Leaving the rent from land for charity could land you in front of a government select committee, as Willows Priest Old Tommy Sherbourne found out...

Tommy, the Brindle Will Case and the Law of Mortmain

When William Heatley Esq. died aged 77 on 21 July 1840, he left a large part of his estate to Father Thomas Sherbourne of the Willows Church, Kirkham. Although he died a bachelor he had two nieces, who through their husbands contested the will. The court case made national news; at this time some Catholic Priests were suspected of using their power over 'mind and soul' to encourage people to leave their money to the church.

William Heatley, born in 1765, was the son of James Heatley, the land agent of Lady Stourton. He lived at Barton Lodge until he built Brindle Lodge in 1808. William went to the Douai Roman Catholic School in France and on his return he was commissioned (Major) into the Lancashire Fencibles, a home defence regiment which was disbanded in 1805. William Heatley began to buy land, mortgage property and invest in shares etc., and at the time of his death he was worth £200,000.

Father Sherbourne met William Heatley when he was at Blackburn, and the friendship was to last a life time.

William Heatley had two sisters, one who died young and one who married a Mr Taylor. They had three daughters, Henrietta, Alicia and Catherine.

Whilst Alicia and Catherine were at boarding school their parents died. Their only living relatives now were their Uncle Heatley and their Grandmother, with whom they stayed when not at school. The two girls left school in 1817. The eldest, Henrietta Dease, was married and living in France. Miss Catherine Taylor met Thomas Eastwood at a party at Barton Grange, now the home of Mr Whallacy. William Heatley disapproved of this marriage. Alicia, later married J. F. Middleton. In 1818, Mr Heatley's mother died and the two nieces stopped visiting their Uncle over his disapproval of Alicia's choice of husband.

When the girls stopped visiting, the only visitors at Brindle Lodge were the Catholic Priests, Reverend Dr Youens, Reverend Richard Thompson Reverend Dr Briggs, John Pratt, Thomas Sadler and William Heatley's steward, James Teebay. The resident priest at Brindle was Reverend James Pope.

In 1822, Father Sherbourne left for Spain and didn't return until 1825. During this period (1824) Mr Heatley made his first will which left £6,000 to the two nieces. The rest of his estate he left for Thomas Sherbourne, to do with what he felt was fit. This meant the estate was left for the Catholic Church. Catherine and Alicia's sister also died in 1824 and left her estate of £15,000 to the two sisters. The girls took a dowry of £10,000 each to their marriages; Mr Heatley thought £23,500 was more than enough money.

Long before 1824, Mr Heatley started buying land and leaving the rent for the use of the Catholic Priests, who were his main source of company. From 1826, there was a long bitter correspondence between Mr Heatley, his niece and her husband, Mr and Mrs Eastwood, which was to continue right unto the point of Mr Heatley's death. The alarm bells started ringing for the Eastwoods in March 1826, when William Heatley was thinking of leaving Brindle Lodge to the Salford Nuns. This year William also asked Father Sherbourne to be his sole confessor.

William Heatley had a stroke in 1827 and stopped holding parties, but he was still occasionally visited by his nieces, if they were careful about 'bugs'.

Brindle Lodge, May 5th, 1828.

I RECEIVED your very pleasant letter of the 18th April in due time, and do not delay long in answering it, both to satisfy your wish, and not to keep you in suspense about one principal point in it. You have an idea or plan of coming over to these parts, and doing me the favour of a

> ᴊᴀ
>
> visit. With all sincerity I tell you that I am glad of it, and I shall be
> most happy to entertain you and Mr. Eastwood, and the part of the family
> you may bring with you; and, under the arrangements you propose, I
> foresee no inconvenience, but a great pleasure. There are, however,
> two things which you will excuse me in noticing: first, the idea of bugs
> terrifies me, and we must use caution in introducing trunks into the house.
> Whatever I brought from abroad of that kind has been kept in the
> outbuildings ever since.
>
> **WM. HEATLEY.**

Catherine Eastwood never went to visit her Uncle. She took it as an insult
that he wrote permitting her to visit, but did not extend an invitation.

> Iᴛ is with feelings deeply wounded, my dear uncle, that I sit
> down to acknowledge your letter containing—I will not call it an invita-
> tion, but a permission, to visit you. It is true, towards the end of your
> letter, you say I shall be glad to see you; but I could not help shaking my
> head on reading this, so appalling was the coldness and so affronting the
> reproach contained in the first part. It is certain that, finding it was

In 1827, William Heatley stayed for a few days at the Willows with his maid
Nancy Banks. The servant of Thomas Sherbourne, Betty Jackson, showed
Nancy a vault under the alter in the old Willows chapel. She said, 'The vault
was intended for William Heatley.' After staying at the Willows, William
and his maid continued to Lytham where they stayed for three months.

The following purchases were financed by William Heatley.

He bought an estate in Grimsargh, the annual income of £100, which he
gave to Reverend Dr Briggs and Reverend Thompson. Two small estates
with the annual income of £50 were for the sole use of Reverend Briggs.
In 1832 he gave Mr Sherbourne £8,914, 17 shillings to buy an estate in
Carleton, which was conveyed to Reverend Youens and Reverend Briggs.
William lent his steward Mr Teebay £3,808. £12,500 worth of shares of the
Great Western Railway were purchased, the dividends used by the priests.

To try and bring the family rift to an end, Mr Heatley, wrote a new will,
dated 15 February 1829. In addition to the old will he now left Brindle
Lodge, an adjoining farm, plus all the furniture to his nieces.

When Mr Heatley died in July 1840, he left a further £30,000 to the nieces
and £10,000 to Father Sherbourne.

Both Catherine and Alicia contested the will through their husbands, but Thomas Eastwood was the main driving force. It went before the Court of Exchequer in January 1841. In April 1841, the case was brought to the Liverpool Assizes.

The main points of contest were that Mr Heatley was weak minded, and the priests controlled his thoughts through fear of the afterlife. Correspondents between the two sides were produced and witness statements read out.

The Eastwoods accused Father Sherbourne of expelling the girls from Mr Heatley's House in 1818. He countered this by saying the girls were never treated as daughters but as nieces and only stayed with their Uncle during the holidays. The reason they left was because of Mr Heatley's disapproval of Alicia's marriage. Mr Sherbourne risked his friendship with William by trying to reason with him. Despite his disapproval he gave Alicia a dowry of £10,000 and asked that the bride and groom visited him on the night after her marriage; which they did.

They accused Father Sherbourne of stopping William from hosting parties from 1827, except for those for the priests. Father Sherbourne put this down to William Heatley's health, after he had suffered a stroke. The Eastwoods also accused Father Sherbourne of telling Mr Heatley to dismiss all his servants and to live with him at the Willows, to further isolate him from his family. This was again disproved. He stayed at the Willows for a few days before moving on to Lytham, this was whilst Barton Lodge was being renovated.

Such was Father Sherborne's influence over William Heatley, he encouraged him to hire a former cotton worker Nancy Heyes, to lecture the servants on spiritual matters. This was again disproved. She was employed as a teacher for the poor women and children of Brindle village.

After Thomas Sherbourne's father died, his mother remarried. In 1805, her husband, Mr Swarbrick gained a place of employment as a butler at Barton Lodge. It was claimed that Father Sherbourne worked into Mr Heatley's trust through his stepfather but it was through his brother, Father Irving that the two friends met.

They also claimed Father Sherbourne became William Heatley's sole confessor until his death. This was true up to a point, as he was his sole confessor from 1826 to 1832, because of William's dislike of Reverend James Pope's eccentric manners. This ended in 1832 when James Pope resigned from Brindle Chapel and was replaced by Reverend Joseph Smith. Between 1832 and 1836, Father Sherbourne visited Brindle 8 to 10 times a year and between 1836 until Heatley's death, 4 to 5 times a year.

They claimed the inheritance was rightfully theirs because William Heatley's Father (their Grandfather) left the bulk of the estate, which William only used to live on. After his father died, the inheritance gave William an income of £2,476 against outgoing of £1,646. One of William's first moves was to sell the Brockholes estate for £58,000, which increased his income by an extra £1,400. At the time of his death he was said to be worth £200,000, which would be £20,000,000 in today's money.

The court case centred around Mr Heatley's mental strength. A statement was read out in court from Thomas Latham, who was once Father Sherbourne's gardener at the Willows. He spoke to Mr Heatley when he came in the garden whilst he was staying at the Willows, and he seemed normal. However, if someone came into the garden he would hide behind a tree looking left and right, like a scared child. Thomas claimed he was also terrified of Mr Sherbourne's house keeper, his cousin Nancy Latham.

J. Orrell was William's surgeon for the last sixteen years of his life and he thought that William was a strong willed, independent man. The statement from Thomas Latham was taken lightly because of his dislike of Sherbourne. Thomas's mother and her sister, Mary Penswick were cousins to Thomas Daniel, who had left all his money on his death to Father Sherbourne to build the old Willows school.

The land left to Father Sherbourne gave a yearly income of £517 against £1,000 for the plaintiffs.

Nearing the end of the third day of the trial at Liverpool Assizes, the two sides came to an agreement and the trial was stopped. After feeling that the priests had cleared their names, they offered the two families £6,000, which they accepted, and the Eastwoods and Middletons accepted that William was competent at the time of making the will.

Thomas Eastwood was not happy. He only agreed to the £6,000 because he thought the Catholic Church was too powerful to fight against and endless mitigation stood before him. What he didn't say was that, expecting the will to be challenged, Mr Heatley put in a clause saying that the will must be cleared within twelve months or everything would go to Thomas Sherbourne.

He even wrote a book which he thought showed that Father Sherbourne was guilty. The book, called the 'Brindle Will Cause', was full of statements and letters between the two sides, to prove this point. He was constantly writing letters to the newspapers, insulting and slandering the Catholic priests and faith and was at one time sued for libel. In November 1850, still not happy, he and his family renounced the Catholic Church and converted to the Church of England. Thomas Eastwood of Brindle Lodge, J. P., died bankrupt on Saturday 20 February 1864 aged 72. Catherine and their ten children survived him and he was buried at St Leonard's, Walton Le Dale.

The problem with making wills during this period was the Law of Mortmain. The main purpose of this law was to stop people leaving land to the church. King Edward I created Mortmain because if people kept leaving land to the church it could eventually become more powerful than the monarchy. The law only covered real estate; personal estate 'money' was exempt. Therefore, you could get around Mortmain by leaving the rent from land in trust.

If you wanted to leave money to an unnamed person, mistress, illegitimate child etc. in a will, you left the money to a 'Secret Trust' who passed the money on after your death. The Catholic Church used secret trusts to avoid the aspects of Mortmain which directly affected them far more than the Church of England. William Billington, Green Grocer of Kirkham, was the secret trust for Father Sherbourne.

The Catholic Clergy had a standard form for wills, and the will maker had only to fill in the blank spaces. The clergy were forbidden from receiving any money for personal use and all the money was paid into a general fund called the Clergy Fund. The fund for this area was banked at the Preston Branch of the Lancaster Banking Company. Ann Brettargh left her money to the church when she died.

> " In the name of God, Amen. I, Ann Brettargh, of Kirkham, in
> the county of Lancaster, spinster, do make this my last will and tes-
> tament as follows:—First, I order all my debts and funeral expenses
> to be paid, viz.: I give, devise and bequeath unto William Billington,
> of Kirkham, grocer, his heirs, executors, administrators and assigns,
> all and every my real and personal estates, whatever and wherever, in
> possession, reversion, remainder or expectancy, to have and to hold
> the same real and personal estates unto him the said William Billing-
> ton, his heirs, executors, administrators and assigns, for his own use
> and benefit for ever. Also, I do hereby revoke all former wills by me
> made, and declare this to be my last will and testament; and I do
> appoint the said William Billington executor thereof. In witness
> whereof I have to this my last will and testament set my hand and
> seal this twenty-fifth day of February, in the year of our Lord 1837.
> Signed, sealed, published and declared by the abovenamed Ann
> Brettargh as and for her last will and testament, in the presence of
> us, who, at her request and in her presence and in the presence of
> each other, have subscribed our names as witnesses thereof. *Ann*
> (L.S.) *Brettargh, Thomas Sherburne, John Booth, William Pile.*
>
> Proved in the Consistory Court at Lancaster, on the ninth day
> of March, One thousand eight hundred and thirty-seven, by
> William Billington, the sole executor therein named.
>
> *Wm. Sharp,* Dep. Reg.

William Billington gave the £3,000 to Father Sherbourne, who gave £100
to four of Mrs Brettargh's relatives a brother, two sisters and her brother's
children. The brothers who lived in Liverpool challenged the will and
employed a solicitor to fight for them. The solicitor was Joseph Bray of Preston.

After a visit from a priest, the relatives dropped the challenge. This shows
the problems with secret trusts. Thomas Sherbourne and William Billington
were carrying out Ann's last request, but to the family it looked corrupt.
Dropping the case after a visit seemed even more suspicious.

A slightly different case involved a Miss Frazer who left most of her estate to
her brother. Just before she died she wrote a cheque for £1,000 to William
Billington, to give to Ushaw Collage.

In 1844 Father Sherbourne was called before the select committee, looking
into the Law of Mortmain. This presents an opportunity to hear what he
had to say on the Brindle Case, and those of Miss Brettargh and Miss
Frazer.

The case of Miss Brettargh was this. She had been a servant in the
Eccleston family and desired me to leave the bulk of her money to
Mr Eccleston in whose house she had lived as a servant, but wished
to do so as not to hurt his feeling, and applied to me about it: and I
said that she could leave it to Mr Billington, a person of conscience
and honour, who would apply it as she wished; and that she could

leave something to her relatives in the same way. She did so the relatives received what was left for them. Mr Billington received £1,700; and I received nothing except £5 in lieu of mourning.

Ann had lived and worked for 50 years with the Eccleston family. He continued, As to Miss Frazer, I was never her confessor. She sent to me repeatedly, but I never went, until her brother's wife pressed me to go. She wished to leave a sum of money so that one of her relatives should always be educated at a college; and I recommended her to give a cheque for the £1,000 for that purpose. For some time, owing to Mr Eastwood, it was not paid: subsequently the money was paid, and the boy is at the college. I suggested, at her request, some other charitable legacies. She offered me £20, which I at first declined, and only accepted when she said that, if I did not receive it, she would not leave a similar sum to another priest.

Referring now to the Brindle Will Case he said, As to Mr Heatley, his nieces had an independent fortune of their own of £10,000 a-piece. The first will was made while I was in Spain and was far more advantages for me than the second, which was made when I was at home. The second will was made without any suggestion or proposals from me. In 1832 he made a codicil, increasing what he had already allowed his nieces. The will was disputed by Mr Eastwood; but shown at the trial to be properly executed: and Sir W Follet, Mr Eastwood's counsel declared in court, that his client and counsel were satisfied that there was no foundation for the proceedings that had taken place.

Mr Cresswell said, 'The verdict will be taken for the defendant, and the will be confirmed; and the bill in equity dismissed.' The parties confirmed the will; and I hoped that all heart-burning were terminated. Mr Heatley's further whole income was about £1,646 per annum; and leaves in land to his next of kin about £600 a-year, and a house worth about £20,000, which would be about £1,600 a-year, allowing 5 per cent for the money invested in land. The rest was left to me; the rental not reaching £500 a-year.

Lord Cresswell was the first Judge in the Chief Court of Probate And Divorce, but the first ever case was before Judge John Addision in June 1858 at the Kirkham Court.

Father Sherbourne continued, The Carleton property was purchased with £10,000 he gave me. I was at perfect liberty to apply the property to my own purposes: if I were to spend any part of my income, from whatever source derived, improperly, I should be accountable for it hereafter; but I am at liberty to apply it as I think fit.Whatever Mr Heatley thought, he never opened his lips to me: so far as I had reason to know his thoughts, his design was to leave me at perfect liberty as to the application of the property. He never mentioned any charitable or religious purpose. The bequest had no more of a religious or charitable character in it, than was implied in the supposition that I should dispose of it for good purposes, and in a proper manner. If the mortmain restrictions had not existed, in all probability this money would have been disposed of in charitable and religious purposes, instead of being left personally to me. I never knew anything of the 'spiritual will'. Mr Heatley was in the habit of giving large sums of money to the poor. I should act on the spiritual will, so far as it was reasonable: I should have done as I should have wished another to do for me.

Six years later in May 1851, Preston Solicitor Joseph Bray was called before the select committee. He had dealings in the three cases mentioned above by Thomas Sherbourne. This time however he was speaking on the opposing side to the priest. Being outside of the Catholic Faith, he looked inwards with suspicion, and was asked first about William Billington.

Mr Billington is a small shopkeeper, a grocer who had nothing to do with the will; he did not make it, nor did he want to have anything at all to do with the bequest. When I spoke to him, he said, 'I must go to the priests'. He an honest sort of man, but a creature of the priests.

Mr Bray talked about Ann Brettargh's case. I wrote a letter to the priest, stating that I was referred by the devisee to him to know what had become of the money, the £3,000; to that letter, I believe I got no answer. I reported this to my clients, the nieces and the nephew; they inquired what remedy they had under such circumstances, and I told them that by filing a bill we could get all the facts. But perhaps I might as well state here, that shortly after the death of the testatrix, an attorney called upon the relatives, the nephew and nieces, and said that in the will referred to there was £100 each for the relatives of Ann Brettargh. And he said that the priests told him that if they did not take £100 they would get nothing. They said, "How is that?" The attorney said, "You are not mentioned in the will, but if you will sign a special receipt." (I think that was the expression). "or a release, I will pay you the money." They believed the statement that they were not mentioned in the will. They thought it best to take the money, and I think three or four of them got £100 each.

When asked who the priest was he answered, 'The Reverend Thomas Sherbourne, of Kirkham, the party benefited by the Brindle Will.' He continued, In making preparations for filing the bill I went to Liverpool to see one of the parties who had received this £100 with respect to his joining the rest in the expenses, supposing we should fail in our attempt. The party told me he had no objection, and I think I got a retainer from the party. About a month after the party called upon me in Liverpool at the very time I was trying the Brindle will cause, and stated that he begged that I would stop any further proceeding, for one of their clergy had been at him and at his mother, and if he went any further he did not know what the consequences might be, the clergy has so much power.

I reported this to my other client in Preston, a most respectable gentleman of the Roman-catholic persuasion, and he said, 'Well, I was afraid something of this sort would take place; I should not like to prosecute this suite at my own risk, and as these parties will not join me, therefore you had better drop it.'

Mr Bray was asked who benefited from the £3,000 and replied, The will is dated the 25th February 1837, and it is proved on the 9th March 1837; within a month it was proved by the executor Billington, the person told me that he had no interest in it; I then inquired where the money was placed at the death of the testatrix, but very soon found on going to the bank that the money passed, I rather think between the date of the will and the probate, and the transaction was then completed; it did not require the probate, for the money had passed a few days before her death, I think; she signed a cheque(not being able to write her own name) upon Messers, Pedders & Company of Preston.

He also said, The will is dated the 25th February and we are bound to suppose that that was the day it was signed. The money passed, I think, between the date of the will and the probate, by her cheque upon Messers Pedders. Mr Billington told me the reason the that the money was transferred before probate was to save duty.

Mr Bray was asked if he could trace all the money beyond the payment. Yes, a Lancashire squire of a very respectable family indeed, whose family this Ann Brettargh had resided in, got I believe about £1,000 of it. Mr Sherbourne, on being applied to, stated that she had made all the money in this family, and that she had left word that he was to send what he thought [proper to this gentleman; and he got above £1,000. The rest I could not trace for want of a bill of discovery; but William Billington is the devisee and the legatee. He takes an interest; he proves the will; and the money passes before the death of the testatrix.

Ann Brettargh died after a long illness on 24 December 1837 at the house of Edward Clifton, Kirkham aged 74 years old.

Mr Bray went on to talk about the will of Mrs Elizabeth Fray. Elizabeth Fray was the house keeper for Father Sherbourne. Her will, dated 20 September 1840, left some small bequest to the clergy and the poor nuns of Darlington. There was a cheque paid out her account at Hornby and Company Kirkham for £1,000. Elizabeth's brother employed Joseph Bray to find this money, and he said,

After her death her brother employed me, and a bill of discovery was threatened to be filed to find out what had become of this £1,000. In a couple of months, the brother called upon me and begged that I would proceed no further; that his wife led him such a life; that one of the clergy had been sent to her, and that she had never slept for a month in consequence of this £1,000 going to be stirred into. He said, 'My wife says that it will disturb my sister's soul'; that the priests had told her so. I said, 'Of course I have no control over it; if you really believe that, there is an end of my interference, if it is likely to disturb her soul, I will not be a party to it; but I do not believe a word of it.' He said 'Well, let me know what your bill is; I dare not go further.'

The £1,000 was sent to Ushaw College through Mr Sherbourne.

Joseph Bray clarified with the judges what Elizabeth's brother said.

The brother said, 'I dare not go any further my wife has never slept for a month,' because her confessor had been to see her; he is living within a few miles of that district; that was the second case in which I was stopped making any further inquiries.'

Mr Bray ended with the statement, I would not trust any class of clergy. I am not speaking now as against Roman-catholics, or against Dissenters, or against Churchmen, but I think there ought to be a check where parties in extremis leave money to persons who are not related to them, disparaging their brothers and sisters, or their nephews and nieces; I think that deeds or wills, giving personal estate as well as real estate, ought to be enrolled, and that some public officer should be appointed to be a witness to the document.

Father Thomas Sherbourne was a victim of the Law of Mortmain, which was amended a few times before being finally abolished in 1960. He was also a victim of Thomas Eastwood's greed. Another reason could be the mistrust between the different religions in Kirkham, at a time when your religion defined your life.

The religions could be split into three groups in Kirkham, Church of England, Catholic and Non-Conformists...

St Michael's

The name Kirkham comes from the Saxon word for a church, 'Kirk' and the Danish word for a Hamlet, 'Ham'. It is unknown how long a church has been standing in Kirkham.

The old church had a bone house built in 1679, which was demolished when the new church was built. The old tithe barn formed the west barrier of the

Sixteenth-century St Michael's Church

church, but was blown down in 1799. The old church nearly fell down in 1777, during an earthquake.

" 1770.
" Memorandum.

   On Sunday the 14 Sep. 1777, att 11 o'clock in the fore-noon, in time of Divine service, immediately after the Gospel, which concludes with these words : 'And there came a great fear on all, and they glorified God, saying that a great prophet is come up among us, and that God hath visited his people ; and this rumour of him went forth throughout all Judæa, and throughout all the region round about.' Then was a shock of an earthquake continued about 1 minute, which came on as of a great rain before it fall.[58] After which a second noise as of a coach at a distance, which encreased until as loud as thunder, the earth still trembling. The church being very old, the con-gregation thought themselves safest to be out of it ; they all (fearing this visitation of God might bury them in its ruins) attempted to get out at once, with shrieks and fearful aspects.

Fishwick's history of the parish of Kirkham

The present church was the third to be built since the Doomsday Book was written. The second was built in the sixteenth century and was replaced by the present church during the nineteenth century over a 30-year period. Rev. James Webber gave permission to rebuild the church in 1820. Whilst the new church was being built, services were held in the National School. The body of the church was built in 1822, at a cost of £5,210. In 1837 the old pulpit was given to the new church in Freckleton.

After the main body of the church was rebuilt, the old tower remained in use. People travelling through Kirkham commented on the high church with a low tower. £1,000 was raised by public subscription for a new tower and the old one was demolished in 1844. The new tower was 150 feet tall and was built by Messrs Simpson.

The foundation stone was laid on 21 November 1843 by Thomas Clifton esquire of Lytham Hall. He was given this honour because it was said that his ancestor Cuthbert Clifton had laid the foundation stone for the old tower in 1512.

A bottle with coins and some newspapers of the day were placed in the cavity along with a list of the subscribers. On top of this was placed an engraved plate with the following inscription:

Parish Church of Saint Michael's Kirkham

The corner stone of this steeple, built by public subscription, on the site of the old tower, on the twenty first day of November, in the year of our lord, one thousand eight hundred and forty-three, by Thomas Clifton Esq of Lytham Hall, in the County of Lancaster.

The very Rev James Webber, dd Dean of Ripon, Rev John Pedder, A.M Curate and Chair of the Committee, Charles and Edmund Birley Esqs,

Lawrence Batley, James Jolley, John Parkinson, Churchwardens.

The new peal of eight bells was cast by Mears of London and cost £900. They weighed over 4 tons and were hung by Mr Cooke from Mears. The bells were rung for the first time on 27 May 1846 by the Preston bell ringers. A service was then held. After that, the bell ringers rang a peal of Bob Majors, consisting of 5,440 moves, for over three hours. That evening, the bell ringers were given a large meal and drinks in Mr Dugdale's Post Office Inn. They were rehung in 1922 for £250. The last part to be rebuilt was the Chancellery in 1853, the stone from the old church was used to build the rear part.

The deceased from the Wesleyan Chapel, which had no graveyard, were buried in St Michael's graveyard. On 21 February 1892, Richard Ford aged 65 and his son Richard aged 26, were buried in the same grave together, after dying on the same day. The father died after a protracted illness and his son from consumption. The bereaved family asked their own minister to take the service and asked for the church bell to be tolled. The Vicar's reply was, 'There is no service in the church today, so they could not have the bell tolled.' The old animosity, still rearing its ugly head.

With all these non-conformists filling up the graveyard, a new one was needed. In June 1893, builder Mr Tomlinson started building the wall around the plot for the new graveyard.

Inside the church is a large brass lectern in memory of Thomas Langton Birley. The five-piece stained glass window was given by his son Arthur Leyland.

St Michael's Church

There are memorials from the old church remaining, one to the Buck brothers. Lieutenant Henry Rishton Buck joined the 33rd Regiment in 1809, served in the Netherlands campaign of 1814, present at the siege of Antwerp, wounded at Bergen-Op-Zoom, He was killed at the battle of Waterloo, 18 June 1815, aged 27. His brother Lt James Buck, 21st Light Dragoons, died 7 Jan 1815, at his mother's house in Preston, aged 19.

There are newer ones for Richard Moore and William Segar Hodgson, and one for Dr Thomas Shaw, near the blocked-up entrance to the France's Family Crypt of Rawcliffe Hall.

There is also a memorial tablet with the names of the men of the church who died in the First World War. The tablet was unveiled on Sunday 24 November 1920 by Sir Harry Cartmell. Mr G. Gregson, ex 7th Battalion Loyal North Lancs, played the last post. A collection raised £26. Harry Cartmell was Mayor of Preston from 1913 to 1919.

The graveyard is probably more interesting than the inside of the church. Here you can find the graves of the Bligh sisters, Betty Titterington, and

Christ church Wesham without its tower.

the Hornby, Langton, Birley, King, Harold Kay, Henry Rawcliffe and Shaw families. It's a peaceful place where you can stand at the grave of somebody who died decades ago and still know a little about them.

As Wesham began to expand, the Kirkham Church was overwhelmed. So, to cope, church services were held in the Wesham School until a church was built. The church opened on 30 June 1894 and was consecrated on 27 September 1894. It cost £3,350 to build and was built without a tower but was designed so one could be added later. The bricks were donated free by Lord Derby, on the stipulation that they were left bare inside the church. A spire was built in 1928 and cost £45,000.

St John the Evangelist

During the reformation, the Catholic faith was kept alive in Kirkham by the Westby family of Mowbreck Hall. They prayed in secret with their own priests until after the reformation. After this period of history, Mowbreck Hall was rebuilt, and a permanent chapel was built inside the hall. The Relief Act of 1791 allowed the building of Catholic churches. William Cottam, a former tenant farmer of Mowbreck, left £400. This was sufficient to build a chapel and a presbytery on his family's land.

The Willows
Church

The chapel and presbytery was built as one building down Willows Lane, in 1809. There was also a small cemetery next to the chapel. The church is known locally, as The Willows, because of the trees that grew around it. After the present church was built in 1845, the old chapel was used for children's services, until being demolished in 1883.

The church of St John The Evangelist was built in 1845 under the guidance of Rev. Thomas Sherburne and cost over £10,000. The architect was Augustus Pugin, who built the church with Longridge stone. Augustus Pugin was the architect who designed the interior of the Palace of Westminster. The tower is 110 feet high and has a peal of six bells. The church was consecrated on 22 April 1845 by the Right Rev. Dr David Brown. The ceremony started at seven, with a parade from the old chapel to the new church and the services lasted until twelve. Afterwards, refreshments were put on in the school for 200 people, provided by Mr Dugdale of the Post Office Inn. The churchyard opened along with the church, and the second one was opened across the road in 1880. This graveyard has an underground vault in the middle – steps lead down to it but it was never used.

This section of an 1848 map shows the old chapel and graveyard, the new church and the school.

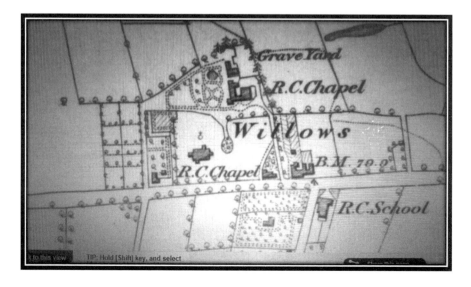

St Joseph's Church Wesham

With the rapid expansion of Wesham, a new church was needed for the 525 Catholic men, women and children who were living in Wesham, but using the Kirkham church. The Rev. Thomas Billington and his sister left £6,000 to build a new church when they both died in 1880. This gave Father Dean Hines of the Willows the chance to build a church in Wesham.

On Saturday 13 July 1884, a parade led by the Kirkham Artillery Band and consisting of 1,000 children and 60 members of the Catholic Brethren, left the Kirkham Catholic School and paraded to Wesham Cross. Here, the Bishop of Liverpool, Dr O'Reilly, laid a foundation stone, under which was placed a bottle and a copy of the Catholic Times. The church for 480 persons, was built on two acres of land acquired from Lord Derby; leaving space for a future school.

The architect was Mr O'Bryne of Liverpool, but the contractor was Mr Singleton of Marsden Street, Kirkham. He employed locals Matthew

St Joseph's Church

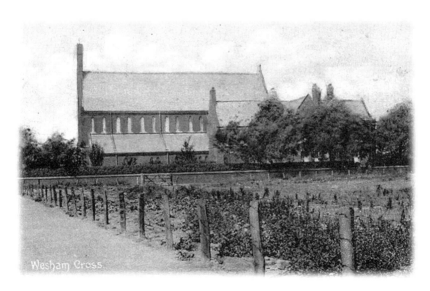

Gardener for the stone work, John Knowles for plumbing, glazing and John Kirby for the plaster work.

The money received from the Billington Family was only enough to build the shell of a church. The church had to collect another £1,000 to finish the inside of the building. The consecration took place on 18 March 1886. It was performed by Dr Cornthwaite, the Bishop of Leeds.

Non-Conformists

The non-conformists were Protestants, who thought the Church of England hadn't distanced itself far enough from the Catholic Church. Their heyday was during the time of the Commonwealth and Oliver Cromwell. During this period, they split into different groups. The two groups, who were to have a future in Kirkham, were the Independents and the Methodists. The Independents later changed their name to 'Congregational', because they were ruled by the congregation.

Kirkham Congregational Church

In the early nineteenth century, the Congregational Church began to expand after years of oppression. Their expansion was mainly in the northern industrial towns of Lancashire and Yorkshire. In places like Kirkham they were considered outsiders. John Bolton at the 'Church Rate' auctions called them 'That Manchester Lot'. He was wrong on that point, because most of the non-conformists' chapels on the Fylde owed their existence to the chapel at Elswick. The Reverend Senier and Reverend Edwards of Elswick had tried to open a station in Kirkham before 1805.

In 1805, Reverend David Edwards of Elswick, and Reverends Walker and Morgan of Preston began preaching alternate weekends in Kirkham.

They met in a building in Slater's Passage off Freckleton Street. This lasted until Spring, when they were stopped from using the room. The following Autumn, they managed to purchase the building. It was a two-storey brick building and the room they used was called the upper chamber, a dismal place, with a dignified name, according to a Reverend Davies.

In 1810, a chapel was built on Back Lane for one hundred worshippers. The land was donated by Roger Charnock. Mr Charnock was the father of Ann, who was married to Reverend John Richards of Walker Fold. They were the parents of R. C. Richards. Roger Charnock was also the great grandfather of William H. Bowdler.

The first preacher at the new chapel was Reverend J. Morrow, who was replaced by the Reverend Capper in 1813. Reverend Capper said about the chapel, 'The Chapel is very badly situated in Back Lane, with a bad road to it and what's far worse, it is so very damp as to endanger any delicate person's life to attend it.' He added, 'We got a stove last week, which we hope will be of service, I sincerely wish we had a better place.' Mr Capper was replaced by Robert Morris Griffiths in 1816.

Reverend R. Griffiths saw Mr Capper's wish come true when a new building called the Zion Chapel was built on the site of the previous one. It opened on 12 August 1818. It was a plain brick building, with small windows arched at the top. It was 46 ft by 65 ft and could hold 350 people. The pews were old-fashioned, deep, and straight backed; about a dozen were family pews. The Bowdlers, Brynings and Crooks all had family pews. There was a large pew in front of the pulpit for the choir and harmonium.

In 1824 a gallery was erected in the chapel, which was used by the Sunday school children. The pulpit was made of oak, later a white marble tablet was erected above it, bearing the following inscription:

In memory of the
REV. R. M. GRIFFITHS,
Who was the faithful, laborious, and successful pastor of this church from 1816 to 1848, and by whose zealous efforts this place of worship was erected.
Died Aug. 2nd, 1859, aged 80 years.
" Looking for the mercy of our Lord Jesus Christ unto eternal life."

Next door to the chapel was an old cottage. In 1834 it was bought and converted into a school, the floor above for the girls, the ground floor for the boys. Rev. Griffiths retired after 32 years' service on 30 April 1848. He died at Kirkham and was buried in St Michael's graveyard.

Mr Robert Best was the successor to Mr Griffiths. Reverend Best was involved in the Church Rate Contest of 1849. Behind the chapel was the graveyard, which opened in 1850. The first person to be buried there was Josias Dagger, the keeper of the chapel, on 7 November 1851. To the right of the Chapel is the Manse (now a nursing home).

The next group of Preachers included Reverend Charles McCordy Davies 1852–1855 and Reverend John Morrison Howie 1856–1860, who was to be replaced by a Mr Parry of Liverpool. Reverend Parry died of fever before he took up the post, his funeral was on the very day he was to start at Kirkham. Mr William Knox took up the post instead and he was to lead the expansion into Wesham.

Zion Chapel 1818

The Independents decided to build a new chapel in Wesham. R. C. Richards donated the land and Benjamin Whitworth paid for the entire project. The building cost £1,000, the foundation stones were laid on Club Day, 7 July 1863. Mr Whitworth laid the foundation stone and Mr Richards placed a bottle, containing coins and some local newspapers inside. The building is now used by Salisbury Electrical.

Reverend Knox left in 1875, replaced by T. R. Davies 1875–1888, Reverend H. H. Theobald, 1889 until 1892, when he left on a missionary to India with his sister.

R. C. Richards bought a piece of land next door to the Manse for a new church, but it was never used. The council bought this land in the early twentieth century to make a new road to connect Marsden Street with Poulton Street, or 'Kirkgate'. In 1896, they decided to build a new church on Poulton Street, on the site of the Bowling Green Inn. The foundation stone was laid on Club Day, 2 July 1896, by Mr James Lever Esq of Thornton Hough. The church cost £3,500 and opened on 19 June 1897.

The Zion Chapel was demolished in 1912 and the site used to expand the graveyard. The stone tablet from the gable end was placed at the end of the graveyard facing Marsden Street. A new Sunday school was built

Laying the foundation stone

Bowling Green Inn Kirkham

in 1913 (now a nursery). In 1972 the Congregational Churches merged with the Presbyterian Church of England to form the United Reform Church.

Wesleyans

In 1841, the Wesleyans of Preston tried to encourage Methodism in Kirkham. The first meetings were held in the ground floor chamber of the windmill on the Wrangway, then later in an empty house on Freckleton Street. They paid a small rent for this house, which could hold 30 to 40 people. They eventually had to leave the house and find somewhere else. This was brought before the preachers in Preston, who all donated £1 each towards a new chapel, and within a short time £46 11*s*. 3*d*. was collected.

A piece of land on Freckleton Street was bought, and two months after laying the foundation stone, the chapel was built. It was built by a Mr Catterall, and cost about £280. This cost was offset by the £46 previously mentioned, and £64 collected at the opening services, along with £142 in private donations. The brick building could hold 200 people and was known locally as 'Tea Kettle Hall', because it stood at the junction of Kettle Well Lane, which branched off Freckleton Street. The first meeting was on 5 September 1844. Reverend John Rattenbury of Manchester was the preacher. In 1887, a new chapel was built on Station Road. The foundation stone was laid on 2 July 1887. The sister chapel was built in Wesham in 1895.

The Church Rates

During the Victorian era, the Church of England was the richest church in the world. Still, parish churches like St Michael's could also raise money for the running costs of a church by levelling a yearly 'Church Rate'. This rate, although small, had to be paid by the entire parish; religious denomination played no part. The non-conformists, who paid entirely for the building and running-costs of their churches and Sunday schools themselves, detested this tax.

In Kirkham, it affected the Methodists, Roman Catholics and the Independents. Most churches didn't raise a rate because it split communities, plus it was proven that voluntary donations raised more money. Kirkham was an exception. The rate (only for the maintenance of the church) could only be raised by the Church Wardens. It had to be passed by a majority vote at a vestry meeting; the date of the meeting had to be advertised for four days. If the vote didn't go the church's way, they could hold a poll.

In May 1849, Reverend Robert Best refused to pay his rate of nine and a halfpenny. He said at the time that he 'could not conscientiously support a system that was full of error.' He was taken to trial along with Reverend Benjamin Whilcock, the Primitive Methodists' minister at Kirkham. The case was tried at the Town Hall, Preston, 14 April 1849, before J. Cunliffe, J. Bairstow and Wm Shawe. Mr Whilcock's rate was 5*d.* They both appeared in court and were ordered to pay the rate plus 7*s.* 6*d.* costs. Edmund Birley and Mr Cornell were church wardens.

Reverend Robert Best recorded the event, in the Congregational Year Book of 1860, it was published in B Nightingale's Book, Lancashire Nonconformity.

We had a fierce conflict against Church Rates at Kirkham. My rate was 9½*d.*, which I conscientiously refused to pay. I offered 5*s.* as a voluntary contribution, but a rate for a religious object I would not acknowledge. I was summoned to appear before the magistrates at Preston and did appear, followed by the issue of a warrant for a distraint upon my furniture. Some of the people thought I would have to go to prison. One farmer's wife came with tears in her eyes and implored my wife to get me to pay, as she did not want her dear minister to go to prison and have his hair cropped. However, it did not come to that. Two policemen came one morning with the superintendent, who was a Roman Catholic. In my absence he expressed deepest mortification and regret at having to make a distraint and politely asked my wife what they must take? She, brave creature, replied that if she told them what to take that would be sanctioning their proceedings. The superintendent then turned hurriedly to his men, telling them to take the chairs from the parlour they had entered. They swept off eight mahogany chairs, valued at £4, leaving Mrs Best, the one on which she sat. These were sold in Kirkham Market Place by a local auctioneer at the very time that I was passing at the head of a funeral to the Church which they were taken to support.

Only six people turned up to the Auction, the rest kept their distance, not wanting to be associated with it.

By 1860, a group led by the Zion Chapel, actively began to resist the Church Rate.

At a Vestry Meeting on the 10th January 1861, the churchwardens, Thomas Langton Birley and James Barrett read out the estimate (below) for the following 12 months.

The Churchwardens' estimate of expenses for the year.			
Wine for Holy Communion		£2	0	0
Bread do.		0	10	0
Moore Michael, Copying Parish Register		1	10	0
Gas Company's Account for lighting		6	0	0
Vestry Clerk		3	3	0
Oakey, Rate book		0	5	0
Coal and Coke for heating Church		7	10	0
Jno. Ward for Candles, Brushes, &c.		2	5	0
Swarbrick, Washing		1	12	0
Jno. Wray, Salary		7	10	0
Do. for heating the Church		2	10	0
Do. for winding Clock		1	5	0
Do. Sundries		0	15	0
Ringers		13	4	0
Wardens for collecting Rate, and other expenses		2	14	0
Sidesmen		1	2	6
Court Fees		12	10	0
Davis, repairing Organ		3	0	0
Guardian Assurance Office		4	2	6
Rd. Lund	0 16 9			
Roberts	0 13 1			
Winstanley	0 11 6			
Ward (Smith)	0 12 10			
Catterall	5 8 7			
Ward, Rd.	0 14 5			
		8	17	2
		70	8	0
		3	3	0
		£67	5	0

At the meeting chaired by Reverend William Law Hussay, a motion was put that the church rate be set at 1½*d.*, which was seconded. Another motion was then put and seconded, that the heating of the church be taken out, however the vicar refused. The £3 3*s.* for the Vestry Clerk was not allowed to be part of the rate. Thomas Langton paid this at the meeting out of his own pocket. The rate was put to the vote and was voted down.

The Vicar then organised a poll to be held on 14 January. At the poll Michael Sharry was refused a vote because he had never paid his church rates (he had a private arrangement with his landlord who paid it for him). The poll was 198 for the church rate and 156 against. The rate of 1½*d.* was levied and ninety people refused to pay it.

On 20 March, the Anti-Rate Group held a meeting in Mr Worsley's Railway Hotel; Reverend J. Hines of the Willows was in the chair.

The following resolutions were passed:

1. That this meeting resolves to resist, the enforcement of church rates, in this parish by every legitimate and constitutional means in our power.

2. That a fund be raised to defray any expenses, which may be incurred in carrying out the proceeding resolution.

3. That the form submitted by Mr Bowdler, for raising the necessary expenses be adopted.

4. That a committee be now appointed, consisting of the following gentlemen: Father Hines, Reverend B Knox, Messrs B Whitworth, R C Richards, James Wilcock, R Bilsborough, Robert Catterall Jnr, Richard Bowdler, John Henry Bowdler, James Leeming, R Gillett.

5. That, R C Richards is treasurer, and Messrs John H Bowdler and Robert Catterall Jnr, are secretaries.

The meeting closed with Reverend Knox, congratulating Father Hines, on his valuable services in the chair.

The people who refused to pay were summoned to Kirkham Court, before Reverend Richard Moore. The first up was John Brindle 8*d*., Joseph Woods 8½*d*., Thomas Gillett 9½*d*., William Worsley 7*s* 6*d*., John Butler 10½*d*., Thomas Wilson 10½*d*., William Fleetwood 8*d*., Mary Livison 3*d*., Richard Bowdler 2*s*., John Whitgreave 4*s* 6*d*., Robert Lawton 4½*d*. The others were

—Messrs. John Wilkin, Thomas Parr, Edward Fleetwood, John Bagshaw, John Woods, Richard Dewhurst, Richard Stanhope, Jonathan Harrison, William Ainsworth, R. C. Richards and Co., George Rogerson, John Danson, Thos. Danson, Richards, Holding, and Co., George Rawcliffe, John Woods, Thomas Dewhurst, Edward Fleetwood, John Brindle, Thomas Appleton, James Duckett, Thomas Ireland, Peter Mc. Villa, Thomas Salisbury, John Nixon, Richard Gillett, Richard Gillett (gardener), John Hornby, Thomas Ogden, Thomas Crane, Richard Charnock, Richd. Billington, Thomas Whalley, Edward Ward, William Whiteside, William Woods, Joseph Woods, Henry Higham, William Birch, Thomas Hornby, Thomas Dirling, Edward Jameison, Thomas Moon, John Moon, William Shaffrey, Robert Moon, J. Barnes, Thomas Simpson, William Billington, Richard Bilsborough, George Hodgson, Cuthbert Catterall, Robert Blacow, William Martin, Richard Walker, John Ainsworth, John Postlethwaite, Henry Nottingham, Henry Moon, Peter Hawthornthwaite, John Butler, William Buckley, William Sanderson ; Revs. W. Knox, and F. Hines ; Ann Billington, Elizabeth Billington, Elizabeth Adamson, Alice Wilkinson, Ellen Wilkinson, and Margaret Rainford.

The Judge Moore thought he wasn't in a position to comment on whether the rate was legal or not and most of the above didn't pay. R. C. Richards and William Bowdler, who at the time were coal merchants together, contested the legality of this rate, on their business premises of 9½d. Their case went to the Chancery Court at York.

Even before the case at York, the wardens tried again in March 1862 to raise a new rate for the following year. When the Vestry meeting was announced, a large group turned up, split into two opposing sides. On one, the members of the Church of England, on the other, the anti-church-rate league, led by the Zion Chapel. The chairman was Vicar Hussay.

Mr Langton Birley read out an item on the estimate, for the next year's rate demand. The Reverend W. Knox of the Zion Chapel would then propose it be struck out. This was then seconded by one of his followers, usually, Richards, Bowdler or Whitworth. It was then put to the vote and put back in by the Chairman. The Reverend Knox would challenge the legality of everything mentioned at the meeting. After the church rate was set, he demanded a poll be held. The poll would always support the rate, as the pro-church-rate group was greater in number.

The hearing at the Chancery Court of York was held on 29 May 1863, the Churchwardens against Richards and Bowdler. The Churchwardens lost the case, for refusing Michael Parry a vote, for recording incorrect minutes, and because the rate included items which were not permitted. Although Mr Richards and Bowdler won the case, the Judge didn't award costs. The Judge thought the Churchwardens were right to bring the case to court. Richards and Bowdler had to pay £10 costs. They then appealed to the Privy Council over the decision not to award costs. At the hearing at the Privy Council in February 1864, the judgement not to award costs was overturned.

In 1865, the vicar was Reverend George Richard Brown, and the church-wardens were Henry Langton Birley and William Harrison. A vestry meeting was held, but none of the anti-church-rate league turned up and the rate was passed unanimously.

Seven members of the anti-rate group refused to pay it. They were summoned to Kirkham Court in April 1866. R. C. Richards was one of the judges, and stood down because of a conflict of interest. Another judge was Thomas L. Birley, who also stood down because his son Henry was one of the churchwardens. They were ordered by the judges, Edmund Birley and

Reverend Richard Moore, to pay the rate. They refused this order and the judges then demanded that goods be taken from their homes and auctioned off.

The people who refused to pay were Richard Bilsborough of Bradkirk Hall, a Roman Catholic, James Thompson, Roger Charnock Richards, Reverend Knox, Cuthbert Catterall, Robert Catterall and Roger Charnock – all non-conformists. Somebody paid the church rate secretly for the Reverend Knox, who had threatened to take it back to the Chancery Court at York.

The first two to have goods seized were James Thompson for 7½*d.* and Richard Bilsborough for £3 0*s*. 11*d*. Six chairs, an armchair and barometer was taken from James Thompson's house. A sofa, an eight-day clock and another barometer were taken from Mr Bilsborough's house. The auction was to be held outside the New Inn on Thursday 3 May 1866.

The Church advertised the auction by placing posters around Kirkham.

The non-conformist created a dummy called 'The Wesham Warden' near the railway station. It held a banner saying, 'Chairs, chairs, more chairs, seizure for church rate, the sale is to take place at Peter Hornby's New Inn, on Thursday next at 4 p.m. Auctioneer not known. Rev S R Brown, H L Birley, Wm Harrison Church Wardens, Richard Moore Solicitor. After the sale, a meeting will be held in the Market Place and speeches made on the old proverb 'That man as not got all his chairs at home'. NB Should the weather prove unfavourable, the meeting will be held in the new school room.'

Mr Topham, the Kirkham auctioneer refused to take part and a Mr Robertson of Poulton held it instead. He suffered a lot of abuse in the way of banter from the large crowd, but everything was auctioned off. The people who bought the goods gave it back to the original owners and it was taken back on a large cart decorated with ribbons. The non-conformist then held a meeting on the Market Square.

This meeting was constantly interrupted by a large group of mill girls from Flaxfield Mill, who constantly screamed out. Later, the National School Pipe and Drum Band came along Church Street and played next to the speakers to further disrupt the meeting.

The next auction was two weeks later.

The first to have their goods taken was Mr Cuthbert Catterall, who was in his eighties. A Police Sergeant and two Constables turned up at his farm in Wesham, where a cart was waiting. They took a clock, a night commode, a gun cupboard, two mahogany tables, a sofa and a parlour carpet (he owed 9s. 11d. plus 14s. costs). The cart then left the goods at the New Inn and proceeded to Mr Catterall's son's house. Goods were seized to cover the 1s. 10½d. rate, plus 14s. costs. Mr Catterall lived on Church Street at the time. When his possessions were being loaded onto the cart (a sofa, a cart saddle, a writing desk, a clock) the Vicar and a few of his congregation walked past. The *Preston Chronicle* reported, 'The Vicar and part of his Flock, who had been to prayers, had the gratification of beholding how the law co-operated in supporting and maintaining the prestige of the establishment'. The goods were again taken to the New Inn.

The last load was taken from Roger Charnock's house, for rates of 7½d. plus 14s. cost, included a looking glass, two mahogany tables, a mahogany sofa and a music stool. Mr Charnock had framed his court summons, but he couldn't get the Police to take it for the auction.

The auctioneer was again Mr Robertson, and there were two main bidders, a Mr Richard Robinson and a man called John Bolton. John Bolton was just bidding because he was drunk.

The auction was recorded in the *Preston Chronicle*:

At three o'clock Mr Robinson mounted his podium, the first up were Mr Catterall's goods.

"A round table, what for it?" said the auctioneer.

"5s." was the first bid;

"That's not reet" cries another.

"It's not in the catalogue," called out a third.

"Where's the clock?" cried out a fourth.

"keep to the rules, or they'll tek advantage on you like they did afore, the Manchester fellows," bawled out a fifth, amid much laughter.

"Any advance," said the auctioneer "on five shillings?"

"Three sovereigns" called out a gentleman and it was knocked down.

"Here's the money, my name's Richard Robinson, auctioneer, formerly of Darwin, and give me a receipt."

The auctioneer hesitated to receive the money or give a receipt and seemed for some time nonplussed. At length, a policeman received the cash but declined to give a receipt.

Mr Robinson told the auctioneer that he had received more than the amount of rate and costs and warned him against going on with the sale at his peril. The auctioneer, who seemed somewhat "bothered", now scarcely knew what to do, but Mr Clarkson, superintendent of the county police of Kirkham told him to go on and never mind, so he invited bids for the sofa, amid calls of "You've not given a receipt," "It's not in the catalogue,"

"yo'r rang," and "Are yo bawn to be baffled o' this road?"

The Auctioneer asked, "Am I to go on Mr Bradley?"

Mr Bradly, vestry clerk said, "Yes auctioneer."

"What for the sofa?" called auctioneer.

"5s." a voice.

"He's not given a receipt." another voice.

"The goods are a receipt." replied the auctioneer.

J Bolton called, "15s. auctioneer."

A voice, "you've got enough money auctioneer."

He replies, "I'm employed to sell all. No advance on 5s." (It was knocked down to a man named John Bolton, who was in a tolerably advanced state of inebriation.)

A voice "Why 15s. was bid for it auctioneer."

Auctioneer, "Well, but Bolton bid it, I could not let him bid against himself."

Bolton, "It's mine."

A voice calls, "Put it up again."

The auctioneer accordingly puts it up again.

Auctioneer, "Well what for it?"

Mr R Robinson called, "Ten Shillings."

The hammer falls, and the lot was given to Mr Robinson.

Bolton claimed, "Its mine, we'll have a law suit about this." (crowd laughs)

The third lot, a dining table was brought out. Auctioneer calls, "What for it? 5*s*. 6*s*. 7*s*., an excellent article, no advance, going, 8*s*., going, going 8*s*., 9*s*., 10*s*., 14*s*." It was sold again to Mr Robinson.

Bolton shouts, 'Don't be done by the Manchester club."

A gun was offered, it started at 5*s*. and ran up to £1, 1*s*., when it was also knocked down to Mr R Robinson, he next purchased a carpet for 26*s*. The next lot was an American clock.

"What for it?" called the auctioneer.

"10 shillings" said Bolton, "I'll make them Manchester folks smart."

The lot was knocked down to Bolton, just as the superintendent of police, whispered to the auctioneer not to take his bid, amid some grumbling at his whispering.

Bolton, on being declared the purchaser said "But I men hev the squab(sofa) wi' it"(roars of laughter).

"No, you must not," said the auctioneer.

"then I wan't hev' th'clock" said Bolton, amid much laughter, and a cry "You're in a fix now."

A night commode was put up at 10*s*. and sold at 13*s*., a cupboard at 1*s*. and sold at 3*s*. 6*d*.; both being bought by Mr Robinson, who it appeared bought them as he had done the other lots, to restore them to the owner. This completed the sale of the goods taken from the house of Mr Cuthbert Catterall, of Mill Farm Wesham for a rate of 9*s*., 11*d*.

The next lots were taken from the house of Mr Robert Catterall. The first lot was a sofa.

"The catalogue says a clock" said Bolton, and "Where's that cart saddle?"

Auctioneer, "Come on what for it? 5*s*., 6*s*. 8*s*., 9*s*., three sovereigns."

At this sum, it was knocked down to Mr Robinson, who again tendered the money, which he declared was more than was necessary for the debts and costs and warned the auctioneer against offering the other articles. No notice was taken of this warning.

A clock was offered next, auctioneer, "What for it? 5 shillings,"

Bolton offered, 10 shillings, and then said, "they'n a club to buy em, where's my squab? What's he selling."

15*s*. was the bid and the clock was knocked down to Mr Robinson.

The Auctioneer, "Now what for this dining table."

Bolton, asked "Where's the cart saddle? Is there any brass nails in it?"

"Any offer? 3*s*." called the auctioneer, at which it was knocked down to Mr Robinson, as was another dining table for 5*s*.

"Now what for a writing table?" asked the auctioneer.

Bolton shouts, "7*s*. 6*d*. Auctioneer."

"I shall not take your bid Bolton." He replied.

"Where's that cart saddle?" asked Bolton.

The desk was ultimately bid from 5*s*. to 9*s*. at which it was knocked down to Mr Robinson.

Bolton, "Come now, sell the cart saddle." (laughter).

A lot of linen, about 120 yards was offered.

Bolton, "5*s*. for it, ha mitch is that a yard."

"10*s*. 15*s*. 20*s*., Mr Robinson again," said the auctioneer.

"Fourteen sacks?" offers auctioneer.

Bolton, "How monny in count?"

Auctioneer calls, "10*s*. 11*s*., a shilling a piece."

Mr Robinson bid 12*s*. and they were knocked down to him.

Bolton, "There's mine, it's a robbery."

A voice "Thaure reet lad it is."

The long asked for cart-saddle was at length brought out.

Auctioneer, "What for it?"

Bolton, "a pound, where's the brass nails."

Auctioneer, "I shall not take your bid."

Mr Richards junior, bid 30s. for it and had it knocked down to him.

Bolton, "Has it brass nails in? I bout it and I mon't hev it."

This closed the sale of Mr Robert Catterall, which had been seized for a church rate of 1s. 10½d. and costs.

The next goods offered were those seized from the house of Mr Roger Charnock of Kirkham, for a rate of 7½d. A sofa was knocked down to Mr R Robinson, for 6s., a mahogany table, £2 to Mr Jacob Sellers, and a table Mr Robinson 8s. 6d. A painted chest of drawers was offered. After an altercation between Mr Bradley, the Vestry Clerk and Mr R Robinson, and between sundry ejaculations of "I'll liver 'em up" from Bolton, they were knocked down at 6s. 6d. to Mr Robinson.

A looking glass(mirror) was offered next.

"You look weel naew" was the cry to the auctioneer, as he held it up to the company and looked at himself in it, and "you've a nice job." This was bought by Mr Robinson for 5s. 3d., as was a music stool for 6s. 6d., amid cries from Bolton that he would "come on 'em for damages." The clock knocked down to Bolton was then put up and re-sold for 7s. The auctioneer stating that Bolton was liable for 3s. loss on the re-sale and 1s. for selling it.

Bolton, "It were noon o mine, mine wur a sqab."

Auctioneer told him, "I shall make you pay!"

John Bolton, spent 4 shillings at the auctions and went home with nothing.

This closed the proceedings at which point Reverend Knox addressed the crowd, this time without the mill girls and the school band. This is the motto of the churchwardens according to Mr Knox:

You shall you shan't, you can, and you can't, you will, and you won't, you'll be seized if you don't.

The stance of the non-conformists was to try and shame the vicar and wardens into ending the compulsory church rate. Stories about the two auctions had been published in most newspapers across the United Kingdom and it wasn't positive for the Church of England.

The last person in the dock was R. C. Richards, who had asked for his case in May to be adjourned. He'd done this because a bill to abolish the compulsory church rate was going through Parliament. It had seemed destined to be passed without any objection, but at the last minute it was rejected. R. C. Richards was summoned back to Kirkham Court in June. In front of Edmund Birley, Mr Kemp and Thomas L. Birley, his fellow judges, he was asked if he would pay the rates of £1 3*s*. 1½*d*. He said he 'would not do so, but would leave it to the magistrates and officers of the court.' R. C. Richards and Thomas Langton Birley had worked together for years. They were on the board of health, board of guardians, both were mill owners, both supported their respected schools, churches and the communities. I wonder if they looked across that packed court room at each other and thought, 'Was it worth it?'

After that day in court the church rates were never mentioned again in Kirkham. Either the wardens had given up and the rate had become voluntary or the Non-conformists just decided to pay. That part of the story has been lost in time.

William Gladstone, the leader of the Liberal Party (whom most non-conformists supported), again put a bill through Parliament in 1868; this time it succeeded. The Compulsory Church Rate Bill brought about the end of the church rates in July 1868. Benjamin Disraeli was still Prime Minister (a Conservative who most of the Pro-rate group supported) but in November of that year he lost the election to the Liberals.

In later years, the Right Honourable William Edward Baxter, a Liberal MP and Privy Counsellor, met Richards Junior. He told him, 'It was the force of your Father's contests at York and the Privy Council that strongly influenced Mr Gladstone into carrying "The Church Rate Bill"'.

The respected churches established some of the first school in Kirkham...

Schools

GRAMMAR SCHOOL

The grammar school was the first school to be established in Kirkham, the date unknown but sometime before 1549. It stood at the side of St Michael's graveyard. Judge Benson, of the Drapers' Company, thought the school was the third oldest in the country, after Winchester, 1387 and Eton, 1441. It was a small clay walled building with a thatched roof, which was run by The Thirty Men and the Vicar. The school being endowed, was free. In 1621, Isabell Birley innkeeper (at the Eagle and Child), walked into the church and gave The Thirty Men £30 towards the school. This was thankfully accepted and encouraged The Thirty Men to ask for more donations.

Sir Cuthbert Clifton gave £20, Mr Westby of Mowbreck Hall £10, Mr Parker of Bradkirk £5, Mr Langtree of Swarbrick £5, Mr Hesketh of Mains 40*s*., Kirkham Vicar Greenacre £4. The townships of Kirkham also donated £170 14*s*.

Most of the gentlemen who gave money were Catholic, except Mr Parker, and there was a struggle about the new headmaster in July 1628. Isabell Birley and her friends wanted a Mr Dugdale to be headmaster, The Thirty Men wanted a Mr Sokell, a Roman Catholic. They asked the Bishop of Chester Johannes Cestrensis, for advice.

> "Apud Wigan 31 July 1628.
>
> "At what day and place divers of the town and parish of Kirkham appeared about the ordering of a schole master thereof for the tyme to come. At their request it is therefor ordered that the whole parish, or so many as shall appear at some day prefixed, after public notice given the Sunday before, shall elect six or nine lawful and honest men feofees for that purpose, whereof a third part to be chosen by the towne of Kirkham and the two other parts by the parishioners generally, of which feofees Isabell Wilding's husband[8] and her heirs, because she gave 30*l*. to the schole maister, shall be one.
>
> JOHANNES CESTRENSIS.   EDW^D BUSSELL."

Fishwick's history of the parish of Kirkham

Mrs Birley lost, and Mr Sokell was made the headmaster. Isabell Birley was the daughter of John Coulbron and the wife of Thomas Birley. After he died she remarried John Wilding. The Eagle and Child was thought to stand in the corner of the Market Square, which was called Eagle's Court. When Henry Fishwick wrote his history of Kirkham, this building was used as the town hall and was the old court house.

In 1655 Henry Colborne, a former Kirkham man who made his fortune in London, left a legacy for the school. The money was invested in land, and the rents were used to finance the school. For the next 170 years, the school was directed by the Drapers' Company of London.

The old school was demolished in 1809, and the gap in the graveyard wall bricked up. The flags from the school were used to pave the path from the vicarage to the church. A replacement building was built opposite the vicarage, on land called the Nearer Church Croft. The building had four classrooms, two on the ground floor and two upstairs. Later, a school house was built, and a school hall was added in 1870.

Although the school was free, the entry requirements were such that the poorest children could not attend. With its classical education, the school

The old Grammar School

was also unsuitable for most local children. In addition, it was being badly run and with the new National School next door, pupil numbers declined.

In 1840, another trust, 'The Baker's Trust' gained more control of the school, the trustees being local and less remote. The Baker's Trust was a legacy left by Rev James Baker, who died in 1670, a former pupil of the Grammar. The school improved after this, with a more fitting curriculum for the area.

In 1879 school fees were introduced, £6 to £12 for children outside of Kirkham and £4 to £8 for children from Kirkham. Children boarding were to be charged £40 to stay in the hostel, or £50 in the master's house per year. To offset these fees, 10 scholarships were offered worth £100, £150 for exhibitions and £200 for girls' education. This put the school completely outside the average family and was strongly opposed. Two public meetings were held, to no avail.

———◆◆◆———

Nearing the end of the nineteenth century, the school was performing well and was financially secure. The main problem was that the school buildings were not fit for purpose. In 1908, plans were made for a new school.

Ten acres of land was purchased off Ribby Road. The foundation stone was laid on 26 July 1910 by the chairmen of the governors, Rev. W. T. Mitton. The Drapers company gave £3,000 towards the new school, which cost £10,000 to build. The new building, for 120 pupils, was opened on 29 September by Judge Benson of the Drapers' Company.

In 1938 the school was extended, adding an oak-panelled library, gymnasium, physics lab, geography room and an art room for £16,160. The school became independent from the Drapers' company in 1944, but a representative stayed on the school board.

KIRKHAM EDUCATION FOUNDATION

The Drapers' company and the Baker's Trust were not the only charitable trusts associated with the Grammar School. There was also the Dr William Grimbaldestone Trust that gave funds for both Treales School and the

Kirkham Grammar; Dr Grimbaldestone's family came from Treales. The three funds, except the Treales part, were combined with the girls' charity school fund, which became one organisation called the Kirkham Educational Foundation in 1894.

Girls' Charity School

In the early eighteenth century, there was no school for girls in Kirkham. In 1760, after they were refused entry into the Grammar school, John Langton of Ash Tree House and Ann Hankinson decided to endow a school from land bought in Freckleton. Thomas Langton, William Shepherd and John Bannett were the trustees. It included two pieces of land, Bannister Croft and Freckleton Croft (1½ acres), plus 12 beast gates on Freckleton Marsh. A site for the school was found at the corner of Moor Street and Orders Lane. This is where the council offices now stand, but at that time this was a piece of waste ground owned by the town.

The Trustees built a small school with bricks from Bradkirk Brick Works. It had a small garden, a house for the school mistress and a turf house. At the school gates, there was a poor box for donations. The girls were taught reading, writing, account keeping, knitting and sewing by a school mistress. The education and uniform, which included clothing, shoes and the blue cloak, was free. On average, 40 girls attended the school, depending on the funds available. The school's direction was driven by the Langtons, free from church involvement. Captain Langton appointed the teachers and decided which girls could enter, based on reading and poverty levels of the parents. The girls were chosen from a list sent to Captain Langton, on 25 December and 24 June.

> ## WANTED,
>
> A MISTRESS for the GIRLS' CHARITY SCHOOL, KIRKHAM. She must not be under Thirty, nor exceeding Forty-five Years of Age,—a Member of the Church of England—a good Needle Woman—and thoroughly acquainted with the National (Dr. BELL's) System of Instruction.
>
> Salary, £25 per Annum, with Apartments in the School House.
>
> The Candidate must address a Letter, post paid, in her own Hand Writing, stating her age and circumstances, and enclosing testimonials of character and qualifications, to THOS. LANGTON BIRLEY, Esq., Kirkham, before SATURDAY, the 21st of MAY.
>
> The appointment will be on WEDNESDAY, the 25th of MAY, at the Girls' Charity School, Kirkham.

Advert from 1836

Between 1761 and 1772, more money and land were donated to the school:

	£.	s.	d.
Of which sum there was given by the trustees of the free-school - -	100	–	–
Mrs. Jane Hornby - - - - - - - - -	100	–	–
Mr. John Langton's legacy - - - - - - -	100	–	–
William Shepherd - - - - - - - - -	50	–	–
Ann Hankinson's legacy - - - - - - - -	40	–	–
Richard Cockin - - - - - - - - -	50	–	–

Joseph and Constantia Brockholes left a legacy worth £425 to the school. It included two cottages with gardens in Freckleton (36 perches), land at Brick Meadow (80 perches), and one cow gate on Freckleton Marsh. Further pieces of land were also in Freckleton, called Two Bakers Meadow, Two Lamma Leches and the Bank (6 acres).

Further money donated between 1772 and 1813 included:

	£.	s.	d.
Amongst others, the Rev. Zachary Langton - - -	50	–	–
Mrs. Abigail Langton's legacy - - - - - -	45	–	–
Mrs. Crook's legacy - - - - - - -	50	–	–
Mrs. Eccles's legacy - - - - - - -	10	–	–
Mr. William Langton's legacy - - - - - -	20	–	–

The expenditure of the school in 1825 was as follows:

	£.	s.	d.
Schoolmistress's salary - - - - - - - - -	20	-	-
Allowance for firing - - - - - - - - -	4	4	-
Clothing for the girls, about - - - - - - -	55	-	-
Books and stationery, about - - - - - - -	2	-	-
£.	81	4	-

In 1860, the old school was abandoned after a new school was built by Thomas Langton Birley of Carr Hill House on Poulton Street. Mrs Ann Birley had managed the old school by herself since 1839.

By 1892, the school had closed, and the building was used as a community hall, until being converted into a savings bank. When it closed, the remaining charitable funds were transferred into the Kirkham Educational Foundation, along with £500 when the old building was pulled down in 1895 and the land sold.

The plan in 1895 was to leave the Grammar School for Boys and build a new school for 100 girls. In 1900, the Drapers' company offered £4,000 towards

Girls Charity school

the new girl's school, which was to be built on Station Road. The school was to be called the Colborne High School for Girls, but the trust had insufficient funds to run this school and the Drapers' company withdrew their offer. This ended the story of the Girls' Charity School.

National School

Due to the expansion of Kirkham at the beginning of the nineteenth century and the failure of the Grammar School to teach the poorer children of Kirkham, a new school was needed. A petition was sent in 1813 to Christ Church by the Curate P. G. Slater. It was signed by John Birley, William Langton, Jas Fox, Thomas Hornby, William Hornby and Vicar James Webber. The request was to build a two-storey building, on a quarter acre site belonging to Lord Clifton, next door to the Grammar School.

Lord Clifton refused the request, but after an intervention from the Dean and Chapter of Christ Church he relented. The school opened in 1815 and was governed by the vicar and the churchwardens. The boys were taught on the ground floor by the headmaster, the girls upstairs by a headmistress.

The school was a subscription school, paid weekly with the 'school penny', until the education act of 1903. It was supported by the Langton, Birley and Hornby Families who, every January, held a charity ball to raise funds. Mrs Langton Birley visited the school at Christmas time to hand out toys and oranges to the children. In 1874, the school was reorganised after the education act. The infants were taught with the girls, and the boys stayed separate; this stayed in place until 1954.

In 1891, plans were put in place to build a new school or convert the old workhouse on Marsden Street into a school, but sufficient funds were not raised. Plans were submitted again in 1904 to renovate the school, but these plans were held up by a group supported by the non-conformists, who wanted a council school to be built. The Vicar suspected them of wanting to close all faith schools in Kirkham and Wesham, and to open one large council school.

In January 1907, the Education Board ordered the school to be called the Kirkham Church School. This year finally saw alterations to the school costing £600 to accommodate more pupils. Another £600 was spent on land for a playground. The architect planning the alterations, was amazed that a school of this size had never had a playground.

The school became a primary school after Carr Hill opened and was extended in 1963, when a gym, assembly hall, cloakrooms were added. The old school building was demolished in 1980 and a new school built.

The managers of the St Michael's school and the Vicar were the force behind the building of a new school in Wesham. It was the second school to be built in Wesham, after the Congressional School opened in 1864. The land was purchased from Lord Derby in 1878 and the school was built in 1881, leaving an extra piece of land for a future church. The building could hold 120 girls and infants, but within a year was found to be insufficient. A bazaar was held raising £713, and the school was extended in 1882 to hold 270 girls and infants. When the infant boys became old enough, they were sent to the National School in Kirkham. This practice ended in 1905.

Willows School

In 1826 Thomas Sherbourne built a Catholic school on the corner of Ribby Road and Bryning Fern Lane. The school, along with a master's house, was built with money left from Kirkham clock maker, Thomas Daniel.

In 1840 the school was being guided by a Mr Townley. It had day pupils and a small number of boarders. The children's education cost 20 guineas per annum, which was paid quarterly. Pupils had to give three months' notice to leave. The focus of the school was preparing the children for an ecclesiastical education.

In 1870 Father Hines, reacting to the Elementary Education Act of 1870, (that made education compulsory for all), expanded the school. Work was started on a new wing in February 1871 and cost £400. A classroom and a large school room was added, plus a cloakroom and lavatory. The girls used the new class room. In the old part of the school, the infants were taught downstairs and the boys upstairs.

In 1894 the school was again extended when a new classroom with a cloakroom was built next door to the school. In the old school new windows were fitted and a new heating apparatus was installed. This work was done

The Old Willows School 1971

when the Irish population was at its peak, and just after St Joseph's school had opened. The new classroom closed in 1900 and was converted into a club.

The building was in use for 150 years, until a new one was built at the end of Victoria Road. The old school then suffered the same fate as Mowbreck Hall, a building closely connected to the Catholic faith in Kirkham. It was left derelict, attacked by vandals, set on fire and finally demolished. Houses now cover the site.

In 1890 a new Catholic school was built in Wesham, attached to St Joseph's church. This could hold 192 children, but in 1905 this averaged about 112.

KIRKHAM AND WESHAM SCHOOL

In 1902, the Education Act provided funds for non-denominational schools. After this date, a group in Kirkham pushed for a council school to be built, which could offer an education without an enforced religious view. This group was mainly led by the Non-conformists.

In 1909, two sites were found in Kirkham, both situated on Station Road, one near the railway and the other where the school is now. The building cost £4,000 to build, of this £2,500 was provided by the government and the rest from the rate payers. It opened on 29 August 1910, with 38 pupils and 12 infants. By 1912, this had reached 80 children excluding part timers.

The school closed on 4 October 1915 at 11:45 a.m., during the First World War. This was to allow the children to say goodbye to their fathers who were leaving for the front.

In 1917, Major Dowling from the Fylde Military Hospital visited the school. Plans were put into place to move the children into the Methodist Chapel opposite, and use the school as a 120-bed military hospital.

The school closed on 28 March 1918, and the Easter Holidays were spent moving into the Independent Sunday School on Marsden Street instead of the Methodist Chapel. The school re-opened on 27 October 1919.

In August 1939, the school was used as a reception centre for evacuee children and parents from Salford. A new classroom was built in a prefabricated building in 1948, and when Carr Hill opened in 1957, the school was reorganised into infants and juniors. The new kitchen and dining room were built in 1960. A new infant school was built in the recreation ground by the graveyard in 1973. This burnt down on 17 May 1980. Parents were asked if the school should be re-built or the two schools joined together by extending the Nelson Street School. The latter was chosen, and it opened on 9 December 1983.

The last major change was when Carr Hill School was built. There were three potential sites under consideration in Kirkham. Ribby Hall Estate was rejected because the children from Kirkham and Wesham would have to cross a busy main road. Milbanke Estate was also rejected, because the site needed much work to clear it for building. In 1954, a 13 acre plot of land was purchased, part of it belonging to Carr Hill Estate and the rest from the council. Fylde Divisional Education Committee held a meeting to decide the name for the new school. The choices were Kirkham and Fylde Secondary Modern, Dowbridge School or Carr Hill Secondary Modern. The final name was chosen. The school for 450 pupils opened in September 1957. The official opening was on 22 of July 1958, when the Duchess of Kent unveiled a plaque. The event was filmed and can be viewed at the Central Library of Manchester.

Another School not mentioned was the Catholic School at Mowbreck Hall. This closed when the new Chapel at the Willows opened. Mowbreck Hall was the grandest of the large homes surrounding Kirkham. The cloth merchants also began building large homes as their wealth increased…

MOWBRECK HALL

The most interesting historic house in the Kirkham area was Mowbreck Hall, the seat of the Westby family. Originally from Westby in Yorkshire, the family settled in Mowbreck in 1233. The original hall was a wooden building, surrounded by a moat, set in an estate of 331 acres. The first recorded occupant of the hall was William Westby, who was the Sheriff of Lancashire in 1345.

John Westby lived at the Hall during the reformation in 1530–91. He was a staunch Catholic who refused to adhere to the new religion. As a famous recusant, he gave sanctuary to travelling priests, who in turn held Mass in secret. He was arrested twice for his beliefs and imprisoned, and at one time he had two thirds of his land confiscated.

On the 'wrong' side again during the Civil War, another John Westby (1608–62) supported King Charles I. One of John's sons, Thomas, died fighting for the King. The hall and land were confiscated after the war, the family having to pay £1000 to regain its property, the deed of conveyance being signed by Oliver Cromwell.

The family was also suspected in the Lancashire Plot to restore James II. Although they took no part in the later Jacobite Rebellion, the field in front of the hall was known as Martyrdale. A fight was supposed to have taken place there during this rebellion.

In 1730 after the restoration, Robert Westby rebuilt the hall, which included a chapel and priest's room. This was the place of worship for Catholics,

Mowbreck Hall front entrance

until a new chapel was built at the Willows in 1809. Reverend John Jones 1760–75, Reverend Robert Banister 1775–1803 and Reverend William Irving 1803–09 were the resident priests during this period.

Robert Westby died on 23 June 1762, but despite being married twice, he had no children to take over the hall. For the next one hundred years, the house was occupied by tenant farmers and the priests until they [the priests] left for the new chapel at the Willows.

In 1862 Captain Jocelyn Tate Fazakerly-Westby moved into the hall with his wife Matilda Harriet. Captain Fazakerly-Westby was a former officer in the Scotch Greys and the Lancashire Hussars. He was a J.P. and Deputy-lieutenant of Lancashire.

Mrs Fazakerly-Westby died on 3 November 1875, after returning home from a party at Ribby Hall. She suffered an attack of paralysis on her left side (a stroke), whilst in her bedchamber and died two hours later. The funeral was a large event, attended by all the main families of the area and the streets from Wesham to Kirkham, were lined with local well-wishers. Matilda was buried in St Michael's Graveyard, aged 44.

Captain Westby had been declared bankrupt on 28 June 1870. When Matilda died in 1875, she left all her estate in trust and the rents and profits of the estate for the sole use of her husband. He could also use and occupy Mowbreck Hall on one condition. 'That he did not marry, or make a contract of marriage, with his cousin Miss Kate Westby, or hold or maintain, any intercourse with any member of her family.' This gave him a home to live in and an annuity of £200 a year.

Captain Westby never married his cousin but he did marry Miss Beatrice Jervis of Ambleside in 1879. Mowbreck Hall and the estate were sold to Lord Derby in 1894. Mr Fazakerly-Westby died on 23 July 1925.

Lord Derby's agent, Alderman Windham E. Hale (1864–1958) lived in the hall with his wife Sara Kezi (1862–1920). When the Hales left, this began the slow death of what once was a great house.

Later in the 1940s, the hall became a residential hotel. In 1962, it was turned into a country club, with a restaurant and ballroom by Kenneth Newby. In 1968, Ellis Kit bought Mowbreck and turned it into a night club with strippers and musical acts. After this, the house stood empty and was attacked by vandals and later set on fire. The Hall was demolished in the early '80s and the grounds are now a caravan park. Nothing remains of the house, but the Coach House and the East Lodge are still standing.

Mowbreck Hall 1845

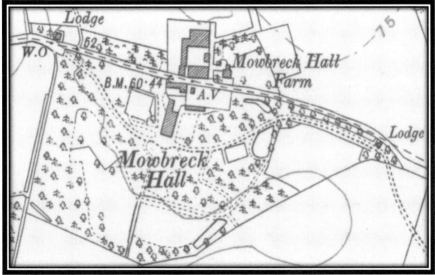

Mowbreck Hall was famous for ghost stories and legends. One was a secret tunnel from the Hall to St Michael's Church, which the priests could use to escape through. This is highly unlikely, as it would be a great feat of engineering to build this tunnel and also the last place a priest would want to escape to. One ghost story was about a White Lady, who was supposed to haunt Mowbreck Lane, maybe Mrs Fazakerly-Westby.

Another ghost story was 'The Gory Head of Mowbreck Hall', a story about the appearance of a bloody head above the alter in the chapel. The head – if true – belonged to a priest called George Haydock, who had been executed for his beliefs in 1584. It was seen by his father Vivian Haydock, a Priest staying at Mowbreck, just after his son's execution. Vivian was said to have collapsed on seeing the head and later died. Along with other sightings of the head, ghostly figures of priest appearing and disappearing have over the years also been reported.

This picture shows Alderman Windham E. Hale, on the balcony, addressing Lord Derby's tenant farmers from Preston, North Lancashire, and Bispham. This was to celebrate his fifty years' service with Lord Derby in 1935.

Milbanke House

Milbanke House was built in 1808 by Thomas Birley in on what was then the outskirts of Kirkham. The 20 acres estate stretched along Station Road from Coronation Road to the Wrangway Brook. Most of the stone boundary wall of the estate is still standing. Thomas lived together with his wife Ann in the house which overlooked his factory, Flaxfield.

Thomas died on 1 April 1847 aged 65, and his son Arthur Leyland inherited the house. Arthur Leyland was born at Milbanke in 1820, the sixth son of Thomas. He married Jane Addison in 1855, and they had two children, John Leyland, born 1857 and Edith Jane, born 1861. John worked in the family mill, Flaxfield, with his brothers but left in 1867 and lived a private life until his death in 1877. Jane lived at Milbanke until her death on Christmas Day, 1889.

Milbanke House in 1845

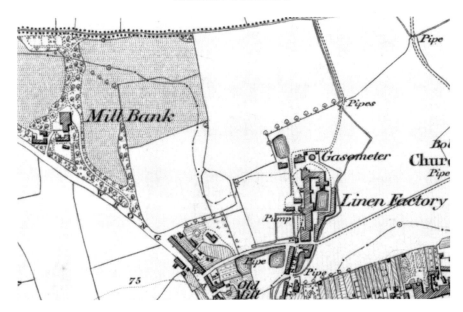

Their son John Leyland inherited the house. John was a steam enthusiast who built a ½-mile-long narrow-gauge railway in the grounds. He also built a steam engine and two carriages in his workshop at Milbanke. He later added a large ornamental pond with model steam launch. There were six tennis courts, where Fylde Tennis Club played, and a small golf course. The house and grounds were opened for Lytham school children, for their annual day trips. John Birley who spent most of his time at Hastings Place Lytham, came back to Milbanke House for his final few days before his death. He died on 16 March 1906. John died a bachelor and the house passed to his brother-in-law, Horace Mellor, who had married John's sister Edith Jane Birley.

Horace Mellor played cricket for Lancashire and along with his brother owned Stourton Cotton Spinning Mills in Preston. John and Edith had one child. Edith died at the age of 32, on 8 June 1894, whilst on holiday at St Augustus in Scotland from Syncope, from loss of blood pressure. The coffin was conveyed in a private carriage, attached to a train to Lytham Station. Edith was buried in St Cuthbert's graveyard.

Milbanke House

Robert Lund, of 10 Birley Street was John Leyland Birley's coachman for many years. He died on 27 December 1925 aged 71; two days later his wife June Fleetwood Lund died.

Even before John Leyland's death, the house was rarely lived in. He spent more time at his residence in Lytham and Horace seemed to have done the same. Horace gave us the name Mellor Road, when land belonging to the estate was built on. The contents of the house were auctioned off in August 1908. The farm belonging to the house was kept going as Milbanke Poultry Farm by John Hull, who lived in the lodge, until he passed away in 1935, aged 83.

"MILBANKE," KIRKHAM.

MESSRS. E. WILSON and SON have received instructions from the owner, to Catalogue and Sell by Auction, at the above Address, on WEDNESDAY and THURSDAY, August 5th and 6th, the Whole of the Valuable HOUSEHOLD APPOINTMENTS contained therein:—Fine Dining-room Suite, in mahogany; superb Sideboard, in mahogany; large Dining Table, carved old oak Chair, five old Chippendale Chairs, Grandfather Clocks, Display Cabinets, Mantel Clocks, Mirrors, China and Glass, magnificent Bookcase; Turkey, Brussels, and other Carpets; quantity of Musical Instruments, Music, large quantity of Books, occasional Tables and Chairs, superb Bedroom Suite, in maple; other Suites, in mahogany; full-sized Billiard Table, excellent Feather Beds and Hair Mattresses; about 500 bottles of Old Port and other Wines, kneehole Writing Tables, in mahogany; Bronzes; and a large quantity of other Lots too numerous to mention.

SALE TO COMMENCE EACH DAY AT 10 30 A.M. PROMPT.

The Contents of the above Residence will be on View, Tuesday. August 4th, from 11 a.m. to 4 p.m.; by catalogue only, for which a charge of 3d will be made, and which may be had from the Auctioneers, Lytham, or at Milbanke, on August 4th.

Horace Mellor died in 1942 aged 91, on the Isle of Man; the same year the house passed into history. The military took over the estate and the house went up in style when the Royal Engineers blew it up. The farm and lodge were demolished, and the grounds formed part of Brookwood POW camp. Nothing remains now of Milbanke House, except the stone boundary wall running along station road. Station Road was later diverted through the former front gardens of the house, to avoid the sharp corner at the bottom of the railway bridge. The house was never sold, so there are no newspaper adverts describing the inside of the house. The contents were however auctioned off in August 1908, and the advert gives you some idea of the grandeur of the place.

Carr Hill House

Carr Hill House was built in 1780 by Thomas Langton for his son William Langton. The estate consisted of a large house set in nine acres of gardens and woodlands, stables, shippons and loose boxes. There was also a coach house, three cottages and later South Farm with 34 acres of land. When William died on 7 May 1814 aged 56, the house passed to Edward and Dorothy King, relations of the Langtons.

Edward King esquire, of Hungrill in the county of York, was the Vice Chancellor of the Duchy of Lancaster and Bencher of Grays Inn. His brother, Captain James King, sailed with Captain Cook on his last ever voyage and his other brother Walter King, was Bishop of Rochester. Dorothy died in 1816, and Edward died in 1824 aged 71. Both were buried in St Michael's graveyard; their tomb is a grade two listed monument.

After Edward's death, his eldest son took over the house. Edward Bolton King was known as Mr Bolton King, and was a Liberal MP for Warwick (1831–37) and Warwickshire South (1857–59), when he retired from politics. He was also a Lieutenant Colonel in the Warwickshire Yeomanry. A keen horseman, he was the Kirkham Harrier's hunt master jointly with Mr Langton Birley. He was married twice, firstly to Georgina Knight, who died, and secondly to Louisa Palmer, who died in 1920. Bolton King died on 23 March 1878 aged 77, at his residence, Chashunt in Warwickshire.

Christopher Waddington of Glebe Windmill complained to Georgina King in 1838 about the estate woods blocking the wind and preventing him from milling. It was all to no avail, and he later lost the windmill after getting into debt.

Thomas Langton Birley and his wife Ann bought the house from the Kings in the mid-1840s. He bought the Lordship in 1870 and became Lord of the Manor. He also bought the Glebe Land from the church, which made up South Farm, and the lease on the windmill.

When Thomas Langton Birley died in 1874, the house passed to his son Henry Langton Birley. Henry died a bachelor, on 4 January 1920, at the age of 82. Later that year, the estate was auctioned off into lots. Richard Haighton Penny bought the house and Manorial Rights. The farm was sold separately to James Ainsworth, who built the present farm house.

Richard Penny came from Nelson and was involved in the cotton trade. At one time he had 116 looms running in Sunnybank Mill. He was involved in a car crash with Arthur Ainsworth (of Station Road), who was driving, near Galgate, Lancaster. Richard suffered serious head injuries, and two months later, on 14 August 1931, suddenly died. Richard, who was a town councillor for Kirkham, is buried in the old Zion Chapel Graveyard. Edward G. Sergeant bought the House from Penny's family.

Carr Hill House

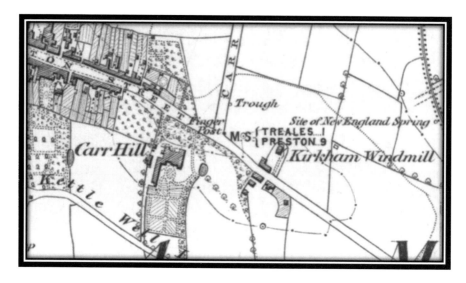

Carr Hill 1845

Later, in 1934, he also bought South Farm. He turned the house into an hotel. Part of the farmland was turned into a horse racing course, after at first being blocked by the local council.

The track was three laps to the mile and the first race was held on 31 March 1934. It was a success, and the track was extended in May that year, to one and a half miles long.

The hotel closed when it was commandeered by the military as an Officers' Mess, immediately at the outbreak of the Second World War. The race course also closed when the War Agricultural Committee took over the land. The military left in July 1946. Carr Hill reopened as an hotel and restaurant. Part of the grounds became Kirkham Caravan Park, used mainly as temporary accommodation, for RAF families.

In 1947, Edward Sergeant put in plans for a £240,000 sports stadium and greyhound track, but the council refused. He reverted to horse racing, but it didn't last long and soon closed. In 1957, Carr Hill School was built on the site. The playing fields are on the site where the track used to be.

The hotel became a night club, 'The Lower Deck Club' which closed in 1963. The building was demolished that year and houses now cover all the former estate.

Ribby Hall

Ribby Hall was built in 1799 by Joseph Hornby. Joseph was a local flax and linen merchant who, in partnership with his brothers Thomas and William, owned three mills in Kirkham. The family were the biggest land-owners in the area. The hall was part of a 771-acre estate.

After Joseph Hornby died in 1832, his son Hugh Hornby, with his wife Ann, lived in the Hall. They had three children, Margaret, Mary and Hugh Hilton. When Hugh died on 25 October 1849, the hall passed to his son Hugh Hilton Hornby. Hugh Hilton died on 6 September 1877 at the age of 39. He was playing croquet on Ribby Hall lawn during a party, when he collapsed and later that evening died. His widow Georgina later married the vicar of St Michael's, Henry William Mason. She died on 21 December 1906.

Hugh Hilton's mother Ann died on 21 December 1878, leaving her two daughters in the hall. They left Ribby in 1890 and moved to Norbreck, near Bournemouth. Margaret Ann Hornby died an invalid after a four-year

Ribby Hall in Hugh Hornby's day

illness, on 14 May 1899. Mary Alice Hornby died on a visit to Scarborough, on 5 July 1907. The maid found her unwell in a chair, and went to call a doctor. When the maid returned, Mary had died. She like her sister, was conveyed by train, in a coffin back to Kirkham and buried in St Michael's. None of the children of Hugh Hornby, known locally as 'Squire Hornby', had had children and the family line ended with Mary's death. They are all buried together in St Michael's graveyard, except Georgina, who is buried in the new graveyard with Reverend Mason.

After the Hornby sisters moved to Bournemouth, Robert Fitton and his wife Margaret moved into the Hall. Robert Fitton was the head of Richard Fitton Cotton Spinners and Manufacturers of Oldham and Manchester. They lived there until his death on 29 February 1904, aged 54.

The same year William and Emily Duckworth took up the lease and moved into the Hall. William was a successful chemist and water essence manufacturer, owner of Duckworth and Co. in Manchester. The Duckworths were keen horticulturists and opened their rose gardens, greenhouses full of chrysanthemums and formal gardens, to raise funds for The District Nursing Association.

Ribby Hall Gardens

The gardens at Ribby Hall. Kirkham, where the chrysanthemums are making a magnificent display, were thrown open to the public yesterday afternoon by the courtesy of Mr. W. Duckworth.

About 500 people visited the gardens, and paid £25 5s. 6d. for admission, which will be devoted to the funds of the Freckleton. Warton, Wrea Green and District Nursing Associations.

Messrs. T. H. Myles, C. Lyon and J. W. Smith officiated as stewards.

In 1910, the estate was auctioned off into lots by the Hornby's relations. The Duckworths bought the house and gardens. The 54 acres of grounds became a separate farm and dairy. Also sold off were Sand Hole Farm, Little Tarnbrick Farm, Tarnbrick Farm, Hill Farm, Nearer Hillock Farm and Farther Hillock Farm. All the fields either side of Ribby Road and Bryning Fern Lane were also sold, plus, the four cottages, outside Ribby

Hall's present entrance. The Duckworths left Ribby Hall in 1942, to live with their daughter in Knutsford. William died in 1949, Emily in 1951; they are both buried in Wrea Green.

In 1945, the Ministry of Education asked the Mary Cross Deaf and Dumb School to provide spaces for 50–60 new pupils. They bought Ribby Hall in 1946 and the school opened in 1948. The juniors of the Mary Cross School were taught there until 1969.

In 1970, the Lancashire Show moved to Ribby Hall, and at this point the formal gardens were cleared. In the 1980s, the hall was converted into flats and the grounds into a holiday park. Most of Ribby Hall estate remains, including the house and the lawns. The farm and dairy are now the restaurant and family bar. The coach house, which was damaged by fire in 1909, is currently used as a holiday cottage. Part of the walled gardens are now the tennis courts.

Ash Tree House

Ash Tree House, a Grade II listed building, was built around 1750 by Thomas Langton. The house was the second to be built on the site; the original building was owned by the Browne family of Kirkham. The house passed to the Langtons, when John Langton married Elizabeth Browne, in the early part of the eighteenth century. John Langton's son, Thomas, built the present house. The new Georgian house had three reception rooms, seven bedrooms, a brew house, laundry and stables. The last Langton to live there was Captain Thomas Langton, who in 1822 mortgaged the house to Thomas Birley.

Richard Moore, a solicitor, rented the house until Charles Birley sold it to Dr William Wright Shaw in 1888. Dr Shaw, held his surgeries at Ash Tree House; previously he had lived and worked at no. 4 Church Street. When Francis Hudson was killed in the Club Day Disaster, he was taken to Ash Tree House, where he was pronounced dead by Dr Shaw. The building was also where the recruits for the First World War were examined. Dr Shaw

died on 31 May 1915, aged 50, from heart failure. The house became a memorial to the fallen soldiers of Kirkham.

It was bought by the Church of England in 1919 and was renamed Church Memorial House. The first caretaker appointed was met with hostility.

CORRESPONDENCE.

A KIRKHAM MEMORIAL.

To the Editor of The Lancashire Daily Post.

Sir,—It was decided not long ago to build a church house or club in Kirkham, to be called the "Parish Church Memorial House." This was subscribed to liberally by all parishioners, according to means, including many disabled men   The House was nearing its completion, and a few days ago it was stated that a caretaker was required.   The appointment was given to a retired union workhouse master, whilst disabled and limbless men are parading the streets of Kirkham unemployed, and have to exist on the pittance granted by the Government.   Thus they are forced to accept the obvious indignity of what is nothing more or less than living on charity.   Why was this vacancy not advertised, or at least a general committee meeting of the parishioners called, to allow applications from local men?   Please wake up, you who subscribed liberally, and don't let your church affairs be run by a few whose sole motto is always "self."—Yours, &c.,

PARISHIONER.

Kirkham, September 21st.

The building was opened by the Bishop of Whalley and Vicar W. T. Mitton, on Saturday 18 October 1919. It contained a reading room, a billiards room, a ladies' room and committee rooms. During the Second World War, it was the HQ for the Local Volunteers' Force. Later, it became the offices of the Labour Exchange, before reverting to a Doctors' Surgery in the early 1980s.

Hillside House

John Birley built Hillside House for his son Edward. Edward died in 1811, before it was completed, and his brother William moved into the house. The Grade II listed building is two storeys high, with cellars and an attic. The ground floor had three entertaining rooms; upstairs were nine bedrooms. It had a large garden, with a tennis lawn, greenhouse, vinery and vegetable garden. Two stable wings, with carriage doors and lunettes above, flank the house; the right-hand wing is now 'The Stable Bar'. There were two houses attached to Hillside for staff.

William Birley died on 28 May 1850, aged 70, whilst living in London. Hutton Birley moved into the house with his wife Alice. Alice died in August 1875 aged 31, a week after giving birth. Hutton moved to Wrea Green in 1890, where he died in 1921.

After Hutton left, Helen Maud Birley Matthews moved into Hillside with her husband, Gervaise Arthur Matthews. Helen's sister Ada also moved into the house. After Helen died in 1915 and Gervaise in 1918, Ada Birley took on the house. Miss Birley was President of Kirkham and District Nursing Association. She was the first ever female town councillor, and Justice of the Peace. When she once advertised for a gardener, she stipulated that he must have one hand. This was part of a campaign to get injured First World War Veterans into work. Ada died a spinster, on 8 March 1934, the last Birley to live in Kirkham.

Captain B. Robertson moved into the house next, a former soldier of the Manchester Regiment and leader of the Kirkham Royal British Legion. The last person to live at Hillside was F. Harris, a chemist. The building was converted into a hotel in 1956 and later became a restaurant. Recently it was converted into a night club, 'The Cube', but is now derelict.

Glebe Mill

There has been a Windmill on Carr Hill for centuries, but the present one – what's left of it – was built in 1812, replacing an old wooden windmill; which itself was dismantled, sailed across the river Ribble, then re-built in Southport. Christopher and John Waddington bought a forty-year lease, for a rent of ten pounds a year, from Lord Clifton of Lytham Hall. They had to build the windmill, various drying rooms, and install all the machinery themselves. The mill had to be given back in a good condition, after the agreed term.

In 1821, Christopher saw a greyhound in danger of being hit by the sails, and on rescuing the dog, he was struck on the arm by one of the moving sails, which came within one foot of the ground. His arm was sliced from the elbow down to the fingers, and he had to have his arm amputated. There was another accident on 27 January 1847, the inquest was reported in the *Preston Chronicle*.

> ACCIDENTAL DEATH.—An inquest was held yesterday, at Kirkham, before R. Palmer, Esq., coroner, on the body of John Ormond.—Robert Ormond, of Ribby-with-Wray, said the deceased was his nephew, and was about 16 years old. He worked at a mill in Kirkham, and on Wednesday morning last, about ten o'clock, as he was going out of the mill, one of the sails of the mill hit him on the head and knocked him down. Witness went up to him and lifted him up, when he found that he had received a severe wound on the right side of the head, from which the blood was flowing. The mill was stopped, and the deceased carried into it. He did not speak, but was quite insensible. Mr. Gradwell, a surgeon, attended him, and bled him; but he died at about nine o'clock on Wednesday evening, from the injuries which he had received. A verdict was returned of " Accidental death."

By 1838, the Waddingtons were in debt, for which they blamed Mrs King of Carr Hill House, whose woods blocked the wind. Christopher Waddington claimed to be losing £80–£100 a year due to not being able to mill when the wind blew from the west. They also complained of paying ten pounds' rent, when a similar sized mill in Lytham was only paying seven. Christopher asked Mr King to chop his trees down, but he refused. He petitioned Lord Clifton, stating his wife had left him, he only had one arm and would end up in the workhouse, all to no avail. They lost the mill the following year, owing £411.

An advert was placed in the *Preston Chronicle* on 4 September 1841, selling the lease. From this we know what the mill consisted of the wind corn mill, a drying kiln, one pair French stones, one pair meal stones, one pair shelling stones, a groat machine, flour machine and dust sieve.

The mill was re-let to a Mr Hudson for £41 a year, and in 1854, the mill was again let to the new owner of Carr Hill House, Thomas Langton Birley, for £21 per annum. In 1863, George Wilkinson of Wrea Green Steam Corn Mill* took over the Kirkham windmill. He refitted the stones and built a warehouse in Wesham, which could hold 3,000 sacks of corn, meal and flour. The mill by the turn of the century was disused and left to crumble. In the 1970s the tower was incorporated into part of a house.

This aerial picture of 1932 shows how the woods of Carr Hill House blocked the wind. There was a second corn mill in Kirkham, built towards the end of the eighteenth century. This mill stood just off Station Road and was called the New Mill. It became disused in the early nineteenth century and was being used as a pot store in 1850. The Methodists' first Sunday school was held in the ground floor chamber.

*George Wilkinson had fitted a steam engine into the Wrea Green windmill, instead of relying on wind. Unfortunately, the boiler blew up on Tuesday 22 November 1861, after the boiler had run dry of water. Undeterred, he later built a four storey steam mill with a four storey warehouse next door, separated by iron fire proof doors on Whitworth Street. Along with the mill, he also built a large six-bedroom house. The high-pressured steam engine powered four pairs of French grinding stones and made the local windmills defunct.

If Christopher Waddington ended up in the workhouse it wasn't all doom and gloom. There were three groups in the workhouse, the old, infirm and the children, whose lives were made as comfortable as possible, the second, people who fell on hard times, who were helped to help themselves and finally the hated vagrants whose lives were made as hard as possible, Christopher being disabled, probably belonged to the first group...

The Workhouse

In June 1726, the town's bailiff, John Langton of Ash Tree House, went from home to home to ask the Kirkham residents about building a workhouse. The answer was yes, and a workhouse was built on Back Lane, which is now called Marsden Street.

In 1834, the government passed the Poor Law Act, which prevented people receiving poor relief unless they entered a workhouse. They would be clothed and fed, and the children would receive some schooling. In return, all must work several hours a day. It was designed to reduce the cost of looking after the poor, take beggars off the streets and encourage people to look after themselves.

In 1837, there were two workhouses on the Fylde, Kirkham and Poulton.

The large three-storey building on Marsden Street was the workhouse. When this picture was taken in the 1950s it was still being used as a boarding house

The Poulton workhouse was closed and plans were put in place to build a single large workhouse in Kirkham. Until 1837, the Kirkham Workhouse was governed by a body of men called the 'Select Vestry', who were appointed at each vestry meeting. After 1837, it was governed by 'The Guardians of the Fylde Union', who held their first meeting on the 1st February 1837. Robert Thompson was the first clerk, elected in 1843, and didn't retire until February 1898, after 55 years.

In 1844, a new workhouse was built on Moor Street for £5,399. The building could hold 200 inmates; this number was often exceeded. It wasn't classed as full if everybody was in a bed. The building was badly designed, with small windows, high up in the wall. The floors were flagged with stone, which made the building cold and damp. The inmates shared large iron beds, with straw mattresses; the vagrants slept on boards.

FYLDE UNION.
To Contractors and others.

PERSONS desirous of CONTRACTING for the various departments of Work in the ERECTION of the NEW UNION WORKHOUSE, at Kirkham, in the County of Lancaster, may inspect the Plans and Specifications, at the Office of the Clerk to the Guardians, Freckleton-street, Kirkham, on and after Monday next; and sealed Tenders (endorsed Tender for Building) will be received there, addressed to the Clerk, until Wednesday, the 4th day of October next. The Contractors will be required to enter into Bond, with sufficient sureties, for the due performance of their Contracts.

The Guardians do not pledge themselves to accept the lowest tender.

By order of the Board,
ROBERT THOMPSON, Clerk.

Kirkham, September 15th, 1843.

The old workhouse on Marsden Street was sold by the guardians, and then it was used as a boarding house until being demolished in the 1960s.

To be Sold, by Auction,

At the house of Mr. John Barnes, the Black Horse Inn, in Kirkham, on Tuesday, the 7th day of October next, at Six o'clock in the Evening, subject to such conditions as will be then produced,—

ALL that Freehold MESSUAGE or BUILDING, situate in the Back Lane, in Kirkham, in the county of Lancaster, lately used as a Workhouse, and late in the occupation of the Guardians of the poor of the Fylde Union, with the Garden, Yard, Stable, Shippon, Outbuildings, and Appurtenances thereto belonging, containing, in the whole, in statute measure, 1 R. 11 P. of Ground, or thereabouts.

The Building, which is a very good one, and in substantial repair, is 22½ yards in length, and 11 yards in breadth, and is capable by a very trifling outlay, of being converted into a convenient Manufactory.

The premises may be viewed on application to Mr. John Brindle, or Mr. Richard Rawcliffe, the Overseers of the poor for the Township of Kirkham; and further particulars may be had on application to Mr. JOHN BRINDLE; or Mr. RICHARD RAWCLIFFE; or to Mr. RICHARD MOORE, Solicitor, Kirkham.

Kirkham, Sept. 24th, 1845.

In 1864 a new ward was built; the workhouse could now hold 260 paupers. This also gave the guardians the chance to split the children from the adults and re-arrange the inside of the building.

Room no. 1, on the men's ward, which was being used to store potatoes and straw, was to be cleaned and used as a workroom. The potato store was moved into a building in the gardens. The old police cells became the men's washrooms. A new shed was built next door to the piggeries. This shed became the store for the straw and where the men could break stones in wet weather. A room on the boy's ward, which had previously been used to break the stones, was now to be used as the boy's play and washroom. The door between the men's and boy's wards, was to be constantly locked, apart from when the boys went to school, or at meal times.

At the end of the new women's ward, a partition wall was built, to create a room for the school teacher. The girls and the women exchanged wards. The adjoining door was to be locked, just like the door between the boys and men's wards.

This union of workhouses gave the name Fylde Union Workhouse and was governed by 25 guardians, who met once every two weeks. The number of guardians depended on the size of the town's population. Kirkham and Poulton both had two guardians, the rest just one. These figures changed over the years, especially on the coastal towns. The guardians were elected every year until 1882, when it was changed to triennially.

A governor and matron, usually husband and wife, a nurse, school mistress and medical officer (Dr Thomas Shaw) looked after the inmates.

The 26 townships covered were split into three districts, each with a relieving officer and medical officer.

The Kirkham district covered: Kirkham, Weeton with Preese, Greenhalgh with Thistleton, Medlar with Wesham, Treales, Roseacre and Wharles, Clifton with Salwick, Newton with Scales, Freckleton, and Ribby with Wrea.

The Poulton district covered: Poulton, Carleton, Hardhorn with Newton, Great Marton, Layton with Warbreck, Bispham with Morbreck, Thornton, Singleton, Little Eccleston with Larbreck and Elswick.

The Lytham District covered: Lytham, Little Marton, Westby with Plumpton, Bryning with Kellamergh and Warton.

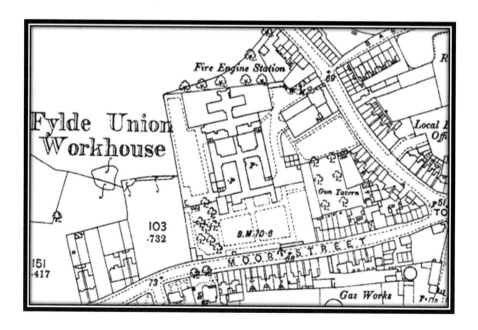

Picture post card of Moor Street workhouse

To enter the workhouse, or receive medical care, you had to apply to the relevant district relieving officer. If you qualified (deserving poor) for help, he gave you a ticket, which you took to the workhouse to gain entry. If the head of the household went in, so did the entire family.

In August 1852, Owen Llavalla, a labourer from Ireland, tried to enter the workhouse. He told the Kirkham relieving Officer, Mr J. N. Davies, that he had hurt his groin making hay on a farm in Marton, and was unable to work. On entering the workhouse, he refused to remove his boots. The officer being suspicious, pulled his boots off and a purse with 19*s.* 6*d.* rolled out. He was sent to court and Judge Edmund Birley sentenced him to 14 days in Preston Prison. He also had to pay expenses from his funds.

The workhouse tried to be self-sufficient. The women sewed clothes, baked, tended the gardens and orchards. Pigs were bred and sold. It had its own bake house and kitchens. The old and infirm carried manure for the vegetable garden and did the hoeing. Some supplies had to be bought in.

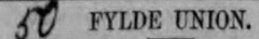

FYLDE UNION.

CONTRACTS FOR PROVISIONS, CLOTHING, BEDDING, &c.

THE Board of Guardians for the Fylde Union are desirous of Contracting for a Supply of the undermentioned Articles for the Union Workhouse, at Kirkham, from the 25th day of September inst., to the 25th day of March next, namely:—

Beef, Flour, Oatmeal, Coals, Cheese, Milk, Butter, Sugar, Treacle, Tea, Coffee, Tobacco, Salt, Hard and Soft Soap, Candles, Clogs, Cotton, Fustian, Barracan, Linsey, Sheeting, Flannel, and Blankets.

Persons wishing to Contract for all or any of the above Articles, are requested to send Sealed Tenders, marked "Tender for Provisions, Clothing, or Bedding," as the case may be, addressed to the Clerk to the Board of Guardians, at his Office, in Kirkham, on or before MONDAY, the 24th of SEPTEMBER instant.

All Tenders must be accompanied by Samples, or particularly specify the Quality of the Articles to be contracted for. The Contractors will be required to deliver the Goods at the Workhouse free of Expense, at such times and in such quantities as the Board of Guardians, or any other competent Authority, may from time to time direct; and also, to enter into formal agreements, and give Security, for the due performance of the Contracts, if required.   By order of the Board,

ROBERT THOMPSON,

Kirkham, 11th September, 1849.   Clerk.

The men broke stones, which were used to pave the streets and the roads. Some of the able-bodied men were sent out to work on farms. The farmer then paid any wages due, directly to the guardians. R. C. Richards used the inmates on his farm. In June 1864, he handed over £8 to the board; about a thousand pounds in today's money.

During the Cotton Famine in 1862, the workhouse was full, so extra work was found oakum picking at the Freckleton Street Mill. Oakum picking was when old rope was cut into two foot lengths and beaten with a wooden mallet to remove the tar. It was then split into single fibres and cut into small pieces. The fibres were then mixed with tar or grease to produce oakum. The oakum was then used as caulking to fill the gaps between the wooden planks on ships to make them watertight.

In January 1869, the board asked Mr Hibbert of Preston to draw up plans for a new infirmary. The infirmary was to be built separate to the rest of the workhouse, but with easy access to the kitchens. It could hold forty patients – twenty of each sex – and was divided from the rest of the workhouse by a wall. The building also had a Dead Room (morgue). The building cost £2,575 and was completed in nine months.

In the workhouse, there was a vagrants' ward, where tramps could get overnight accommodation, after being given a ticket from the police. The tramps first had to break a set amount of stones in return for a bath, food and a bed. The one problem was that the workhouse gates were locked at 9 p.m. each night. The tramps were then taken by the police and put in one of the town's lodging houses, at a cost of four pence to the guardians; sleeping rough was illegal. So the tramps waited until after 9 p.m. to report to the police to save being put in the workhouse. This however was remedied in 1879 when the guardians gave Police Inspector Stafford a key for the gates.

This worked for Kirkham, but the guardians were still paying to put vagrants into the lodging houses in Blackpool and Poulton. Blackpool was exceptionally bad, especially during the summer. The Board called this the 'Tramp Season' and in 1881 was costing the Fylde Union 30 shillings a night.

In 1882 a new Vagrants' Ward was built, along with a porter's lodge for £1,600. The first porter, John Clay, could now let the tramps in at any time during the night. The ward had separate baths and sleeping cells for the men and women. There was also working rooms in which to break the stones.

The vagrants were often called casuals and stayed anywhere between 1 and 14 nights. In the first 6 months of 1895, there were 91 casuals (85 males, 4 females and 2 children). During this period, they broke 29 tons, 2 c.w.t of stones. The stones cost 2*s*. 3*d*. per ton to buy and the broken stones were sold for £3 5*s*. 9*d*. per ton. The large stones were broken with a sledge hammer by the inmates. The casuals then broke them down into smaller stones. The average casual broke 6 c.w.t, 3 q.r, 12 lbs of stones during their stay. The workhouse master reckoned his old men could sledge hammer 13 c.w.t (660 kilos) in two hours. The four women had done nine hours of scrubbing and cleaning of the vagrant's ward. The children didn't work. The money spent on their accommodation and food during the six months was £4 1s. 4d.

In 1882, the guardians were being encouraged to build a new infections ward but were reluctant because all cases of infection in Kirkham would be burdened onto the Union. They did however extend the women's part of the infirmary in 1884, which was struggling to cope. New toilets were built jutting out of the ward, with side windows for ventilation. Two small buildings were attached to each end of the ward, connected by a glass corridor. In one went the fever cases, the other became the 'Lying in Ward' (confinement).

The true victims of the early workhouse system were the children. There were different reasons for children to be in the workhouse. Some came in with their families, but there were also abandoned children, illegitimate children and orphans.

In the early years of the Moor Street Workhouse, the children shared the wards with the adults and went to the Kirkham Schools. They were vulnerable in the workhouse and stigmatised in the schools. This however changed in 1861, when a classroom opened inside the workhouse. The first school mistress appointed was a Miss Cooke, who received a salary of £30.

Things improved further when the children were split from the adults inside the wards. The boys stayed in the workhouse until thirteen and then were found an apprenticeship.

The girls followed a similar path; in 1884, Mrs Birley, Mrs Richards and Miss Shaw asked permission to go into the workhouse and read to the girls; which was granted. When they felt the girls were ready, they would take it upon themselves to find them a position of employment in the outside world.

The children were lucky in the sense that some of the guardians and the chairmen were from Kirkham; Charles Birley was chairman in the 1850s and William Segar Hodgson was the chairman for 28 years.

The workhouse children had a yearly day trip to Blackpool and took part in the Club Day Parade. The appearance of the children during these events were recorded in the newspapers; the reputation of these powerful men depended on the children's appearance. The workhouse children were invited to shows at the Co-op hall and similar events in the town.

Christmas was celebrated by decorating the dining hall and having a meal of roast beef and plum pudding. Gifts of sweets, fruit, toys were routinely donated by the wealthy, and tea, tobacco and snuff, for the older residents.

The Children's Act of 1889 allowed neglected and abused children to be taken from their parents and placed in the workhouse.

In 1895, Inspector Dawson of the NSPCC, sent 13 children from two families in Kirkham to the Union Workhouse, all in a starving and destitute condition. Some of the children were from a family called Murphy. Their parents had just been released from prison after a two-month sentence for child neglect. The others were from an old man called Atkinson and his young wife, whose children were barefoot and starving. Police Sgt Callard found the children and informed the NSPCC.

Timothy Murphy was summoned to Kirkham Court for neglecting his children, Patrick 12, John 10, Mary 9, Jane 7, Timothy 5 and Ann 2. He lived on New Row, Kirkham, but worked at Fleetwood docks, where he lodged. His lodger said, 'He came home in drink every night.' Inspector Dawson found the children with insufficient food, badly clothed and living on the mercy of their neighbours, even though the father earned £1 a week. Dr Shaw examined the children. He said, 'They had no bruises, but were thin and had a hungry look. They had vermin but were not covered, were below par and covered in sores from living in poor conditions.' The children were placed in the infections ward, their mother was also removed into the workhouse. Murphy, who pleaded guilty, was sentenced to another two months' imprisonment, with hard labour. The children from the Atkinson family were suffering through destitution, not neglect and were not charged.

The care of the young girls was often undertaken by volunteers. They lost the protection of the workhouse guardians at the age of 16. Miss Shaw suggested that this be raised to 18, to which the board agreed. Interventions like this encouraged the board to accept female guardians. In 1892, Mrs Ashworth, Mrs Sharples and Mrs Baxter became the first female guardians.

People on the Fylde with mental health issues were assessed at the Kirkham Workhouse. If somebody was sectioned, they were sent to Whittingham or Winwick Asylums. The patients stayed under the protection of the Fylde guardians, who had to pay the expenses of the patient to the asylum. The guardians also sent a visiting committee every six months, to check on their charges.

In 1894, the question arose again about expanding the Workhouse. The plan was to build a new board room and use the old one for the expansion projects. They first asked the Local Board of Health, if they could move the fire station and town yard, possibly to the site of the old charity school. The board could then build the new boardroom on that site. They agreed in principle but said it would take years to arrange. They then looked at buying some cottages and land from Mr Birley, next door to the fire station. The price he wanted was too high.

Even if they carried out this work, it wasn't the answer to the solution. When the Moor Street Workhouse was built, the population of the Fylde was 20,000. In 1895, it was 60,000. Under the Union Laws, the workhouse had to accommodate 1 per cent of the population (600 paupers), plus the population of the Fylde was not going to stop at 60,000. There were other points:

1. Apart from the vagrants' ward and infirmary, it wasn't worth spending any money on the buildings.

2. It was important to totally separate the children from the adults.

3. Even if the children were removed, there was still not enough space on the existing site, to rebuild a workhouse sufficient for present needs and future enlargements.

4. There was no adjoining land which could be procured, except under restrictive covenants which would render it useless, for Poor Law purposes.

The board of guardians was offered land by Lord Derby at £150 per acre. In February 1896, the Board accepted his offer. The plans for the new workhouse were agreed in January 1897. It was to be built in Wesham, capable of holding 300 inmates, but with the space to hold an extra 500. The old workhouse was to be used only by the children. After the plans were agreed, the project was put on hold. The numbers in the workhouse were averaging 130 paupers and the board was split on whether to build the new one.

In the meantime, the old one was connected to the National Telephone Company System. A new horse ambulance was purchased. The old paupers' ward had new windows fitted. They stopped breeding pigs and auctioned the Tamworth Boars at the Kirkham auctions. The board of guardians numbered 40 in 1899. Blackpool, which was now the biggest town on the Fylde, asked for more representation. It was agreed, and an extra 6 guardians were elected onto the board, taking the number to 46.

In March 1895, Father Hines of the Willows asked for the Catholic children between the ages of two and seven to be sent to the new Catholic orphanages, St Vincent's School, Preston for boys, and Leyfields School Liverpool, for girls. The board felt it might be an advantage to some, but not to all. The request was refused.

In August 1896 they provided the old ladies with serge skirts and bonnets to wear at the Willows Church. Mrs Sharples organised a new matron to look after the young children, who had been previously looked after by the young female inmates and who had been caught teaching the children to swear. The men received boots, instead of clogs.

The board on Mr William Segar Hodgson's guidance, as previously mentioned, bought 10 acres of land in 1896 from Lord Derby, plus another 10 acres in 1899 costing in total £3,099 for the new workhouse. Whilst waiting to start the building, they used some of this land to grow wheat and to employ the able-bodied inmates. The wheat was then sold at the Kirkham auctions. Part of the land was also leased out.

SALE OF WHEAT, at WESHAM (three minutes from Kirkham Station).—Mr. E. G. HOTHERSALL is favoured with instructions to Sell by Auction, on TUESDAY NEXT, July 30th, about four acres of Well-grown WHEAT, the property of the Fylde Board of Guardians. —Sale at Three o'clock (after the Fat Sale at the Kirkham Auction Mart).
E. G. HOTHERSALL, Auctioneer.

The old arguments for the new workhouse remained. In January 1902, it was decided to commence building the new workhouse, with immediate effect. The loan for the land had been paid at this point, another credit for Mr Hodgson, who stepped down as chairman in April 1901, after 28 years. He'd been elected a guardian in 1861. He stayed on the board and became the chairman of the building committee, taking responsibility for the erection of the new workhouse.

The foundation stone was laid on 2 July 1903 by William Segar Hodgson and the building was to be completed by 1 June 1906.

In 1904, the old workhouse had a fire inspection. The inspector advised on three points. The two vagrant wards only had one exit into the main building. If the main building was on fire, there was no escape route. He advised that doors be put in at the ends of each ward. The tramp cells were locked with keys. He advised that bolts be fitted instead, as it was quicker to slide a bolt across, than to go along the cells unlocking doors. The third point, the other doors had two bolts, top and bottom. He suggested they removed one and moved the other to the centre of the door.

In the last few years, a dentist was appointed to the Union. The organist Mrs Trickey, it had been discovered by the board, had been playing every Sunday Service for ten years without pay. It was decided to pay her £5 a year. Thanks to the proximity of Blackpool, some unusual people appeared at the workhouse gate. One night an injured acrobat from Kensington and eight Piccinini Minstrels from Philadelphia turned up. Complaints arose about the children being sent to the outside schools, infected with ring worm and sore heads. This was put down to the Medical Officer being off sick.

The new workhouse was finally opened on Wednesday 27 March, 1907. Mr W. Hodgson, Chairman, opened the building with a golden key. It was meant to be William Segar Hodgson, but he was unavailable.

The buildings cost £45,129 3s. 9d. The water tower cost £1,910 3s. 9d., which was £295 3s. 9d. more than planned, but the well had to be sunk deeper to obtain more water, and this could now supply 1,000 gallons an hour. It was built so high to provide the necessary pressure in case of a fire. The boundary wall cost £615 15s. 3d., architect £2,652 14s., special items £6,014 18s. 2d. and £3,500 for furnishings. The total cost was £59,823 8s.; the budget was £60,000.

On 20 June 1907, the adults were transferred into the new workhouse. The board moved into the new boardroom on 17 July 1907.

The paupers were buried in unmarked graves in the Wesham churchyards. Children born inside the workhouse were given the address 1 Derby Road on their birth certificates to avoid the stigma of being born in there. The infirmary was also used as an emergency ward for accidents outside of the workhouse, just like the old Moor Street workhouse.

James Proctor, aged 72, was one of the first people to die in the workhouse, in 1908. A veteran of the Indian Mutiny, with the 18th Staffordshire Regiment, the Workhouse Master, Mr Perry, organised a military funeral for him. A gun carriage with six horses, was borrowed from the Artillery, at Fulwood Barracks. The 1st Battalion LNL provided a firing party. The parade left the workhouse at three. The Loyals led the parade with their guns at the reverse, followed by the gun carriage with the coffin covered by a Union flag and six inmates. Sgt Butler, Private's R. Cross, S. Blacow and W. Fisher joined the Parade. The Grammar School provided the guard of honour. After the service led by Rev. T. Walton, James was placed in his pauper's grave.

James Proctor was not the only link to the army. In November 1916, the Fylde Auxiliary Military Hospital opened on the site, with 120 beds for injured soldiers.

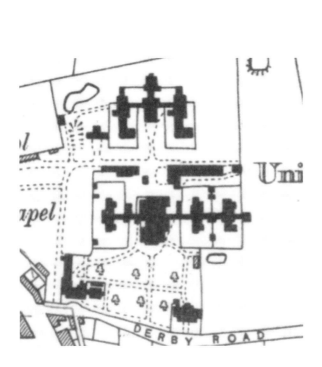

The building had central heating and was lit by gas.

Sewing, baking and cleaning the workhouse was still done by the female inmates and the men still tended the 100 pigs and 2 heifers and gardens, but the days of breaking stones were gone.

In September 1925, the workhouse was full with 303 inmates and 98 casuals, the guardians looked at expanding the male accommodation. The options were to build new wards, erect ex-army huts, or transfer some men to the old infirmary on Moor Street. The Ministry of Health refused permission for any of this. The ministry said that the spare capacity in other workhouses must be used up first. In December that year, 50 inmates were transferred to Chorley Workhouse. The following November it was again full, but there was no space at Chorley, Preston, or Garstang. After this winter, the numbers in the workhouse reduced back to normal levels of about 220 inmates and 50 children in the home.

Christmas in the workhouse infirmary Wesham 1913

The doctor on the left is William Wright Shaw, who died in 1915. He was replaced by Wesham Doctor W. A. Smith. Doctor Smith, who later joined the Royal Field Artillery as Medical Officer, was killed in June 1917, whilst serving in France.

The year 1929 was the beginning of the end for the workhouses. Until this point the Fylde board of guardians could set rates to pay for the costs of poor relief. This was now to be undertaken by Lancashire County Council. The Lancashire C. C. created new ratable areas and combined the old boards with urban district councils. Blackpool created its own assessment committee, but still sent people to Wesham and the Kirkham homes. The Fylde and Garstang Guardians Committee was formed with 18 members shown below.

FYLDE AND GARSTANG AREA.—Including Lytham St. Annes Borough 3, Fleetwood U.D. 2, Kirkham U.D. 1, Poulton-le-Fylde U.D. 1, Thornton U.D. 1, Fylde R.D. 2, Preesall U.D. 1, Garstang R.D. 2, Fylde Guardians 2, Garstang Guardians 1, County Council 2 ; total 18. Meet at Kirkham and Garstang.

The two boards worked together through a transitional period. The first meeting of the new committee was held on 12 February 1930. There was some continuity with William Hodgson remaining as chairman and some former guardians staying on the committee. The guardians held their last meeting on 26 March 1930. On the wards, each bed was fitted with a wireless with headphones. Mr Hodgson switched the system on and broadcasted a message to the inmates, thus ending the 90 years' service of the Fylde guardians. Mr William Hodgson came from Poulton le Fylde and joined the board of guardians in 1881. He became the chairman in 1904 and held the post until his death in 1945. He was also a county councillor, J. P., and was knighted in 1935. The workhouse now became the Wesham Public Assistance Institution.

By now, less able-bodied people entered the institution and it was mainly filled with sick and infirm patients. Work such as cleaning the wards, laundry and cooking was now undertaken by staff. Extra nurses were required to care for them. The costs spiralled and so did the death rate. On average 20 people a month died in the Wesham Institution.

During the 1930s, the infirmary was used to assess people who were suspected of having mental health problems. Two men were brought to Wesham in June 1935, both for a 14-day assessment, William Alan de

Prez aged 38 of New South Promenade, Blackpool and John Kirk aged 61 of Henry St, Blackpool. They both shared a two-man room and for some reason, Alan de Prez barricaded the door and beat Mr Kirk to death with an iron fender. William was sent to trial at Manchester Assizes. Dr Higson thought that 'he was insane, and a dangerous lunatic.' He was declared unfit to plead.

In October 1939 a 98-bed emergency hospital was built at the rear of the institution. The Fylde Emergency Hospital was mainly used to house old and infirm evacuees from April 1941 to the end of the war.

The National Assistance Act of 1948 finally abolished workhouses, the year the NHS was created. The Wesham Institution now became Wesham Park Hospital. It was used as a geriatric hospital with two wards (46 beds) kept for patients with mental health problems. The hospital came under the authority of the Blackpool and Fylde Management Committee. In 1953 it was extended further, with new wards for the chronic sick; it now had 346 beds. Around this time the infirmary ended its role as an 'Accident and Emergency Unit'. The hospital closed in 2002, and the remaining buildings are currently used as offices for the NHS.

The Fylde Union was known as the 'A1 Union', as it had been classed as the best union in the country for most of its life. William Hodgson gave three reasons for this, one being its unique geographical position, another the growth of the residential population, and the last and most important, the administration by excellent officials throughout the time he had been there.

The Fylde union had two chairmen for 56 years and only two clerks for over 98 years. This continuity helped the union to slowly evolve with the changing world.

In 1859 William Segar Hodgson joined the board of guardians. In April 1873 he replaced R. C. Richards as chairman. He resigned as chairman in 1901 but stayed on the board until his death. Mr William Hodgson joined the board of guardians in 1881, and was elected chairman in 1904, a post he held until the board of guardians was disbanded in April 1930.

On 1 February 1837, Preston solicitor Robert Thompson became clerk, and stayed in the post until 1898, when he was replaced by Fred Brown. Mr Brown had worked as a boy for Mr Thompson since 1882 and retired as clerk in January 1935.

Compared with life outside the workhouse, the elderly inmates had fresh fruit and vegetables, baths, medical care, and tended the gardens in the fresh air as the workhouse in those early days was in open countryside. Richard Townsend of Freckleton was 97 years old when he died on 10 November 1879. He was in the workhouse for nearly 20 years and was said to have thoroughly enjoyed it.

Cottage Homes

When the adults left the old workhouse, the old infirmary was cleaned and painted. This now formed the main accommodation and the children were moved into it. The straw mattresses were replaced with fibre ones, unused furniture was sold and a new piano was bought. A nurse and two foster parents, husband and wife, looked after the children. The parents in the workhouse could only visit their children once every three months; the board thought this was the best way to stop the children becoming like their parents.

When the children turned up at the workhouse, some were in a terrible state. They were bathed and cleaned at the Wesham House, before being sent to the Kirkham Home, as the board now referred to the two buildings. The dirty laundry was also sent up to Wesham to be cleaned.

The board couldn't decide what to do with the children. Some wanted to board them out (foster), but this only worked if they had the parents' permission and the children were over three years old. Even if 'Boarding Out' were at its maximum potential, children would still remain in the home.

In May 1911 the Local Board Inspector demanded something be done with the old workhouse. The guardians appointed an architect in August that year, who presented plans for a 'group system' children's home. The board again was divided.

There were two types of children's homes, the group system and the scattered system. The scattered system was the cheapest; the home had a central administration hub and rented homes in the town for the children and a foster parent. More homes could be rented or unrented depending on demand. The down side was that the neighbours could become hostile to the children, thus enhancing the stigma of workhouse children.

The group system involved building semi-detached houses. Each house could hold 10 to 12 children. This was more expensive, but it kept the children in one area. The group homes system was adopted. Three semi-detached homes were built on Moor Street and a superintendent's house on Station Road.

The old workhouse was demolished except for the infirmary. The foundation stone for the new homes was laid on 23 July 1913 by Mr William Hodgson, chairman of Fylde guardians. They built three semi-detached houses and an administration block. It cost £10,000, could accommodate 72 children aged between 3 and 18 and was opened early 1914. The infirmary was later taken over by the army and became a military hospital during the First World War.

The children used to receive a penny a week pocket money, but the new committee gave them a rise in November 1930. Children under 10 still received a penny, those aged 10 to 12 two pence and over 12 three pence. The children must have trusted the first two superintendents Mr and Mrs Magson. The boys who left the home usually ended up going to sea, and the girls into service. The boys used to leave their bank books with the

superintendents until they returned to port. The children ended up all over the world. Some though never forgot the home.

> " Once again it is Christmas time, and I enclose my donation for the children at the Homes. I trust that you will see that it is distributed among the children for spending money, so they may spend it as they want. I know that children spend money on silly notions, but at the same time a silly notion often brings a lot of sunshine to a little child."

Part of Mr Whittle's letter

One of the old boys ended up in New York, working as a bus conductor. Every year, he sent a gift of £2 for the children. He once wrote; 'My, how I remember Blackpool Day, the days I spent at the home are buried in my memory and I still take pride in saying that I am a "Home Boy"'.

The infirmary was demolished in 1941. The cottage homes were also nearly demolished that year by the Luftwaffe when a bomb was dropped in one of the yards. The children's homes closed in 1957 and the buildings were used by the NHS and social services.

Just the boundary wall remains of the old workhouse, but in some places in Kirkham you can still see the stones used to create pavements that the inmates broke.

One of the soldiers at James Proctor's military funeral was Private Cross, a Kirkham Footballer. He, along with Kirkham reservists, Privates Woods, Gallagher, Worthington, Cummings and Sgt Harrison of the Loyal North Lancashire Regiment, were called up for the Boer War in November 1899. After being entertained on the previous Thursday at the Queen's Hotel, they left for the front on Saturday 18 November. The Kirkham Subscription Band and the Kirkham Artillery Volunteers escorted the men to the station. They travelled in a decorated cart, cheered on by the crowds lining the streets.

This was another episode in the long history Kirkham has had with the military, starting with the Romans.

Military

Kirkham has had connections with the military for over 2,000 years, from when the Romans built an outpost on Carr Hill. The oval wooden fort straddled the Roman road travelling from Ribchester to the Roman port at Fleetwood. Situated near the windmill, it was built around 70 A.D., and was later rebuilt using stone. The fort was in a line of forts that could be supplied by ships. In Roman times the sea levels were higher and without land reclamation the River Ribble would have spread closer to Kirkham.

There have been numerous finds, the most important being an umbro of a Roman shield. This was found by schoolmaster Mr Whalley, in Mill Hey Field, near Dow Brook in 1793. An article in the *Preston Chronicle* 9 May 1868 claims that he thought it was a piece of brass and sold it to a travelling Scotsman for 30 shillings. The Scotsman sold it to C. Townley, who deposited it in the British Museum.

The Saxons also visited, leaving a church and the name Kirkham. In Wesham, there is the remains of a Saxon animal enclosure. The Danes also passed through using the old Roman road as a path into North Lancashire. The Roman road is known as the 'Danes Pfad'.

Both sides of the English Civil War passed through Kirkham. After the Siege of Preston in 1643, the Earl of Derby garrisoned his troops in Kirkham. Whilst staying at Lytham Hall, he ordered all men over 16 to appear before him with their best weapons. The following year, the area was again filled with Royalists, who escaped over the River Ribble, to avoid a battle with Sir John Meldrum's Parliamentary Army.

After the Jacobite Rebellion, some troops passed through Kirkham on their way back to Scotland. One legend is that a rebel carrying a bag of money for the troops became scared and tried to give it to some inhabitants. They refused to take it and in the morning John Loxham was seen taking a bag off the Market Cross. The bag was suspected of containing the rebel's gold, but Mr Loxham said it only contained yellow buttons. He was, however, able to afford to buy Wesham Hall a few years later. The Thirty Men recorded the event.

> **" 1746.**
> " 28 March.   Paid for hiding registers, vestments, plate &c. at the rebels coming, 2s: 6d. ; same day paid for ringing when the duke of Cumberland came to Preston, and when he retook Carlisle, 6s.

In 1751 the 1st Lancashire Militia was formed from soldiers recruited from the Fylde. Kirkham was represented by the Loyal Kirkham Volunteers, until the Militia was disbanded in 1816, after Napoleon was defeated.

The early nineteenth century was an unsettled time for Lancashire with regular riots, as hand looms began to be replaced by powered looms. The authorities were expecting riots in Preston during the 1826 election. It was therefore decided to billet a detachment of the 1st Dragoon Guards at Kirkham. The rioters knew the troops were at Kirkham and expected a three-hour window of opportunity, before a runner could arrive in Kirkham and the Dragoons could get to Preston.

When they started to riot, they were surprised to see the Dragoons appear within 45 minutes. They'd done this by placing a soldier with a flag in a church tower in Preston, and a lookout at Carr Hill House. When the flag was raised at 5:10 p.m., the lookout dispatched the Dragoons and they arrived to disperse the mob, forty minutes later.

In response to the threat of war with France in 1859, and with the British Army spread across the Empire, a new Volunteer Army was created. On 15 March 1860, the 10th Lancashire Artillery Volunteers were raised in Kirkham, and came under the umbrella of the 4th Administrative Brigade LAV in 1863. Their headquarters were in the drill hall on Birley Street. The 80 man-battery had a rifle range on Carr Lane and its own brass band. The embankment from the range is still visible. Captain Charles Birley was the commanding officer and Dr Thomas Shaw the medical officer.

The 10th LAV used a firing range at Guide near Warton, where six artillery guns were permanently positioned during the summer months. Four belonged to Preston LAV and two to the Kirkham LAV. Both units fired the guns every week, at a target 1,700 yards away, in the Ribble Estuary. They both fired shot or ball at the target and usually held bets on who would hit the target first. They held their two-week annual camp at Euston Barracks, Fleetwood, meeting the gunners from Preston at Kirkham Station, and travelling by a special train to Fleetwood.

In 1880, the Corps was reorganised. The 10th Kirkham (senior) became no 1 battery. The 21st Preston (five batteries) became no. 2, no. 3, no. 4, no. 5 and no. 6; the 21st and 25th Lancaster batteries became no. 7 and no. 8; the 26th Blackpool became no. 9. The brigade was renamed the 5th Lancashire Artillery Volunteers and its HQ was at Fulwood Barracks. In 1908, it was again renamed as the 2nd West Lancashire Brigade, until being disbanded the following year.

CARBINE CONTEST AT SOUTH SHORE.—A carbine contest took place on Saturday afternoon, at South Shore, between ten of the 25th (Blackpool) and ten of the 10th (Kirkham) Artillery Volunteers, both of the 4th Administrative Brigade. The distance was 100 yards, ten shots each, Altcar scoring. The following were the scores :—

10TH.		25TH.	
Capt. C. A. Birley	33	Lieut. Gorton	36
Asst.-Surgeon T. Shaw	39	Lieut. Stead	28
B.S.M. T. Gardner	40	B.S.M. Parkinson	31
Sergt. Barlow	40	Sergt. Drummond	37
Sergt. Coskson	33	Corpl. Cardwell	39
Bomr. O. Fleetwood	35	Corpl. J. Dewhurst	40
Gunner S. Rainford	33	Bomr. Stirzaker	35
Gunner Turner	38	Gunner L. Hall	36
Gunner J. Fleetwood	31	Gunner W. H. Bell	43
Q.M.S. W. Whiteside	32	Gunner J. Walkden	41
Total	354	Total	366

The contest ended at 4·30, just before the drizzling rain came on. The contending parties afterwards dined at the Albion, Blackpool, and the evening was passed in a most enjoyable manner, toasts, songs, and sentiments being given in quick succession.

Article published in the *Preston Chronicle*, October 1879

As well as the LAV, there was the Lancashire Rifle Volunteers. The 29th Lytham Rifle Volunteers were raised on 28 January 1860, and formed part of 3rd Lancashire Volunteers, who held their annual camp at Lytham. The 29th eventually became the 4th Battalion Loyal North Lancashire Regiment, the territorial unit that men from Kirkham would join.

The local regular infantry regiment which recruited in the area was the Loyal North Lancashire Regiment, which formed in 1881, during the Cardwell Reforms. The Regiment was formed by the amalgamation of the 47th Lancashire and 81st Loyal Lincoln Volunteer Regiment of Foot. Two battalions of the 3rd Royal Lancashire Militia (Duke of Lancaster's Own) completed the Regiment. The 3rd Lancashire was one of the few militia units kept, when the local militia units were disbanded in 1816.

Every year, the Territorial Regiments held a two-week summer camp to practise their basic training, although most soldiers used it as a summer holiday. In August 1912, 9,000 territorials from the entire West Lancashire Division held their annual summer camp in Wesham. This camp was used to practise for war, with the troops split into two opposing armies.

The Division camped on Lord Derby's land in Wesham and along Mowbreck Lane. As well as the Infantry, there was an Artillery, the Royal Engineers, a Telegraph Company, a Field Ambulance Brigade (camped at Weeton) and the Royal Army Service Corps (camped at the railway station).

During the First World War three military hospitals were opened, one at the Wesham Workhouse, one in the old part of the Children's Cottage Homes and one in the Nelson Street School.

In 1931, the LNL opened an HQ for two platoons on Freckleton Street, to save the soldiers having to travel to Lytham. At the start of the Second World War, the 4th Battalion became an Anti-Aircraft Unit and was absorbed into the Royal Artillery 62nd Searchlight Regiment in 1939.

Troops on a route march passing Bradkirk Hall

During the Second World War, thousands of Allied troops passed through Kirkham. Carr Hill House was compulsorily purchased in October 1939 and was used as an Officers' Mess. Brook Mill became a transit camp and was later incorporated into 168 Brookwood POW Camp, when Milbanke House and grounds were compulsorily purchased in January 1942.

In 1940, the Royal Air Force built the no. 8 School of Technical Training on land belonging to Guild Farm. The camp RAF Kirkham covered over 220 acres and trained over 72,000 people, covering 21 trades, with over 86 courses, mainly in armaments. The school trained pupils from all over the world including America, the Commonwealth countries, Holland, Free France, Norway, Belgium, and Czechoslovakia. The camp had ten hangars, along with an 800-seat cinema and a hospital.

After the war, the school became 101 Personal Dispersal Centre and a training centre for RAF Boy Entrants. The first man to be demobbed was Sergeant James Bird of Morecambe on 18 June 1945. The second was W. O. James Spalding of Blackpool, after 27 years' service. James flew in 'The Great War' in Belgium, France and Germany, as an armaments' specialist. The camp closed in 1957, and later in 1962 part of the camp became HM Kirkham Open Prison.

Thousands of Axis troops came to Kirkham...

168 POW Camp

During the Second World War, a prison camp was built in Kirkham to accommodate 2,000 prisoners. Most were German and Italian prisoners of war, although other axis prisoners were held there. The main accommodation was inside the disused mill called Brook Mill. The outside areas were formed in the former grounds of Milbanke House. Milbanke House was blown up by the Royal Engineers and demolished to make room for the army barracks, which consisted of wooden huts. The mill and the grounds were secured with barbed wire, and additional guard posts with search lights surrounded the mill. The wire ran along the top of the old stone wall on Station Road, and a fence was built inside the woods. The prisoners

This picture shows the wall of Milbanke House opposite the Old Derby Arms, with the house in the distance. The wall topped with barbed wire formed part of the prison boundary.

crossed from the mill, into the woods at the bottom of the slope near the Railway Hotel. Guards were also posted at the bottom of this slope, and it (the slope) was blocked off with a wooden gate.

The prisoners lived and slept in the mill. A two-storey building was attached to this which included a Medical centre and vehicle bays. The medical officer was a German doctor, who was praised for preventing a fire on 10 December 1945. He noticed the fire in the first aid room and organised the Italian, Austrian and German prisoners to fight it. The fire was under control by the time the NFS arrived.

The prisoners were taken out daily to work just like most POW camps in Britain. A Hungarian called Tako Lorinc escaped from one of these working parties but was arrested after 12 hours. The green prisoner's uniform had given him away. This was in April 1946, one year after the end of the war, and he said he just wanted to go home.

Another group held at Kirkham were 226 Spanish Anti Fascists. Most of these escaped to France after the Fascists won the civil war in Spain. In the Second World War, they were arrested by the Vichy government and sent to Germany as slave workers. On being liberated by British troops, they were further interned at the Kirkham camp. The reason given was that they only had their word who they were, and the British required a secure guarantee that Franco's government would treat them well on returning to Spain.

Augustin Sola was dismayed to find himself a prisoner after being 'liberated' in Europe. He committed suicide on 11 July 1945 by jumping out of a second-floor window of the mill. His friend, the leader of the Spanish Floor, Gregoric Segura, said they'd been prisoners since 1939 in France and Germany. Augustin was shocked to find himself again in prison alongside some of the Fascists, who had originally incarcerated him.

Sergeant Desmond K. W. Bowes found the body on the west side of the mill, after being alerted by Pte Henry John Belbin. John had been on guard duty when he heard a window being smashed. When he shone his searchlight on the window, two men were shouting, 'man out the window'. The Spanish were later moved to Chorley POW camp, which was not fenced in and was less repressive.

Thomas Clarkson (49) of Freckleton Street worked at the camp in the coal compound with an 18-year-old Hungarian. The lad had lost his mother, brothers and sisters in an air raid on Budapest. Thomas out of sympathy had passed him three letters from his homeland, and sent two for him, which was illegal at the time. After being caught Thomas was fined 20 shillings.

By mid-1946, the council was pushing to close the camp in order to use the mill for employment purposes. Part of Sunnybank Mill was also being used as an army store. In December 1946, all the prisoners had left and a working party of 300 POWs cleared the site. The only things remaining of the camp are the concrete bases from the fence posts in the woods, and the U-bend nails and bits of barbed wire along the remaining stone wall.

Even the Luftwaffe paid a surprise visit...

Kirkham Bombed

On Sunday night, 28 September 1941, a lone German plane dropped four bombs on Kirkham, killing two people and injuring ten. One bomb was dropped in a field, and one in the children's cottage homes' garden. The blast smashed windows. A wall was demolished, and the building peppered with shrapnel. Luckily none of the 80 children was hurt – all were asleep in their beds at the time. One bomb dropped on cottages on Moor Street, damaging six homes, and one dropped on the gas works, which didn't explode but set fire to the works.

From this, it sounds like the plane flew along slightly to the left of Ribby Road and Moor Street, and if the bombs were dropped in succession, the field would be where the houses on Aikin Court now stand.

The two people killed were Gilbert Eadon, aged 68 of 11 Rawlinson Street, Wesham – a retired railwayman doing his fire watch duty at the gas works. The other was Harold Kay, aged 4, who died later in the workhouse

Cottages on Moor Street

infirmary. Harold had a severe scalp wound; his sister 11-year-old Irene Kay suffered from shock and had minor injuries. Slightly injured were three elderly spinsters Mary, Annie and Elizabeth Monoghan, also Harry Woods, Gerald Mcsperit and a Mrs Dickenson.

They all suffered from shock, and cuts from glass splinters. Most of them lived on the opposite side of the street, where the glass was blown inwards by the blast.

The worst damage was on the houses, but luckily the bomb landed on the high dividing wall keeping the explosion high up. Richard Kirkham, a First World War veteran was just going upstairs with his wife Margaret, when the bomb went off. Their 16-year-old son appeared from under the rubble, dirty but unhurt.

Eighteen people had to be evacuated to friends and neighbours. The children in the cottage homes helped clean up the glass and damaged furniture, and the event was said to be more exciting than scary. The bomb that was dropped in the field killed two cows and 20 hens. It is still possible to see the repaired brick work on the cottages, and the patched-up shrapnel marks on the wall behind Moor Street Clinic.

Kirkham was probably not the intended target; the plane could have been lost on the way to Liverpool or Barrow. The planes did not have enough fuel to fly back to Germany with the bombs still on board, so pilots usually dropped them in the countryside. Maybe the pilot thought Kirkham was open countryside or he dropped the bombs on purpose, after seeing the glow from the gas works furnace.

Kitchener's Army

On Monday 31 August 1914, the Army held a recruiting day at the Market Square. The meeting attracted over 1,200 residents.

There were speeches made by the Vicar Rev. W. T. Mitton, Rev. T. C. Walton (Headmaster KGS), Mr Windham, E. Hale (Mowbreck Hall), Mr

R. L. Birley, Mr W. Duckworth (Ribby Hall), Mr Leslie Duckworth and the Preston Councillor Frederick Matthew.

At the close of the meeting 100 men had signed up to join the 7th Battalion Loyal North Lancashire Regiment. The men had their picture taken in front of W. H. Bowdler's old house on the Market Square.

A penny gazette was published in Kirkham and Wesham in 1914 and 1915. As well as letters and articles, it contained the lists of every soldier who had volunteered, here are the names from 1915.

NAVY—KIRKHAM.

R. Dale, Church St., H.M.S. Warspite
W. J. Bath (Leading Signalman), 21, Fylde Street, H.M.S. Iron Duke.
H. Cryer, Kirkham, Royal Marines.
D. Kirby, H.M.S. Circe.
J. Redman, Ward St., Australian Navy.
H. Boothby, Sen., Kirkham, H.M.S. Benbow.
H. Boothby, Kirkham, H.M.S. Clio.
S. Cunningham, Kirkham, H.M.S. Invincible.
R. Taylor, Kirkham, H.M.S. Indefatigable.
E. Ward, Barnfield, H.M.S. Skirmisher
E. Boardman, Kirkham, H.M.S. Indefatigable.
R. F. Ashton, Kirkham, H.M.S. Canopus.
F. Rennison, Kirkham, H.M.S. Worcestershire.
J. Gregson, Kirkham, H.M.S. Indefatigable.
J. Rennison, Kirkham, H.M.S. Indefatigable.
E. Birket, Treales, H.M.S. Devonshire.

ARMY—KIRKHAM.

Cavalry.

2796 W. H. Rogerson (Corporal), 22, Poulton Street, Duke of Lancaster's Own Yeomanry.
4787 T. R. Riley, Preston Street, 15th Hussars.
10430 P. Cullen, Preston Street, 12th Lancers.
11807 J. Ridgeway, Preston Street, 18th Hussars.
13011 G. E. Stacey, 6th Dragoon Guards.

Royal Horse Artillery.

59341 G. H. McCauley, 106, Marsden Street.

Royal Field Artillery.

W. A. Bowdler (Lieutenant), The Square.
A. R. H. Bowdler (Lieutenant), The Square.
W. M. Mitton (2nd Lieutenant), The Rectory.
57158 J. Plant, Orders Lane.
1355 Joseph Hill (Gunner) 3, South View.
1311 John Hill (Gunner), 3, South View.
1310 F. Hill (Bombardier), 3, South View.
R. Pearson, Station Road.

Royal Garrison Artillery.

43862 F. W. Whamsley, 3, South View.

Royal Engineers.

60268 J. Woods, Station Road.
60348 F. Kearns, Preston Street.
5576 P. Corrigan, Orders Lane.
45108 J. A. Sharples, Church Street.
50797 T. Fowler (Corporal), 2, Ward Street.
62098 M. Caraher, Birley Street.

Royal Engineers—Continued.

55167 J. A. Gardner, Sunny Bank.
70771 E. Burrows (Despatch Rider), 20, Church Street.
T. Rawsthorne, Freckleton St.
J. Cartmell, 37, Marsden Street.

Scots Guards.

12222 T. Coulburn, 24, Orders Lane
11915 R. Charnock, 43, Orders Lane.

King's Own Royal Lancaster Regt.

C. Cross, (2nd Lieut.), The Moor
12353 R. Richardson, 34, Freckleton Street.
12567 J. Richardson, 10, Stanley St.
8424 M. McHugh, Dobson's Court.
1534 T. Walker, 22, Marsden Street.
14978 A. Swann, Station Road.
12458 D. McCall, 116, Marsden St.
12546 T. Aspin, 2, New Row.
12556 J. Wilby, 1, Chapel Walks.
3235 G. Lewis, Freckleton Street.
3238 R. D. Wilby, Freckleton Street.
3263 J. Shore, Freckleton Street.
3236 J. R. Taylor (Band), Freckleton Street.
3214 J. A. Tracey, South View.
3218 J. H. Woods, Preston Street.
3208 F. C. Cookson, Freckleton St.
3213 G. H. Salisbury, 13, Clegg St.
3266 H. Bolton, Station Road.
3268 A. Pomfret (Band), Victoria Rd.
3292 W. Singleton, Freckleton St.
3291 J. Singleton, Freckleton Street.
3287 J. Cottam, Freckleton Street.
3278 H. Thomas, Freckleton Street.
3312 W. Livingstone.
3315 T. McCall, 116 Marsden Street.
3333 J. Woods, Station Road.
3330 J. Hornby, South View.
12733 F. Sandford, Eagle Court.
17752 C. Sandford, Eagle Court.
3205 J. Anderton, Orders Lane.
1766 J. Livingstone, 20, Mill Street.
14629 J. Coulburn, 20, Marsden St.

King's Own Regt.—Continued.

3358 J. Singleton, 32, Preston St.
3374 J. Barnes, Orders Lane.
3421 A. Rose, 49, Poulton Street.
3206 J. Bamber, New Row.
3412 T. Critchley, 114, Marsden St.
3430 J. Carten, 4, Houghton Court.
3456 J. Tyson, 32, Station Road.
3459 A. Webster, 49, Freckleton St.
3458 G. Webster, 49, Freckleton St.
3434 T. Donnelly, Station Road.
3436 J. Entwistle, Freckleton Street.
3450 W. H. Riley, 1, Chapel Lane.
3449 J. Riley, 1, Chapel Lane.
3443 J. McCall, 116, Marsden Street.
3435 J. Dugdale, Freckleton Street.
3455 W. Townsend, 48, Station Rd.
3484 J. Crane, 5, Old Row.
3496 P. Woods, Marsden Street.
3495 T. Ward, Barnfield.
3586 Robt. Hall, Marsden Street.
3498 J. Higham, New Row.
2706 R. Singleton, 13, New Row.
3513 M. Livingstone, 13, New Row.
3514 J. Lund, 13, New Row.
3517 J. Wilson, 1, Chapel Lane.
3512 A. Edwards, 110, Marsden St.
3515 H. Singleton (Band), 93, Preston Street.
231 J. Larmour, Mill Street.
R. Worthington (Sergeant), Kirkham.
12503 T. Bunce, 10, Marsden Street.
P. English, 9, Orders Lane.
3211 J. Lawrenson, Mill Street.
3497 R. Hall, 11, Mill Street.
12304 R. Reid, Hornby Square.
H. Bramley, 75, Marsden St.

Liverpool Scottish Regiment.

4340 W. B. Rawcliffe, Poulton St.
4390 B. Lockey, Grammar School.

Liverpool Irish Regiment.

3326 C. Lewis, Freckleton Street.

Lancashire Fusiliers.

15474 R. E. Fox (Bugler), 17, Church Street.
4049 W. Beckett, Freckleton Street.
3327 C. Tattersall, Preston Street.
15480 W. E. Turner, Station Road.

East Lancashire Regiment.

7053 P. Murray, 11, Ward Street.
8652 T. Dixon, 51, Freckleton Street.
2250 J. Moran (Sergeant), 35, Station Road.

Border Regiment.

9690 B. Cartmel, 4, Chapel Walks.
13201 S. W. Kirby (Quartermaster-Sergeant), Preston Street.

Border Regiment—Continued.

17511 R. Woods, Ward Street.
17512 W. G. W. Kirkham, Freckleton Street.
17513 H. C. Crane, Church Street.
6612 A. E. Wilkinson, 37, Marsden Street.

South Lancashire Regiment.

10237 H. Cookson, Poulton Street.
R. H. Ashton, New Row.

Oxford and Bucks Light Infantry.

3457 R. Charlton (Lance-Corporal), Poulton Street.

Notts and Derby Regiment.

17584 R. Charlton, Burley, Oakham.

Loyal North Lancashire Regiment.

12821 W. Roberts, Moor Street.
12994 W. Hudson, 12, Mill Street.
12769 J. Crook, 14, Station Road.
12784 Alick Danson, 62, Preston St.
12822 W. Dodd, 3, Ward Street.
3941 J. Reynolds, Station Road.
12814 J. Parkinson, 76, Station Road.
12356 C. Widdows, Preston Street.
12795 L. Gardner, Ribby Road.
12794 A. Willacy (Band), Birley St.
13922 R. Harris, Poulton Street.
13946 J. Murray, " Annandale."
12989 A. Pearson, Church Street.
12749 T. Gardner, Preston Street.
960 F. Woods (Corporal), Preston Street.
12826 T. Ireland, 93, Station Road.
12780 J. Brown (Band), 70, Station Rd.
12800 J. H. Pearson, Poulton Street.
13992 A. G. Littlefair, Station House.
13910 F. Holden, 81, Freckleton St.
13798 H. Fox, Church Street.
12812 J. V. Wright, Dean Terrace.
3904 O. Gallagher, Station Road.
12821 W. Bradshaw, 68, Marsden St.
12998 C. Saunders, 74, Marsden St.
12788 L. Haslam (Band), 35, Park Rd.
12796 T. Woods (Band), 11, Freckleton Street.
12993 R. Jackson, Poulton Street.
12987 J. C. Parkinson (Corporal), Stanley Street.
13935 J. Clarkson, 47, Freckleton St.
13893 J. Fisher, 45, Willow Terrace
12821 W. Bradshaw, 68, Marsden St.
17207 G. H. Oxley, Mill Street.
19654 J. Hudson, Stanley Street.
12988 H. Parkinson (Corporal), Station Road.
12990 E. Gardner (Band), Ribby Road.
12087 J. McCall, 116, Marsden Street.
1396 E. Jolly, Preston Street.
13307 J. Cookson, 76, Marsden Street.

Loyal North Lanc. Regt.—Continued

12996 R. Tyson, Station Road.
13952 H. Clarkson, 29, Fylde Street.
13926 J. B. Porter, Poulton Street.
13909 D. Powell, Marsden Street.
30386 W. Fisher, 7, Clegg Street.
13033 W. E. Crossley (Lance-Corporal), Ribby Road.
13140 W. Gastrell, late Railway Hotel
13015 R. Warburton (Lance-Sergeant), Poulton Street.
12999 J. Fox, 17, Church Street.
17400 J. Danson, 62, Preston Street.
17580 Arthur Danson, 62, Preston St.
14003 J. R. Fishwick, 64, Station Rd.
13904 R. H. Anderton, Orders Lane.
3971 J. C. Lewis, Preston Street.
12993 J. Foreshaw, 1, Houghton Court.
17401 J. White, 6, Fylde Street.
13269 J. Leonard, 1, Orders Lane.
6029 M. Downey, 3, Houghton Court
19655 E. Taylor, Freckleton Street.
17395 R. Birch, 4, Dyer Street.
13554 M. McGinty, Marsden Street.
17397 G. Gregson (Band), Birley St.
10048 John Tinsley, 54, Station Road.
10792 Joe Tinsley, 54, Station Road.
W. Chillingsworth, Elswick.
17581 H. Shuttleworth, 89, Poulton St.
17399 J. T. Gregson, Birley Street.
12598 E. Moran, 13, Orders Lane
1035 John Jolly (Corporal), 57, Preston Street.
2101 James Jolly, 57, Preston Street.
247 J. Whiteside, 16, Smith Street.
1075 T. Whiteside, 16, Smith Street.
1091 J. Gardner, Ribby Road.
1033 G. Wilding, Marsden Street.
1090 B. Hodgkinson, Ribby Road.
234 J. Hudson, 8, Barnfield.
235 W. Woods, 54, Freckleton St.
236 B. Lewis, 44, Freckleton Street.
1004 R. Rawsthorne, 95, Preston St.
246 W. Bourke (Corporal), 2, Dobson's Court.
240 M. Gallagher, 24, Station Road.
230 E. Lester (Sergeant), 5, Orders Lane.
1029 T. Anyon, 22, Marsden Street.
1043 F. Matthew, Freckleton Street.
2602 C. B. Salter (Corporal), 25, Sunny Bank.
13967 J. Donnelly, 22, Mill Street.
1078 R. Yates, Church Street.
19653 W. Godfrey, Marsden Street.
19652 J. Gorman, Moor Street.
3664 J. Jeffrey, 3, Preston Street.
3965 J. Barnes, 13, Orders Lane.
3764 G. Parker, (late) 22, Preston St.

Loyal North Lanc. Regt.—Continued

3604 W. Wilkinson, Preston Street.
244 J. McQueen, 52, Station Road.
3636 F. Kirby, 80, Preston Street.
13904 R. H. Anderton, Orders Lane.
3971 J. Lewis, 18, Preston Street.
13865 R. Anderton, Orders Lane.
19103 H. Yates (Drummer), Church Street.
4274 W. McNamee, Marsden Street.

Duke of Wellington's Yorkshire Regt.

2621 W. Yates, 9, Dyer Street.

Middlesex Regiment.

2064 F. G. French, Grammar School.
A. T. Whitelock (Machine Gun Section), Grammar School.

Manchester Regiment.

1668 W. Bates, 75, Marsden Street.
J. Westby, Marsden Street.

Yorkshire and Lancashire Regiment.

J. Tracey, South View.

Royal Irish Rifles.

S. Larmour, Stanley Street.

Army Service Corps.

28046 J. Parkinson, 20, Fylde Street.

29956 F. Butler (Corporal), Station Road.
34692 A. W. Firth, Poulton Street.
02263 E. Whalley, 65, Preston Street.

Royal Army Medical Corps.

C. Yates, 9 Dyer Street.

National Reserves.

15856 J. Penketh, Freckleton Street.
P. Mulligan, Station Road.
E. B. Higham, Post Office.
T. Mansfield.
O. Gallagher.
R. McGinn.

Canadian Contingent.

5513 J. Murray, 11, Ward Street.

Australian Contingent.

W. Beeston, Station Road.
G. Sowerbutts, Freckleton St.

ARMY—WESHAM.

Royal Field Artillery.
86343 H. Butler, Porter Street.
12257 W. Woods, Garstang Road.
1040 J. Hudson, 11, Albert Street.
12890 S. Gorton, 1, Station Road.
75015 W. Bee, 74, Garstang Road.

Lancashire Fusiliers.
5066 T. Rigby (Sergeant), West View.

Liverpool Irish Regiment.
3359 B. T. Cook, 24, Garstang Road.

Royal Engineers.
50391 C. Charnley, Station Road.
32902 W. Harris, 11, Whitworth St.
68567 T. B. Sanderson, 8, Whitworth Street.

King's Own Royal Lancaster Regt.
12356 J. Whiteside, Garstang Road.
11764 J. Clarkson, Garstang Road.
3447 J. Rossall, 19, Weeton Road.
3446 E. Pearson, 18, Garstang Road.
3420 W. Rossall, 19, Weeton Road.
10108 E. Butler, Porter Street.
3431 W. Cook, Railway Terrace.
W. Hogarth, Porter Street.

Army Service Corps.
E. Smith, 25, Garstang Road.
E. Lees, 5, Garstang Road.
025822 C. Shorrock, 17, Rawlinson St.

R. Army Medical Corps.
W. Sanderson, 5, Garstang Rd.

Border Regiment.
17508 J. Quin, 72, Garstang Road.

Loyal North Lancashire Regiment.
12810 F. Littlefair, 45, Garstang Rd.
12813 J. R. Ingham, 38, Garstang Road N.
12811 W. Lang, 86, Garstang Rd. N.
12781 J. Sanderson, 5, Garstang Road.
R. Sanderson, 5, Garstang Road.
13306 W. Leigh (Corporal), Fern Bank, Garstang Road.
13894 W. Kelly, 4, Porter Street.
13934 W. Ball, 4, Albert Street.
14010 W. E. Coady, 14, Porter Street.
12824 J. S. Bamber, 2, Railway Terrace.
12832 J. Fenton, 6, Railway Terrace.

Loyal North Lanc. Regt.—Continued
13313 G. Bowshear, 10, Garstang Road N.
13927 W. Kent, 45, Garstang Rd. N.
13381 J. Lingard, Catherine Street.
R. Benson, Garstang Road.
19334 R. Willacy, 28, Garstang Rd. N.
W. Alston, 15, Whitworth St.
17578 W. Benson, 50, Garstang Road.
17582 E. Singleton, 19, Whitworth Street.
17584 J. Poole, 1, Catherine Street.
H. Lee, Railway Terrace.
S. Camp (Nat. R.), 20, Railway Terrace.
14826 H. Winkley (Sergeant, Nat. R.), 1, Garstang Road N.
17396 J. Swarbrick, 17, Whitworth St.
13892 F. Fox, 11, West View.
13827 J. Edwards, 12, Railway Terrace
13989 J. Hodgson, 59, Garstang Road N.
12388 J. Gallagher, 31, Whitworth Street.
13937 W. Devanney, 22, Railway Terrace.
13930 W. Kirby, Fern Bank, Garstang Road.
12999 R. Kirby (Lance-Corporal), 55, Garstang Road.
13932 J. Redman, Garstang Road N.
H. Clarke, 80, Weeton Road.
14009 R. Christopher, 7, Porter St.
14011 A. W. Woods, 1, Whitworth Street.
M. Roskell, 3, Segar Street.
14007 A. H. Forshaw, 4, Market St.
14005 D. Forshaw, 4, Market Street.
14360 E. Forshaw, 4, Market Street.
14010 R. Hodgson, 59, Garstang Road N.
O. Gallagher, 1, Whitworth St.
14389 A. Boulton, 1, Station Road.
16331 F. Taylor, 3, Station Road.
2829 J. Crane, 4, Billington Street.
1059 J. Butler (Colour-Sergeant), Market Street.
1092 W. Carr, Garstang Road.
233 G. Kent, Garstang Road.
1075 J. Smith, 14, Albert Street.
291 J. Woods, Station Road.
14267 R. Balshaw, 7, Porter Street East.
J. Hudson, Albert Street.
W. Green, Garstang Road N.
M. McCaffrey, Porter Street East.
49263 J. Whiteside, Garstang Road.
242 T. Whiteside, 21, Whitworth Street.
17585 John Whiteside, 21, Whitworth Street.

The Future King met the soldiers on a visit in 1921...

Royal Visit

Club Day of 1913 was the most colourful in terms of the town's decorations. The town was covered in buntings and flags. At either end of the town large

This arch was erected on Preston Street, with words to welcome the King and Queen.

The Royal Car coming down Poulton Street, on Tuesday afternoon, on the 7th July 1913. It was a flying visit and the car didn't stop, but it still gave people a chance to see the Royal Couple.

The Willows Church, under the guidance of Monsignor Gillows, stole the show with this imitation stone Triumphal Archway, on Ribby Road.

decorative arches were erected. All this was to welcome King George V and Queen Mary, who were travelling from Preston to Blackpool.

Large crowds lined the route of the royal entourage, which went via Preston Street, Poulton Street and Ribby Road. A stand was built and covered with decorations in front of the Children's Cottage Homes to give the orphans and workhouse inmates a chance of seeing the royal couple. Children from the different schools were also placed along the King and Queen's route.

On Friday 8 July 1921, Kirkham had another royal visit when the Prince of Wales travelled from Blackpool to Preston via St Annes, Lytham, Wrea Green and Kirkham. Prince Edward, the future King, briefly watched a group of children dancing around the May Pole at Wrea Green, before proceeding to Kirkham. After a short stop at the Grammar School, the Prince had lunch at Mowbreck Hall, where he inspected some local ex-servicemen. Afterwards he travelled back through Kirkham to Clifton and then on to Preston.

Kirkham Memorial Park

In 1898, an unknown benefactor left five acres of land between St Michael's Church and Mill Street. The land called 'The Close', or locally 'The Cloise', was accepted by the council. Paths were built and trees and shrubs were planted to create a miniature park. A play area was also built and Kirkham Recreation Ground or 'The Rec' was born.

This is how it stayed until 1925, when a War Memorial Committee was set up, chaired by Rev. G. Strange, Headmaster of Kirkham Grammar School. Money was raised, and work began on the grounds on Monday 22 March 1926. After a parade led by the Kirkham Subscription Band, Mrs Duckworth of Ribby Hall cut the first sod of earth.

The ground at the time was a plain grassy hill in the middle of the recreation ground. 105 lime trees were planted to represent each fallen soldier from the First World War. Where possible, the planting was done by the soldiers' families. A terrace was built, and gardens containing lavender, rosemary and roses were planted. A cenotaph was built out of ashlar stone, with a brass plaque containing the names of the fallen soldiers. The designer was a Mr E. Prentice Mawson of Lancaster, who also donated the brass sword on the rear of the cenotaph.

The parade was filmed and was shown in the Kirkham Co-op cinema. The film survived, and can be viewed in the Central Library of Manchester.

The Memorial was unveiled on Remembrance Day afternoon, Sunday 7 November 1926 by Lt General Sir Richard H. K. Butler KCB/ KCMG, General Officer Commanding in Chief Western Command. A parade led by the Police, ex-Captain Duckworth, a detachment 4th Loyals, Kirkham Subscription Band, 1st Kirkham Rangers, Local School Children, St John's Ambulance, Postmen, Firemen, Women's Institute, The Memorial Committee and Town Council paraded to the Memorial.

Sir Butler spoke with the guard of honour, formed by ex-service men. He stopped to speak with Mr W. Benson, who lost both legs in the war, enquiring if his pension was sufficient. General Butler loosened the flag covering the memorial, and after a speech, the buglers from The Loyals and

The re-built park in the 1970s, Flaxfield Mill in the background

East Lancashire Regiment sounded the last post. After a short silence the reveille was sounded. A telegram from the King, was read out and various wreaths were laid to end the proceedings.

In 1930 the recreation ground was further developed, when the council borrowed money from the unemployment grants committee. Some tennis courts were built on the right-hand side of the war memorial, and a play park was built on the left-hand side.

The park consisted of a paddling pool, a children's sand pit, slides and swings. A football pitch was also built. The scheme cost £1,000. At some point this was removed, and the play area was rebuilt adjacent to the tennis courts, where it is today.

For the ones who never came back, the last view of Kirkham was from a railway carriage...

Railways

In 1834, Sir Hesketh Fleetwood came up with a plan to build a railway from Preston to the mouth of the River Wyre, where a new port was to be built. This would enable the industrial counties of Lancashire and Yorkshire to use a port with direct sea access to Scotland and Ireland. A meeting was held in the Black Bull Inn, Preston, to raise the £130,000 capital with shares at £50 each. He only had one backer from the Fylde, as most people thought it was a wild adventure. At that time the area was a wild and desolate place with only a couple of houses.

Hesketh Fleetwood raised the capital and obtained his act of Parliament on 3 July 1835. The Preston and Wyre Joint Railway opened on 25 July 1840. The company ran three trains daily in each direction, with one on Sunday. The railway expanded for the next 90 years and on some summer Saturdays in the 1930s, over 600 trains were passing through Kirkham.

The new railway was 19¾ miles long and cost £260,000 to build. It consisted of a single track with a passing point at Kirkham. The original platform

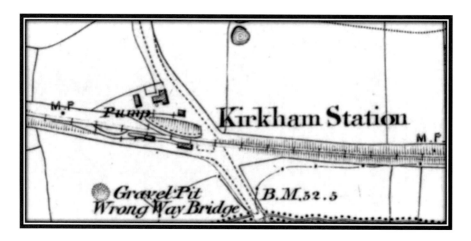

Kirkham Station 1848

stood on the opposite side of the road from today's current platform, the line crossed by a level crossing.

When the railway opened, a special train was put on from Preston to Fleetwood. After an excursion on a steam ship around the port, a banquet was held before the guests left for their return train to Preston. The train left at seven o'clock, but it ended in a disaster when a man fell from the train and was killed. The train had travelled one and a half miles down the track when William Dean from Preston fell whilst trying to climb from the second to the first carriage. He was decapitated. At the inquest the next day, the verdict was accidental death. Dean was intoxicated at the time; no blame was apportioned to anybody connected with the railway.

Before the railway to Scotland was built, passengers travelling from London Euston could catch ships at Fleetwood to take them further north to Scotland. This was how Queen Victoria travelled from Scotland to London in September 1847.

Until 1846, passengers who wanted to visit Lytham or Blackpool caught coaches from either Kirkham or Poulton. On 16 February 1846, the branch line opened to Lytham and on 29 April that year, the branch line to Blackpool opened. The line from Preston to Kirkham was also doubled in 1846, giving an 'up and down' line. The Preston & Wyre Railway and Dock Company, to give its full name, lasted until 1849. In this year, the company was split, one third to London and North-Western Railway Co. and two thirds to the Lancashire and Yorkshire Railway Co.

The original Lytham branch junction was at Bradkirk and because the company's depot was based at Fleetwood, the track curved towards Fleetwood [freight being the priority rather than passengers]. Trains arriving from Lytham had to go through the junction, and after the points man changed the points, the train propelled towards Kirkham Station. To return to Lytham, the driver ran the engine around the train [to put it at the back]. The driver propelled to Bradkirk, passed the junction, the points were changed and now the engine was at the front, on the way back to Lytham.

When holiday makers in Blackpool wanted to visit Lytham, or vice-versa, they had to make a 17-mile journey via Kirkham. The P & W Joint Railway was approached and asked to extend the line from Lytham to Blackpool. This was refused, and a new company was set up with the support of Colonel Clifton. The Blackpool and Lytham Railway obtained its act of Parliament in 1861, and the first sods were cut in September that year. The railway took 12 months to build and now Lytham had two stations, at either end of the town. The opening was delayed until the holiday season started on Monday 6 April 1863.

The freight side never really took off, but the passenger side did, such was the massive growth of the Fylde coast. The railway infrastructure was inadequate and so began the second wave of expansion in 1870.

The line from Kirkham to Fleetwood and Blackpool was doubled, with up and down tracks. A new junction was built at Kirkham for trains travelling towards Lytham. This new junction faced towards Preston, where most of the traffic flowed ,and it joined the old line at Wrea Green. The two separate railways at Lytham were joined together and in 1874 a new station opened. This new track from Kirkham was a double line and connected Kirkham to Blackpool via Lytham. The old Lytham branch was kept in place, as it served Bradkirk Brickworks. This line also saved trains travelling from Lytham, towards Poulton and beyond, the need to run the engines around at Kirkham.

Kirkham, now had a coal yard, a goods shed, a private siding for Phoenix Mill and two sidings for Brook and Selby Mills. The siding for Selby Mill ran parallel to the mill and a turntable to turn railway trucks 90 degrees was built. Single trucks could now be turned and pushed on rails leading into the mill. The old Kirkham station was still in use and was a basic platform without any buildings.

The biggest problem for the railway was the level crossing at Kirkham. Gates operated by a crossing keeper closed the crossing to traffic when a train was approaching. Pedestrians used a wicker gate, but most just crossed whether a train was approaching or not.

On 21 December 1877, Thomas Snape, aged 44, crossed behind a goods train as another train was leaving for Lytham. Thomas, a factory worker, was struck by the 18:10 Lytham train. The train severed both his legs and he died four hours later. In 1880, the railway built a footbridge and closed the level crossing to pedestrians. Nobody used the bridge and more deaths occurred until the third stage of improvements, when the crossings were closed and over-bridges built.

After obtaining an act of Parliament in 1883, the line from Preston was doubled again, giving four tracks to Kirkham. A bridge was built over the railway at Kirkham and the level crossing was closed in August 1887. A new station was built at Kirkham, with a ticket office and waiting rooms, covered with a twin pitched roof. The railway had moved away from points men in track-side huts, and proper signal boxes were built. The local Kirkham signal boxes were Treales, Kirkham South Junction, Kirkham Station, Kirkham North Junction, Bradkirk and Weeton. The private siding at Phoenix Mill was extended into a new coal yard. On Segar Street, cattle pens were built to hold cattle and horses waiting to load/unload onto cattle trucks.

The fourth and final expansion was being planned in 1885, even before the last set of works was finished. This involved building a new express line from Kirkham to Blackpool. Due to restrictions at Poulton, it was decided to build a new line from Kirkham to South Shore. The work started in 1901, and the line crossed Weeton Moss and joined the old railway at Blackpool South. The line, without stations reduced the distance to Blackpool to five miles. In March 1903, the line was connected to the railway at Kirkham, with a junction and a flyover to cross from the fast lines onto the new line. The Marton Line, as it was called came into service at Easter 1903.

The Railway was now at its peak, with trains passing through Kirkham for Fleetwood, Blackpool North and Blackpool Central. It was a large employer with over 170 people employed in Kirkham and Wesham. This is how it

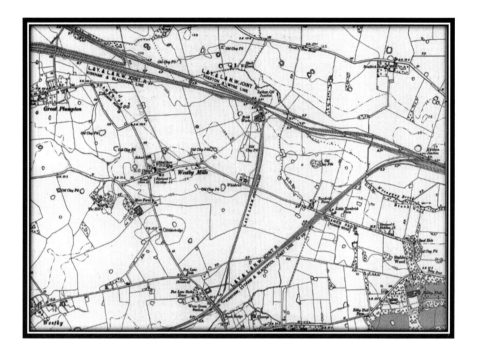

Map showing final layout north of Kirkham

remained until the 1950s, when the slow decline began. The first line to go was the Old Lytham Branch, when the Blackpool Road was widened in the 1950s. The track was taken up and the council used the cutting as a land fill site; the route is still traceable, with part of the line side fence remaining in fields near Wrea Green.

The track between Preston and Kirkham was reduced back to a double track in the 1960s. Blackpool Central and the Marton line closed in 1964. Fleetwood Station closed in 1970, but the Fleetwood branch stayed open until 1993, for Chemical Trains serving ICI at Burn Nase. The Lytham branch terminated at Blackpool South and was reduced to a single line in the early 1980s.

When the railways arrived, large quantities of coal could be delivered. One user of coal was the Kirkham Gas Company, one of the three utilities…

Kirkham Gas Company

In the eighteenth century it was proven that when coal was heated it released gas, which burnt a bright flame. In the early part of the nineteenth century, gas works were appearing in all major towns and cities. The gas produced was called town gas and was used mainly for lighting.

On 26 July 1838, Kirkham Gas Company was formed with a capital of £1,200. The company erected a gas works, with a single gas holder, on the site of the old tanner's yard on Orders Lane. The original gas holder would have consisted of a bell floating in water, but this was replaced with a telescopic gas holder in 1865.

To make town gas, coal was heated in a sealed tube called a retort. The gases, which were mainly hydrogen and carbon monoxide, passed through a water trap. The gas was then cooled in a condenser, where tar and other liquids were removed. The gas then passed through a purifier, to remove sulphur compounds and other impurities, and was stored in a gas holder.

The by-products were sold on by the company (1852 figures):

Lime – 1*s*. 6*d*. per horse load, for use as fertiliser.

Tar –1*s*. per barrel, shipwrights, coarse painting, pavements.

Coke – 7*d*. per c.w.t.

Ammonia Water – was sold for whatever they could get.

In the early days, customers were charged by the number of gas lamps they had in their homes or buildings. They also agreed to use the lights at a set time and a gasman went around Kirkham policing these agreements. Gas meters had been invented in 1817, but they didn't start appearing until the second half of the nineteenth century. In 1870, prepayment or slot meters were introduced, and this gave poorer households access to gas.

With all the mills as well as large and small homes using gas, the gas company prospered and in 1880 the works were expanded. A second telescopic gas container was built, and a steam exhauster installed, to pump the gas into the main systems. All this work cost £4,000 and was completed by 1883.

What followed, was a period of unrest amongst the firm's customers, about the cost and quality of gas.

There were lots of complaints about the quality and cost of gas in Kirkham. The two are inseparable, because the poorer the gas, the poorer the light given out on burning. This meant that customers were turning the gas lights up and burning more gas at a higher price. Perfect for the gas company but not for the customers.

It all reached a head when Mr W. H. Bowdler was driven out of his home on 'The Square'. Mr Bowdler was at this time running Selby Mill. He sent this letter to the Local Board of Health's meeting on 4 October.

"Kirkham, October 3rd, 1881,—Dear sir, I wish to draw the serious and prompt attention of your Board to the poisonous stench my house has been filled with during the past two nights, especially last night. Between eight and nine o'clock last night I had four lights burning in my dining-room, but in about half an hour was driven out of the room by a dense fog, and sulphurous vapour proceeding from the gas, and there was not a room in the house fit to inhabit from the same cause. The damage to picture frames, silver, etc., will be very considerable if this sort of thing is to be tolerated much longer. I have made it my business to see our medical officer of health, who informs me that the gas, at the time I have named, was of a highly poisonous nature and fraught with the greatest danger to health. As I am enclosing this complaint I also take the opportunity of adding that, during the last 18 months, the consumers of gas in this town have, from time to time, suffered great inconvenience, both from the quality and the uncertain supply, whilst their bills have grown heavy ones out of all reason. Your Board would not be doing a greater service to the town at large than by using all the power the law gives them in these matters.—Yours, faithfully, W. H. BOWDLER."—Mr.

The letter was also published in the *Preston Chronicle*.

Dr Walker was also at the meeting as Medical Officer and backed up Mr Bowdler. He stated that, after receiving numerous complaints about the quality of gas, he tested a sample in his own home. It contained sulphurated hydrogen which is poisonous and damages silver. The flame burnt blue, a product of sulfurous acid gas and water. He also went on to say that an outbreak of typhoid fever on Moor Street and Ribby Road a few years earlier was, in his opinion at the time, the effects from the foul gas leaking into the air and not typhoid. The gas company was approached by the board which stated that an accident with the purifier had occurred, and the gas holder holding the impure gas was isolated from the mains. This gas had now been released into the atmosphere. These complaints had now been going on for 18 months and were to continue for years to come. Mr Bowdler was not giving up.

By 1883, Mr Bowdler was the chairman of the Gas Consumers of Kirkham. At the first meeting on 5 February, the group focused on the amount of gas each person had used during 1881, compared with 1882. After reading out several gas statements, it was agreed they were all using more gas than previously, due to the low quality. At the close of the meeting, it was agreed to send a delegation to meet the board of the gas company.

On 22 February 1883, the Gas Board held its half-yearly meeting. Present were President Thomas Shaw, William Houghton, John Gardner, M. Clegg, R. Whiteside, B. Stuttard, J. Bennett, J. Bradly, M. Gardner, William Harrison, J. Ward, J. Whiteside and T. Whiteside.

The board went through the accounts and mentioned that the extension works were now complete. During the extension works, the company had fitted a gas testing machine, which prevented contaminated gas entering the mains. The board also agreed to reduce the price of gas from 5*d.* to 4*s.* 7*d.* This decision had nothing to do with the Agitators, as the board called them.

The gas, measured in cubic feet, now cost:

4*s.* 7*d.* – when yearly consumption was below 200,000 feet.

4*s.* 4*d.* – when yearly consumption was between 200,000 and 250,000 feet.

4*s.* 2*d.* – when yearly consumption was above 250,000 feet.

The company also placed posters around Kirkham, which listed the price of gas in towns comparable to Kirkham, but they withheld the above discount for large users because of the Agitators. Gas tariffs were as complicated then as they are now. Different discounts were offered, depending on the amount of gas used, if bills were paid within fourteen days and if using a prepaid meter.

Before the next meeting of the gas consumers, they wrote to a few towns listed on the poster, in order to compare their gas prices with Kirkham's.

The Gas Consumers of Kirkham were not to be under estimated as they included the mill owners: William Harrison, The Richards Brothers, Thomas Moss and shareholders of Fylde Mill, all leading businessmen and ordinary gas consumers. Their meetings were held in the New Black Bull Inn at Town End.

The next meeting was held on 12 March 1883, with eighty people in attendance. Remembering that the price of gas in Kirkham was 4*s*. 7*d*., with no discount, Mr Bowdler now started to compare the price of gas with other towns. The first figure, from the Gas Board's poster:

Lytham 4*s*. discounted to 3*s*. 9*d*. due to be lowered by 3*d*. in April making it 3*s*. 6*d*. per 1,000 ft.

Fleetwood 4*s*. 7*d*. discounted by 10 percent to 4*s*. 1½*d*. per 1,000 ft.

They also read out the letters from Holme Firth and Carnforth Gas Companies, both cheaper than Kirkham. The quality of gas was measured in candles. Lytham was 20 candles, Fleetwood 18 candles and Kirkham 16 candles. This all proved that Kirkham was more expensive and less luminous.

The group penned a letter stating that from 31 March, they would ask to be disconnected, if gas prices were not reduced. Sixty people signed at the meeting and a further 100 signatures were added the next day, after canvassing the town. The company relented and, on 14 April 1883, reduced gas to 4*s*. 2*d*. for all customers with a discount for a few large consumers.

As well as providing gas, the company was paid by the town to look after the 80 public lamps. They also held exhibitions in the drill hall, showcasing new gas appliances.

KIRKHAM GAS COMPANY, LIMITED.—The Directors of the above Company have pleasure in announcing that an EXHIBITION of GAS COOKING and HEATING STOVES, Gas Engines, Gasfittings, Burners, Globes, and Lanterns, together with other Apparatus for the utilisation of Coal Gas for Domestic and Trade purposes, will be held in the Drill Hall, Birley-street, Kirkham, on June 11th, 12th, 13th, and 14th. —For particulars see catalogues, or apply to
ROBERT PORTER, Secretary and Manager,
Gasworks, Kirkham.
May 19, 1884.

Gas Containers Behind The Fire Station

By 1896, the company had 500 credit customers and 50 'penny in slot customers' and the annual usage was 10,000,000 feet. They were also providing Freckleton and Wrea Green with gas. In 1907, a new gas holder was built and 1938 marked the firm's 100-year anniversary with an exhibition in the Ambulance Hall.

The works were bombed on 28 September 1941, killing Gilbert Eadon, who was on fire-watch duty. In 1949, the company was absorbed into North West Gas, when all gas companies were nationalised. The end came in the late 1960s when North Sea gas was discovered. The gas holders were dismantled, but the retort house remained standing. Henthorn's Building Merchants took over the site and used the retort house as a warehouse, until it was demolished, and houses built on the land.

Fylde Water Company

In 1860, various groups like Kirkham Local Board of Health and the Lytham and Fleetwood Improvement Committees, came together to find a solution to the problem of a clean water supply for the Fylde. The company was based in Kirkham, the offices on the corner of Poulton Street and Birley Street.

The provisional directors in 1860 were Thomas L. Birley, Edmund Birley, Colonel Clifton, Dr Cocker, James Fair, Frederick Kemp, George Murton, E. C. Milne, Edward Pedder, Robert Rawcliffe and Benjamin Whitworth.

The engineer was Thomas Barham Foster, the surveyor Thomas Fair. The banker was Pedder and Co., Preston, the solicitors William, Decon, and Wilson of Preston, and Mr Richard Moore of Kirkham.

The company planned to supply Kirkham, Lytham, Blackpool, Fleetwood and Poulton with fresh water from the edge of the moors, on the Bleasdale Range. The water was to be taken from Grizedale Brook, and conveyed by pipe to Weeton, where a reservoir was to be built. The reservoir would be situated 20 feet higher than any other point and in a central position. The capital needed was £60,000, with 12,000 shares at £5 each. The company gained its Act of Parliament in 1861, and Thomas Langton Birley became the company's director. Work began straight away, but it took nearly 70 years to get the supply right.

A dam was built across a valley at Nicky Nook, through which Grizedale Brook flowed. The dam was 20 feet high, 70 feet thick at the base, and sloped to twelve feet at the top. The water flowed through a culvert on the west side of the dam into a gauge. Here, a stipulated amount was turned back into the brook, the rest flowed into a 12-inch pipe to Weeton.

The pipe left Grizedale to Slack Farm, under the railway and through Greenhalgh Green. It passed through Bowgrave, the grounds of Catterall Hall, east of St Michael's, through Elswick, then to Weeton.

Weeton Service Reservoir was built on Whinprick Hill on Lord Derby's land, built because the pressure would have been too great at Grizedale. The crown of the hill was reduced by 12 feet and the material was used to build the embankment. The thickness of the embankment was the same as at Grizedale, and it could hold 15 million gallons. Weeton Reservoir also became a tourist attraction, the Victorians walking to it in order to stand on the embankment and enjoy the views.

A ten-inch main pipe left from the south end of the reservoir for Lytham and Kirkham, where it later branched off into two nine-inch pipes, one for Lytham and one for Kirkham. Another ten-inch pipe left the west side, for Fleetwood and Blackpool. This pipe branched off at Marton, for Fleetwood via Bispham and Rossall.

The chief engineer was Mr Foster of Manchester; Mr Macguire of Accrington was the contractor at Grizedale, and Messrs Cunliffe and Sons of Blackburn for Weeton. Mr H. Ashcroft laid the pipes from Grizedale to Weeton and from Weeton to Lytham and Kirkham. Mr Bickerstaff laid the pipes from Weeton to Blackpool.

The work took two and a half years to complete and cost £80,000. The opening ceremony was held at Blackpool on 20 July 1864. Almost immediately the supply was insufficient, and plans were put in place for a new reservoir. The Grizedale Reservoir was too small to cope with the population growth on the Fylde, and in addition it leaked. A new, larger reservoir was built. The new reservoir was called Barnacre, and was split into two reservoirs, Barnacre North and Barnacre South. The reservoir was supplied with water from the Calder and Upper Calder Streams. It could hold 156 million gallons and was supplying the Fylde, with water by 1879.

The largest growth in population was around the Blackpool area, and new main pipes were laid from the reservoirs directly to Blackpool, avoiding Weeton. In 1895, a new 15-inch pipe was laid to Blackpool and in 1899, an additional 21-inch main was laid to Blackpool.

This second pipe was the last operation the Fylde Water Company completed, and from 31 August 1899, the company was taken over to become the Fylde Water Board. The committee of the new board consisted of members of Lytham, St Anne's, Blackpool and Fleetwood Urban District Councils. There were no representatives from Kirkham, as the town that had been dominant in the area for centuries was now being over shadowed by the new towns on the Fylde coast.

The new board was again under pressure to provide more water and in 1902, plans were put in place to build a third reservoir. The company borrowed just under £160,000, of which £137,727 was used to build the reservoir,

£20,000 to extend water mains and £1,680 for miscellaneous work. The new reservoir was called Grizedale Lea. It opened in 1919 and could hold 332 million gallons.

The growth on the Fylde coast was relentless:

Year	Fylde Population
1891	71,510
1901	111,258
1911	136,632
1921	163,891
1931	220,000

The daily water consumption in 1897, was 2,268,123 gallons and by 1930, this had reached 7,391,000 gallons.

The board had to deal not only with a fast-growing population, but every year with an extra 160,000 holiday makers (1930s figure) during the holiday season. The board closed the Kirkham offices and moved to Blackpool in 1905. The old Kirkham offices became the Kirkham Institute. In 1912, a scheme was put in place to finally solve the water supply problem.

The scheme involved damming the Hodder to store 3,151,000,000 gallons of water and to build two new service reservoirs. The company obtained its Act of Parliament that year in 1912, but progress was delayed due to the outbreak of the First World War. Work got underway in earnest in 1923. The reservoir, called Stocks Reservoir, cost £1,500,000 to build and could supply 13,000,000 gallons daily. The two new service reservoirs were Westby Mills (which was connected to Weeton) and the Warbreck Hill reservoir.

Warbreck reservoir was a tower standing 123 feet high, which could hold 600,000 gallons. It was built this way to keep the water pressure high.

Westby Reservoir was built at Westby Mills, named after the two windmills that once stood there. The Clifton Arms was demolished and the reservoir was built on top of the old Blackpool main road. The work started in 1925 and the main embankment was built up with broken stones from Withnell Quarry. The stones were delivered by road and moved around the site by a miniature railway. When work finished for the day, the driver took the small engine back to its shed. The labourers used to ride on the engine when they went to clock off. On 9 September 1926, William Townsend of Station

Road, Wesham, was riding on the front of the small petrol engine when he fell off. The wheels didn't pass over him, but he was still crushed and died later of internal injuries.

The scheme was completed in 1932 and Prince George opened the works on 5 July that year. The last major project was to cover Weeton and Westby reservoirs with roofs. The board had to employ a bird scarer and both reservoirs were covered over in the 1960s. In 1973, Fylde Water became part of North West Water; North West Water and Norweb amalgamated and became United Utilities.

Electricity

On 22 July 1925, Preston Electric Corporation officially opened its new power station. The building on the banks of the River Ribble in Penwortham was to supply Lytham, St Anne's, Blackpool, Fleetwood and towns east of Preston with electricity. The electricity was carried to Blackpool, by overhead cables, and in 1926, Kirkham Town Council was putting plans into place to connect Kirkham. It wasn't until Thursday 28 November 1929 that Kirkham finally got its electric supply. Councillor E. Rhodes switched on the supply at Kirkham and Councillor R. E. Kent switched on the Wesham Supply.

Electric supply switch on outside the show room

A sub-station was built at Hall Cross Farm, to connect to the mains, reducing the voltage from 33,000 volts to 6,000 volts. Two further sub-stations were built, to reduce the pressure to 416 volts and 240 volts. They built one on Orders Lane, for Kirkham and one in Wesham. The corporation had asked, that the Kirkham Council could guarantee 250 customers for twelve months, but they had received 383 applicants. The project had cost £18,000 and the work included an electricity show room on Orders Lane, attached to the competitor's gas retort house.

Even before the electric switch-on, Kirkham had two cinemas, the Empire on Birley Street and the Co-op Electric Cinema, on Poulton Street. Both used gas engines to produce electricity. Sport was another pastime. For the upper class, it was hunting...

Kirkham Harriers

The Kirkham Harriers was a fox and rabbit hunting pack, consisting of beagles and harriers, re-established in 1835 by Hugh Hornby of Ribby Hall. Hugh Hornby was master of the hunt for 10 years, and during this time the kennels were held at Ribby Hall. Later, Mr Langton Birley and Mr King

Kirkham Harriers 1902

Mr. Charles Addison Birley, Master Kirkham Harriers.

Charles Addison Birley in his
Kirkham Harriers uniform

hunted the pack jointly. The kennels were now in a field off Bloody Lane End in Wesham. Charles Birley of Bartle Hall, took over from his brother after a few seasons, and by 1900, his son was the hunt master; the kennels now in a building off Carr Lane. The hunts were formed mainly by the local gentry, but often officers from Fulwood Garrison joined in the hunt.

The pack was welcomed on to the land by the farmers, who helped them by marking wire fences with red disks. The country hunted was between the Fylde Coast and the Longridge Fells, the uniform consisting of green jackets and brass buttons with the initials 'K. H'. At the end of each season the group held point to point races. The pack was disbanded shortly before the First World War.

Kirkham Cricket Club

Kirkham Cricket Club was formed in 1830, the ground was in a field off Freckleton Street. Dr Thomas Shaw was the first chairman. Some of the early matches played were against Preston on Clifton Marsh. The area was set up like a country fair with beer tents and food stalls.

```
            KIRKHAM.—FIRST INNINGS.
                                         No. of Notches.
Mr. Gradwell  caught out by Myres..............  10
  ,,  Brown  bowled out by Jacson  ..............   4
  ,,  Anyon  bowled out by Jacson  ..............   0
  ,,  Bawdler  caught out by Woodburne..........   8
  ,,  Birley  stumped out by Jacson  ............   1
  ,,  Williamson  called  out leg before wicket....   0
  ,,  Crookall bowled out by Jacson  ............   4
  ,,  Richards bowled out by Banister............   1
  ,,  Shaw  not  out,................................   0
  ,,  Loxham bowled out by Jacson  ............   0
  ,,  Bennett bowled out by Jacson  ............   0
                                              ____
                                               28
```

These were the scores for Kirkham's first innings against Preston, which was played on Wednesday, 23 August 1837. In the second innings they were all out for 29 runs. Preston were the winners after scoring 108 runs in their first innings.

The other teams Kirkham played against were Poulton Gentlemen's Club, Lytham Cricket Club, Preston Morning Star Club, Preston Brunswick Club, Fleetwood Gentleman's Club, Blackpool Cricket Club and Wrea Green.

In the early days the biggest problem for the local clubs was fielding enough players. In July 1845, Kirkham joined with Lytham, and Fleetwood with Blackpool. The Kirkham Club lasted until 1859, when it was disbanded. In April 1865, a meeting was held in the National School, by Thomas Shaw and R. H. Birley, and the club was re-established. Mr Hornby let the club play at Ribby Hall until they could find a new ground.

In 1876 they were back, playing next door to the old ground on land belonging to Mr Langton Birley. The problem they faced was finding the money to level this ground. Edmund Birley of Clifton Hall was renting the old ground out. He arranged for the tenants to be moved and the club was back at the old Freckleton Street ground. This left them enough money to build a pavilion.

The year 1880 was one of the better ones for the club. They played 16 matches, winning 10, drawing 1 and losing 5. The teams they played against were Preston 2nd Eleven, St Anne's, Pembroke House School, Lytham, St Michael's, Great Eccleston, Blackpool, Eleven of Lytham, Freckleton,

Whittle le Woods, Preston North End 2nd Eleven and Swainson, Birley and Co. Preston, where Kirkham had their highest score of 150 runs. The list below gives the players' average runs for that season.

> George Lewis, 13·5; G. N. Golby, 9·2; James Singleton 7·7; John Carter, 12·3; R. M. Birley, 12·; J. A. Parkinson, 16·4; George Bagot, 5·; Sumner Fisher, 4·7; J. W. Sladen, 5·5; James Foster, 7·1; Robert Parkinson, 4·5; John Kirby, 5; Thomas Lewtas, 3·3; Arthur Rogerson, 7; John Lewtas, 3; William Swann, 4·3; Robert Whiteside, 4; W. W. Shaw, 3·6; George Tattersall, 2·3.

For the 1885 season, the club moved to its new ground on Station Road. In 1890 the club was struggling, and a meeting was held in 1891, to discuss the advisability of continuing playing cricket. At the meeting, chaired by Dr William Wright Shaw, it was decided to continue for one more year. The problem was the scarcity of players but the following season they managed to recruit new young players to the team.

By Saturday 3 June 1892, they had played four games and lost them all. On this Saturday they were beaten by Poulton who were 96 for 6 and Kirkham all out for 13 runs. At the time the cricket pavilion was a marquee, which was uninsured. In the morning after the match against Poulton, the marquee burnt down and all the club's equipment worth £50 was destroyed, except the bats which hadn't been put back after the Poulton game. The club struggled into 1893, with its bank balance of £8.

Since 1883, the Kirkham Lawn Tennis Club had played at the cricket ground. With the cricket club struggling, the tennis club passed a motion at a special meeting in 1890, to separate the two clubs. The tennis club assets included a tennis pavilion and seats. They wanted equal use of the lawn mower and roller, and to pay the cricket club a yearly rent of £3. The motion was voted down.

In 1895, there was a plan to join the cycling, football, tennis and cricket clubs together. This never happened, and the clubs stayed as they were. The cycling club's headquarters were at the Ship Inn on Freckleton Street. They held cycle races, some of which were 50 miles long, from May to September.

In 1899, Kirkham joined the newly formed Fylde Cricket League, which included the teams of Fleetwood, Blackpool, Kirkham, Thornton Alkali

Works, Lytham, Clifton, St Anne's, Ashton on Ribble and Bamber Bridge.

In 1900 the first ever Athletics Event was held on the Cricket Ground. The club was now called the Kirkham Cricket and Athletics Club. This festival, held in July or August, kept growing and became a big event. In 1904 there were 5,000 spectators, cycle races, running races, with over 350 entrants, with the Kirkham Subscription Band providing the entertainment.

> ### KIRKHAM.
> Given fine weather a capital day's sport should be seen on the picturesque ground of the Kirkham Cricket Club to-morrow afternoon. The entries are exceptionally large, and include runners of the calibre of Horne (Cambridge University), Roberts (Sefton Harriers), and Cooper (Manchester University)—three of the finest sprinters in England, whilst the cycle entries contain the names of many well-known riders in the North of England. The total entry of 325 constitutes a record for these sports.

In 1909 the Kirkham Lawn Tennis Club was disbanded. The cricket club stopped playing during the last few years of the First World War; this was a financial struggle because they still had to pay the rent for the field. The club was back playing in 1919, and the athletics events were restarted; but not on the same scale as before the war. The athletics event stopped in 1922 and the club became known as Kirkham and Wesham Cricket Club.

In 1934, Reverend Strange of the Grammar School was the chairman and the club was doing well. A new pavilion was built, and the club was making a profit. It was costing about £300 to keep running and had a bank balance of £60. On Wednesday 13 February 1935, they celebrated 50 years at the Station Road ground. After the Second World War, the club had a helping hand when the William Segar Hodgson Trust bought the ground and donated it to the club.

Football was the main sport for the working class...

Kirkham Football Club

Kirkham Football Club was formed in 1881 and played on what was called 'The Freckleton Street Ground'. This was situated just off Freckleton Street on Guild Lane. Kirkham played in The Lancashire Alliance League in the early days, until the Preston and District League was formed. The Preston and District League was for clubs within a ten-mile radius of Preston, and the League became The West Lancashire League in 1908. Kirkham also played in the Lancashire Football Association Challenge Trophy. The first year in this competition they were knocked out in the first round. They were beaten 14–0 at home by Blackburn on 5 November in the 1881/82 season. Kirkham never won this, but their local rivals Lytham won it in the 1894/95 season.

By 1890, the team was in debt, and even applied to the Co-op society for a £5 loan, which was refused. One member said, 'it's not good use of public money to kick leather about, better spent to cultivate the minds of the community.'

Kirkham gambled on fielding a fully paid team in the 1891/92 season, but it was a financial disaster. The club ended up £111 in debt. Just the players' wages alone cost £93 12s. 10d., to the yearly gate receipts of £56 4s. 10d. The club folded but reappeared in March 1893 to play the last few games of the season as Kirkham Athletic FC.

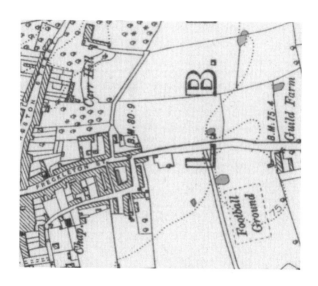

Crowd trouble was common. Even during a friendly match between their local rivals, Lytham, on Christmas Day 1897, fighting broke out. Lytham was winning 1–0, when Kirkham equalised near the end of the game. A player was kicked on purpose and the player's friend hit the perpetrator. The fans started fighting each other, Sergeant S. Wilcock and some Constables broke up the fighting.

The team had mixed success until 1910 when the Lancashire FA ordered the Kirkham ground to be closed from 31 October to 28 November. This was because of crowd trouble between Kirkham and Skelmersdale United on 15 October during the Lancashire Cup. After this season, the Kirkham team was bankrupt again and ceased to be, along with the Freckleton Street ground.

In August 1912, a new club was formed, Kirkham and Wesham F. C. Rev. Yates was the chairman. The new club had no ground but secured an agreement to play on the cricket ground for a rent of £7 10*s*. This agreement was only for one year in case the club caused too much damage to the cricket pitch. The team re-joined the West Lancashire League and ended the season in second place.

At the end of the season the club was in profit with a sum of £9 2*s*. 6*d*. One home game against Fleetwood took gate receipts of £42 4*s*. All this was

Kirkham Football team around 1890

to no avail though as the cricket club refused to let them play there again because they caused too much damage to the pitch. An alternative ground could not be found, and the club disappeared until after the First World War when they re-joined the West Lancashire League in August 1919. The team was now called Kirkham and Wesham United.

Kirkham and Wesham United played a charity match on Christmas Day 1926. This was to raise funds in aid of the family of William Townsend, who died whilst working at the new Westby Reservoir. William, an ex-player, was crushed when an engine fell over on the work site. The game raised £8 14*s.* for his family.

The team did not resurface again until 1946, when some ex-servicemen formed a committee to restart the Kirkham team and re-join the West Lancashire League in the next year's season. The journey takes Kirkham eventually becoming AFC Fylde with a new ground and a bright future.

Everybody enjoyed club day…

Club Day

Once a year, the Kirkham Benefit Societies belonging to St Michael's Church went to the church for a service. Afterwards, they paraded to their respected lodges (one of the town's inns) for a meeting and to go through the accounts. People joined a club and paid in a weekly amount, and when a member became sick the club paid out. The societies also paid towards the funeral costs if a member or one of his family died.

The clubs had strange names, as illustrated in the list of the Kirkham ones below:

Independent Order of Oddfellows, United Order of Free Gardeners, Ancient Order of Druids, Loyal Order of Ancient Shepherds, Ancient Order of Foresters, The Free Mechanics, The Catholic Brethren.

In the early nineteenth century, the Sunday School Children and clergy of St Michael's joined in the parade with the clubs and Club Day was established.

The year of the first Club Day is unknown (probably around 1820), but the first one mentioned by a paper was in July 1846, by the *Preston Chronicle*:

> ## KIRKHAM.
>
> **KIRKHAM CLUB FESTIVAL.** — Tuesday last was the anniversary festival of the benefit societies established in Kirkham. Divine service was celebrated in the morning, and a sermon preached by the Rev. D. Sutcliffe, at the Parish Church. The benefit societies then paraded the town, preceded by the boys and girls of the Church Sunday Schools, headed by their clergymen, the Rev, J. Pedder, the Rev. D. Sutcliffe, and the Rev. J. G. Piccope. The children were afterwards entertained with dinner in their respective schools, superintended by most of the ladies and gentlemen of the town.—The Zion Chapel Sunday School children were also handsomely treated in their school rooms, adjoining the chapel, and a social Tea Party took place there in the evening.—The members of the clubs sat down to sumptuous dinners at their respective houses.—The Wrea Green Sunday School children were treated with a jaunt to Lytham, by the eight o'clock morning train, returning to their school about half-past one, where a substantial dinner awaited their arrival, provided by the liberality of Mr. and Mrs. Hornby, of Ribby.

By 1869, the event had increased in size and was a major event for the area, with lots of visitors arriving in Kirkham, especially from Preston. The parade had increased in size and was a colourful affair. The town was bedecked with flags and the churches and the clubs, started carrying banners. There was also a fair on the Market Square. The fair included, Hobby Horses, Steam Driven Omnibuses, Sway Boats, Shooting Galleries, Half Penny Picture Galleries and Iterant Photograph Studios. There were 'Nut and Gingerbread Stalls' and street entertainers.

The parade of 1869 went as follows:

After the church service at St Michael's, given by Rev G. R. Brown, the parade formed outside the church. They walked along Church Street, up and down Preston Street, then turned left into Freckleton Street. They then went down Marsden Street, up Station Road to Milbanke House, where they turned around and headed back to the Market Square via Poulton Street.

The Britannia Brass Band of Preston led the parade, followed by:

Rev. G. Brown, 360 female scholars from the National School and 200 boys.

Rev. R. Moss, Kirkham Wesleyan School, 80 females and 40 males.

90 members of the Oddfellows and the Militia Band

95 members of the Free Gardeners and the band of the 22nd LRV Church (Accrington).

30 members of the Druids and the band of The Preston Rifles.

22 members of the Shepherds carrying crooks and the band of the 52nd LRV(Leyland).

Last, came 46 members of the Foresters, with the band of Preston Royal Artillery.

The bands formed together on arrival at the square, where they played a selection of music together. Afterwards, the clubs went to their respected lodges, and the National School Children had a meal and a sports afternoon in a field adjoining the school. The Wesleyans also had a meal and later had an afternoon of fun and games in a field lent by John Birley and Sons. The

pubs and inns were kept busy until 10 p.m., when the day's entertainment ended.

In 1870, The United Catholic Brethren joined the parade for the first time, with a flute and drum band. From 1871, the boys and girls from the workhouse started taking part in the parade and walked with the Church of England Scholars. That year, The Free Mechanics didn't take part as they were split on whether to parade in Freckleton or Kirkham.

Club Day slowly grew until 1875, when the day was changed from the first Tuesday to the first Thursday of July. This was to give the mill hands a four-day holiday and to stop them turning up drunk at work on Wednesday morning. The mills were closed on Wednesday night and reopened on Monday morning. This four-day holiday was a blessing in those days and gave Kirkham Club Day a new emphasis.

Kirkham Artillery Band led the 1875 parade, followed by St Michael's Clergy and scholars, the workhouse children, pupils of the Girls' Charity School, Newton Blue Coats, Greenhalgh Brass Band, The Free Gardeners with St Joseph's Band of Preston, followed by The Free Mechanics and The Preston Artillery Band, and for the first time, The Lodge of Orangemen with their Kirkham Flute and Drum Band. Finally, the Oddfellows with the 3rd Loyal Lancashire Militia. Missing were the Catholic Brethren who had been insulted by the Orangemen.

At a meeting, to decide the parade order, it was decided that the Church of England would go first followed by their Friendly Societies. The question then arose of who would go next, Catholics or Orangemen. Both sides being amicable, it was decided to draw straws; the Catholics won. The Catholics would walk to the Market Square and join the parade behind the Oddfellows; the Orangemen would bring up the rear. When the Catholic Brethren arrived at the Market, the Orangemen had positioned themselves in-between the Free Mechanics and the Oddfellows, however. This forced the Catholics to the back of the parade, who, feeling insulted, turned around and marched back the way they came.

The Orangemen never paraded again and the Catholics refused to parade in the 1876 and 1877 Club Days. In 1878, the Brethren returned, though intermittently, but this was mainly due to financial restraints.

From 1878, Club Day now followed a set routine: St Michael's, The Willows and Methodists all held a church service in the morning. Afterwards, the

Church of England scholars, clergy and Friendly Clubs with their bands formed up outside St Michael's Church. When the parade passed Market Square, the Catholic Brethren joined on, and paraded up Preston Street to Carr Hill House. The parade came back down Preston Street, turning left into Freckleton Street. As it passed the Methodist Chapel on Kettle Well Lane, the Methodists joined the parade and it followed the usual route around town back to the Market Square. The C of E children now held their sports afternoons in the grounds of Carr Hill House. The winners of the races received monetary prizes given by Mr and Mrs Birley. In later years, the Birleys opened the house to the public and the brass bands played in the gardens. Tables and benches were laid out and the children were given a free meal. The Birleys' servants and staff served the tables.

The Independent Congregation held their parade in the afternoons. They met at the Manse on Marsden Street at 2 p.m. and paraded with a band to the Independent School in Wesham. The Minister, R. C. Richards, and William Bowdler led the parades. After a meal, the children also held a sports afternoon on land belonging to Mr Richards. The two-pole banner with a picture of the Zion Chapel was first carried in 1878, and is still carried today.

During the last decade of the century, the parade changed again and was split into three separate parades. The Willows and Holy Cross Wesham held mass at 8:15 a.m., then paraded with their Scholars, Church and Catholic Brethren. They met at Townend, and walked around Kirkham, back to Townend, where they split back to their own churches and field days.

The Church of England's parade stayed the same but was now led by the town's horse-drawn fire engine. In 1895, a newly formed group of local businessmen started holding their own parade. The Methodists stopped taking part and joined with the Independents. They paraded in the afternoon and held joint field days. The fair continued to be held on the Market Square. The day after Club Day, people started catching excursion trains for day trips to Keswick and Windermere. The Independents usually travelled to Rivington Pike by train and bus. This was the home of Lord Leverhulme, a supporter of the Congregational Church.

At the start of the twentieth century, the Clubs had stopped walking in the parade and it was revamped. Horse drawn carts started appearing, carrying local dignities, school children and rose queens. It was held on a Thursday for the last time in 1906. The mill workers now received a week's holiday.

From 1907, Club Day was held on the first Monday of July. It was this parade in 1907 that made national news when the fire engine ran away and killed two people who were standing at the Fishstones, and injured four.

The fairground had moved to the recreation ground by 1905, and new steam powered rides were appearing. One of the most popular was called a gondola switchback. In 1906, Elizabeth Boardman, aged 47, of 13 Clegg Street, went to the fair on Club Day night with her friends June Benson and Rebecca Aspin. All three went on the gondola switchback. After paying the attendant, the ride started before Elizabeth could sit down and she was thrown out of the gondola. Her friends called for the engine man to stop the ride, but he wouldn't. The ride continued for five minutes before it stopped. When June and Rebecca got to Elizabeth, some men were bandaging her head. She was taken home and attended to by Dr Shaw. Elizabeth had deep lacerations on her head and a broken spine. These injuries proved to be fatal and Elizabeth died on Sunday night at 11:30 p.m. At the inquest, the ride's operators were found guilty of negligence, for collecting the fares whilst the ride was in motion. It was also recommended that gates or doors should be fitted to either side of the carriages.

Club Day carried on this way until 1915. This was the last Club Day to be held until after the war. The first post-war parade was in 1919, which was part victory celebrations. By the early 1920s, people had a bit more money than previous years and were starting to go away for a week's holiday. Now, when the mills closed on Saturday, many were catching the night boats for the Isle of Man. They had a one-week holiday per year and didn't want to waste two days waiting until after Club Day and travelling on a Tuesday. The parades, although still enjoyed by lots of people, were becoming quieter.

After a meeting with the mill owners, unions and workers, it was decided to move the half-day holiday from September to June. The holidays in Kirkham were now the first week in July, and the September holidays were the first Saturday, Monday and Tuesday of that month. Previously, the September holidays were the first Monday, Tuesday and Wednesday in September. From June 1926, Club Day would now be held on the second Saturday in June as it is today. After the Second World War the friendly societies died away with the birth of the welfare state. Club Day continues as before with the parade and the fairground, not that much different from the parade days of the Victorian times.

Kirkham suffered from low level crime...

Justice

When Kirkham received its Royal Charter from Henry III in 1299, it enabled the town to administer justice through punishment. The town's stocks were in St Michael's graveyard, but they were later moved to the Market Square. The town's gibbet stood at the crossroads formed by Garstang Road, Mowbreck Lane and North View in Wesham.

There was also a cuckstool over a pond on Moor Street; the pond was called Cuckstool Pit. The Town's Court was held in the top floor of the Moot Hall, which stood on Poulton Street next to the Market Square. This building was two-storeys high with steps up to the top floor. The ground floor was used as shops, butcher's etc. The Moot Hall burnt down in the 1790s, and courts were then held in a house on the Market Square.

Order was kept by the town's two bailiffs, a police constable and his sergeant. The town had a police lock-up, which was attached to the workhouse.

KIRKHAM LOCK-UP HOUSE.

[Inspected November 6, 1847.]

This lock-up house and police station is private property rented by the county. It is in a convenient situation in the centre of the town.

There are three cells, and the following are their dimensions:—

Cells.	Length.	Breadth.	Height.	Cubical Contents.
	Feet.	Feet.	Feet.	Feet.
1	7½	7	12	630
1	8⅓	7	12	720
1	6½	7	12	550

There is a resident constable.

The cells have boarded floors and appear to be always dry. One cell has a glazed window opening into a yard belonging to the police station, but the only provision for lighting and ventilating the other cells is two unglazed gratings in each, one in the door and one in the upper part of the cell opening into a passage. These two cells are not well lighted.

The cells are secure. They are warmed by a stove in one cell, and by the smoke pipe from this stove in the other two.

Each cell has a guard bed, but there is no bedding.

There was only one night-vessel for the three cells.

The prisoners have two meals per day, and 3*d*. is allowed by the county for each meal. There is no fixed quantity of food, but the constable said he gave as much as he could afford for the money. Each meal consists of milk porridge and bread.

The place was in good order.

The number of prisoners last year was 101. The greatest number at any one time was four, and the longest period of detention is from Saturday night to Monday morning.

The keeper, who is a county constable, appeared properly qualified for his duties. He is married, and his wife attends to the female prisoners.

This lock-up house appears to be sufficient for the purposes required.

It was stated that there is very little crime in the neighbourhood, and that the offences consisted almost entirely of vagrancy and of disorderly conduct, arising from drunkenness.

In 1854, work was started on a new police station. It was built on a piece of land on Freckleton Street, which belonged to Lord Derby. The new police station had two cells and Kirkham Court was upstairs. Attached to this building was a superintendent's house, with three police cottages in the yard.

The Kirkham Police Division in the old police yard in 1930.

The Kirkham Police Court was held on Mondays. The serious cases were sent to the next court up from this, which was the Preston Quarter Sessions. The Quarter Sessions were held at Epiphany (Winter) Lent (Spring) Summer and Michaelmas (Autumn). The four sessions were to relieve pressure from the Assizes, which were held in Spring and Summer for the most serious crimes. The Petty Sessions Court was held at Kirkham on Tuesdays. These were small cases brought by individuals, the accuser being the prosecutor and the accused the defendant. The cases were brought before two judges, mostly concerning accusations of theft or assault.

The County Court was also held once a month at Kirkham. This made history in 1858 when the first trial in the country for the 'New Court of Probate Act' was held there. The nephews and nieces of Robert Parkinson of Treales contested his will, on 22 June 1858.

Robert Parkinson, was a small farmer from Treales who died in January 1858. He was suffering from palsy, and in 1849, was treated by Dr Shaw for St Vitus's Dance. He lived a chaotic life with his siblings William and Nancy, on their neglected farm. William and Nancy ended up in the workhouse in 1850, and Robert went to live with his other sister Ellen Udale in Kirkham. Robert, a bachelor with no heirs, left his entire estate of £300-worth of property and £200 of personal possessions to Ellen. The case centred on Robert's mental state when he wrote the will in 1849. Although he was disabled, the judge accepted that he was mentally able to produce a will. The nephews and nieces lost the case.

The court closed in 1972 when the government created Crown Courts, and the old police station (which is still standing) was replaced by the new building next door.

The Inns experienced most of the trouble...

Pubs and Beer Houses

In early Victorian Kirkham, the town was full of old thatched inns, modern hotels and beer houses. Below is the list of all the pubs, inns and beer houses in 1895, just before new hotels began to be built.

Robert Wright outside The Gun Tavern where Coroner's Inquests were often held.

Thatched House Tavern, corner of North View/ Garstang Road.

Royal Oak, 14 Garstang Road.

Stanley Arms 8 Garstang Road.

Railway Hotel, Station Road.

Derby Arms, 71 Station Road.

Gun Tavern, 55 Station Road.

New Black Bull Inn, 108 Poulton Street.

Rose Bud, 2 Moor Street.

Old Swan Inn, Town End.

Bowling Green Inn, Poulton Street.

New Inn, 19 Poulton Street.

Queen's Arms 7 Poulton Street, formerly King's Arms before Queen Victoria ascended the throne.

Black Horse Hotel, 35 Preston Street.

Old Black Bull Hotel, 33 Preston Street.

Ship Inn, 8 Freckleton Street, headquarters Kirkham Cycle Club.

Post Office Hotel, Freckleton Street, which replaced 'The Blue Bell' postal inn, 1 Church Street demolished in 1869.

Farmer's Arms, 54 Freckleton Street.

Live and Let Live, 83 Freckleton Street.

Joiner's Arms, 88 Marsden Street.

Royal Oak, 42 Marsden Street.

Britannia Inn, 38 Marsden Street.

By 1900 new large hotels were being built as Kirkham developed industrially. The St George Hotel replaced the New Black Bull Inn and the Rose Bud. The Old Swan Inn was demolished, and the Swan Hotel built on the site. The Lane Ends Hotel replaced the Thatched House Tavern and the Congressional Church was built on the site of the Bowling Green Inn.

Live and Let Live fishing club

By 1940, all the beer houses had closed and some of the inns, leaving the Lane Ends Hotel, Royal Oak, Stanley Arms, Railway Hotel, Derby Arms, St George Hotel, Swan Hotel, Queen's Arms, Black Horse Hotel, Post Office and The Live and Let Live.

Bowling Green Inn

The Bowling Green Inn was a thatched-roof inn on Poulton Street. The inn had two bedrooms, a bowling green, stable and a brew house, covering a site of 1,798 square yards. A favourite haunt of the navvies, who were building the railway through Kirkham, the pub had a bad reputation. This reputation was worsened when landlord Richard Noblett was attacked with a knife by 29-year-old Stephen Rainford. The event happened on 4 February 1845; the day of the old Kirkham Fair.

Rainford was drinking in one of the lower rooms with six friends, when Richard heard him talking crudely to one of the maids, Isabella Wilding. The landlord ask Rainford to leave, but he refused. After being asked to leave again, he drank another man's glass of ale and walked to the front door. Richard followed him to the door and bid him goodnight, at which point Stephen Rainford, challenged the landlord and then struck him in the face with a knife. Rainford at this point ran away and Richard went to Dr Gradwell, to get the wound dressed. It wasn't too badly cut and healed after ten days. Pc Brownhill arrested Rainford, who admitted striking the landlord, but only with his hand, not with a knife.

He was sent to trial at Lancaster Castle, where he was found guilty of Common Assault and sentenced to six months' hard labour in Lancaster Prison. At the same Spring Assizes, Richard Noblett was back in the witness box after being burgled on 21 December 1844 by Charley Swan aged 26, who went by the alias John Johnson.

On Saturday night, after locking up, Richard stated there were three four-penny pieces, two six pences and 20s. worth of copper in the money draw. Amongst this money, there was also a crushed half-penny piece. Standing on the opposite side to the draw was a full cask of gin. The next morning, the landlord noticed slates missing from the cellar roof, which abutted the inn. There was a hole big enough for a man to fit through; the door between the cellar and house was always left open. He discovered the till and gin missing, which he later found outside. The money had gone and only three gills of gin were left in the cask.

Charley Swan was arrested in his lodgings on Marsden Street, by Pc Thomas Barnes. When Pc Barnes entered the cellar where Swan slept, he saw him hiding something in his pillar. In the pillar were found two four-penny pieces, one six pence and some copper. Also, in the bed was more copper, including the damaged half-penny piece. Pc Barnes also found a chisel in the bedroom. The woman owner of the house said, 'the chisel belonged to Swan.'

William Walden shared a room with Charley Swan. William said at the trial, that Swan told him, 'He'd robbed a shop in Garstang of three pounds and 3 lb of tea.' He also said that, 'He could easily break into Noblett's place, through the cellar, he would have the money, or die for it.'

At the trial, Swan tried to put the blame on William Walden, but the Judge found Charley Swan guilty of felony. He was sentenced to be 'Transported beyond the seas, to such a place, Her Majesty may be pleased to appoint, for the term of fifteen years.'

Throwing Jack off the green

In June 1852, Mr and Mrs Noblett were back in court, after being summoned by Betty Towers for assault. Jack Towers, her husband, had been going on a drinking spree at the Bowling Green Inn. Betty was sick of going to fetch him home. Whilst Jack was playing bowls, her temper got the better of her. She went to the inn and attacked him. When he still refused to go home, she began throwing all the jacks and the bowls off the green. Mr and Mrs Noblett at this point ejected her from the inn 'very roughly' according to Betty. Betty then went into the garden next door and started throwing stones and other missiles at her husband and the other bowlers. The judge at Kirkham Court dismissed the case and the Nobletts were exonerated.

The next landlord of any significance was Henry Rawcliffe, who made the ill-fated mistake to move from the Bowling Green Inn to the Swan Inn, six months before his murder.

TO GENTLEMEN, FARMERS, AND OTHERS.

HENRY RAWCLIFFE, of the Bowling Green Inn, Poulton-street, Kirkham, begs to return his sincere thanks to the inhabitants of Kirkham and its vicinity for the kind and liberal support he has hitherto received, and desires to inform them that he is about to enter on those well-accustomed and commodious premises, the Swan Inn, Kirkham.

H. R. hopes, by attention and perseverance, to obtain a liberal share of public patronage, and feels convinced that, with the excellent accommodation he possesses for all classes, together with a choice assortment of wines, spirits, &c., he will be able to give entire satisfaction.

An excellent young boar, of the large breed, kept on the premises. For pedigree, &c., see card, or apply at the Swan Inn.

Kirkham, 24th April, 1862.

By 1892, the Bowling Green Inn was the oldest in Kirkham. With it only having two bedrooms, plans were put forward by Mr J. W. Lawrenson for it to be demolished and replaced with a double fronted inn. The plans were rejected, but the inn was still demolished to make way for the new Congressional Church.

The Bowling Green Inn wasn't the only pub with a bowling green; the others were at The Derby Arms, The Post Office Inn, The Live and Let Live and The Royal Oak (Marsden Street).

Six months after taking over the Swan Inn, Henry Rawcliffe was dead...

HENRY RAWCLIFFE

On the evening of Sunday 28 September 1862, Henry Rawcliffe, aged 36, Landlord of the Swan Inn at Townend, was trying to eject some drunken harvest men from his pub. This event eventually led to his murder.

It was closing time and Martin Garrity, who had been drinking with James Cain, Margaret Cain, their nephew Patrick Cain and Mary Smith, were all drunk and refused to leave. Henry dragged Garrity to the porch, but was over powered by him. He then went into the street to blow his whistle. Pc Fletcher entered the pub, where he saw Garrity strike Henry Rawcliffe in the chest. The policeman then arrested Garrity.

Pc Fletcher took him outside, and was surrounded and attacked by the Cains and some of their friends to prevent him arresting Garrity. Sgt Lofthouse turned up and calmed the situation down. Garrity and Patrick were then arrested and on the way to the cells when Patrick Cain managed to escape. At this point Patrick Cain returned to his lodgings, but later returned to the Swan with an iron poker. On finding the pub locked, he fired the poker 'like a dart' through the upstairs window.

Whilst this was going on Betty Rawcliffe, aged 15, was awoken by shouting and came downstairs to see her father bolting the door. He told her, 'not to mind' and took her upstairs to the club room. They watched from the club room window to see if the mob ill-treated the police, in case they were later needed to give evidence. Henry opened the window and looked out to see the crowd dispersing, upon Sgt Lofthouse's arrival. Sometime later, Betty heard someone strike a lamp post, and saw three men approaching.

The Old Swan Inn Kirkham

Her father closed the window whilst she knelt by him. She then heard glass smashing, and when she looked up she saw a poker sticking out of her dad's eye. He collapsed onto her and never regained consciousness.

Eliza Fullerton, flax spinner, heard a scream and went to The Swan, along with John Smith, a local green grocer. She helped raise Henry's body, whilst John tried to pull out the poker. Eventually, he had to put Henry's head between his knees to do this. Dr Whitgreave arrived in the club room and found Henry on the floor supported by Mr Smith. He had a wound in his right eye – which had penetrated his brain by half an inch. He died two hours later at 1:45 a.m.

Henry Rawcliffe was buried on the following Wednesday in St Michael's churchyard. All the local publicans were present, as well as a large number of the town. He left a widow and five children.

At the trial at Kirkham Police Court, several witnesses said they saw Patrick Cain hanging around the Swan with the poker. Barbara MacConkey and Mary Jane Millar, who had been drinking in the New Inn, saw him on their way home with the poker. Eliza Fullerton saw him with the poker between the pub porch and the end of the house. Mrs Atkinson and her daughter, saw him throw it through the window.

Whilst in the cells at Kirkham, Cain admitted his guilt to Pc Fletcher. At the police court hearing before Thomas Langton Birley and R. C. Richards, he said that he had got the poker from James Cain's house, then went to Rawcliffe's house to find the door and windows closed, that there were no lights on. When he headed home he fired the poker at the window. He thought he had only smashed the window, until Sgt Lofthouse arrested him for murder.

James Cain was charged with assaulting Pc Fletcher and sent to Preston Court, where he received two years' servitude at the Michaelmas Sessions.

Margret Cain was discharged at Kirkham court.

Garrity was fined £10 at Kirkham Court for resisting arrest, but as he could not pay, he was sentenced to two months' hard labour.

Patrick Cain was found guilty of manslaughter at Liverpool Assizes and sentenced to three years in prison.

When is a crime not a crime?

RICHARD BENNET 1836

When Agnes Parkinson rejected the advances of Richard Bennet from across the road, he decided to get revenge by blowing up her dad's house. On the night after her wedding, he placed 30 lbs of explosive in the cellar and set off an explosion.

Mr Thomas Parkinson lived with his family in a three-storey house on Poulton Street. In the early hours of Tuesday 19 April 1836, he and five members of his family were woken at four in the morning by a large explosion.

Ground Floor Plan of House

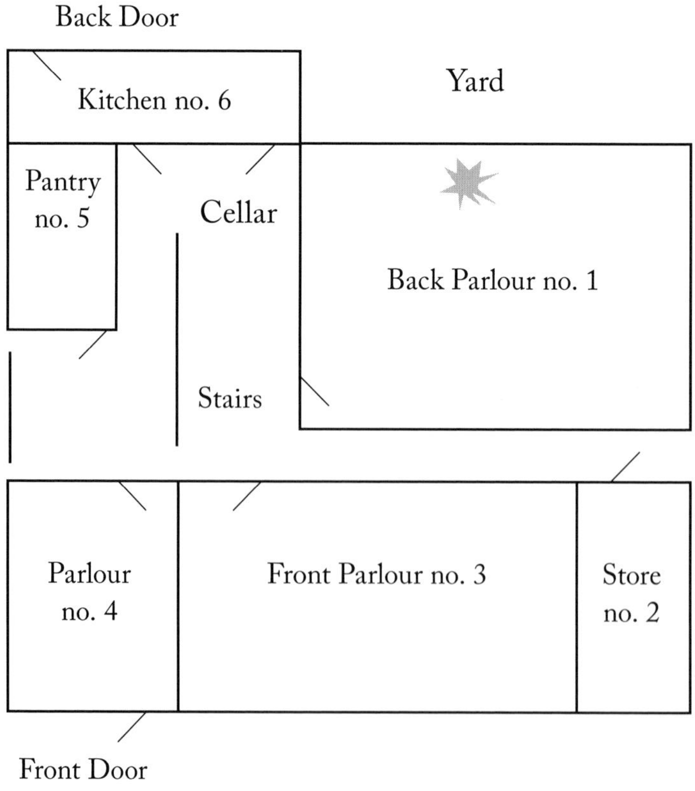

Back Door

Kitchen no. 6

Yard

Pantry no. 5

Cellar

Back Parlour no. 1

Stairs

Parlour no. 4

Front Parlour no. 3

Store no. 2

Front Door

The explosives were left under room no. 1 in the cellar. This floor collapsed into the cellar, destroying all the contents. Half the floor above also collapsed into the cellar, but luckily the remaining floor held the bed with Mr Parkinson's young son and his niece Miss Betsy Parkinson.

In rooms no. 2 and no. 3, the floors were shattered but did not collapse. However, all the contents were damaged. The floor of room no. 4 was damaged, but in the room directly above, in which Mr and Mrs Cummings slept (Mr Parkinson's daughter Betty), was undamaged. In room no. 5, the internal pantry wall was blown down and the contents destroyed. Room no. 6 was the kitchen, and its window and door were blown out. Above this slept Mr Parkinson and his youngest daughter Elizabeth. The furniture was blown over and his daughter's bed was damaged. The blast blew the cellar doors 29 yards across the road, damaging Mr Thomas Hornby's old house.

Luckily, nobody in the house was hurt, but the damage would have been far worse if the explosives had been left in the middle of the room, instead of against the cellar wall.

At first the inhabitants of Kirkham were at a loss as to what had happened, until William Tomlinson reported to the police that he had had 30 lbs of gunpowder stolen from his warehouse. Constable Thomas Buller went to see Thomas Parkinson to ascertain whether he had any suspects. Suspicion soon fell on Richard Bennet (aged 21), the son of a boot and shoe maker, who was arrested.

Reverend Richard Moore led the investigation and began interviewing witnesses. Betty Parkinson said, 'He [Richard] came around six months ago and ask for Johanna.' She had no sister of that name and then Agnes her sister, entered the room. Richard Bennet said to Agnes, 'How long have you been a fortune teller and that she would be his wife.' Agnes left the room and went upstairs, and Richard followed her. Agnes' brother stopped him and threw him out of the house. He returned a month later and this time Mr Cummings threw him out. On leaving he said, 'I will torment you in a different way.' The Parkinson family, thought he had set the explosive to annoy Agnes, who'd married the day before and was not at home.

Mr William Tomlinson, an ironmonger who lived next door to the Bennet family said that he 'had 30 lbs of explosives stolen, from his warehouse behind his shop.' This was stolen on Monday night; it was made up ready in paper and sealed.

Mr Bennet, Richard's father, regularly took in lodgers in a room with three beds, which they shared with Richard Bennet. Several said they saw him in bed at eleven, and again immediately after the blast. His mother Rachel said, 'He went to bed at eleven after having his supper.' A journeyman who shared a room with Richard said he 'often heard him talk romantically of Agnes.' After this evidence, Richard was remanded until the following Thursday.

Richard admitted writing a letter to Agnes whilst she was in Blackburn, and when she returned she smiled at him. This smile made him believe that she loved him, and he also admitted saying that he 'would torment the Bastards in a different way.' The last witness, his father Thomas Bennet said his son 'was often sullen and then the next minute as bright as a button.' He stated that his son was coming upstairs after the blast naked, after going to the toilet. After Richard got dressed they went outside to look at the damage, like the other half of the town.

On Thursday, he was again questioned by Rev. Richard Moore and T. R. W. France, at Mr Pilkington's office. He was asked about his movements between eight and eleven on the night in question. Richard said that he 'had been at the theatre'.

The judges conferred and the only evidence they had was that a trail of gunpowder had been laid, which then ran to a larger amount, which exploded. This was not defined in law as a crime, as igniting gunpowder was not considered arson, no fire was discovered, and no life was lost. Therefore, there was no legal offence and so there was no legal punishment. Richard Bennet was free to go, but it didn't end there.

Nine years later, on 2 August 1845, Reverend Moore was walking along Fishergate in Preston, when someone from behind fired a pistol at him. He then felt something hard hit him in the chest. When he turned around, Richard Bennet was standing there. Rev. Moore apprehended him and Richard was arrested and sent to trial at Lancaster, charged with attempted murder.

At Lancaster Summer Assizes, on 9 August 1845, Richard Bennet pleaded not guilty with intent to murder Reverend Richard Moore.

Reverend Moore stated that he was walking down Fishergate when he heard a gun discharged very close to him. He was enveloped in smoke for a second or two and then felt something hard hit his chest. When he turned around, he saw Richard Bennet standing five feet away and seized him. He called for persons to call the police and a man came up with the pistol and said, 'He shot at you Sir and threw the pistol.'

The man who picked up the pistol was John Harrison. He confirmed what Reverend Moore had already said and added that he 'gave the pistol to Pc Williams.'

A voice in the court room shouted out, 'Ask him where the bullet was found!' The judge replied, 'Who is that … take that man into custody.'

Adam Capstick and William Kirby, both witnesses, confirmed Reverend Moore's statement. Pc Robert Snell Williams was called and he said, 'After a long search the bullet could not be found.'

When the defence began the prisoner said, 'He [Moore] accused me of a crime of which I am not guilty … and I wish to make it known.'

Mr Brandt defence stated that there was no ball, no powder on the ground, no marks on Mr Moore's clothes and so could only be charged with assault, by throwing the pistol. That he will prove that the case is about insanity, not enmity, to Mr Moore.

Dr Thomas Shaw was called and said that he'd 'known Bennet for eight years and found him reserved. He would fall into a state of vacancy for a week at a time, when he would refuse to speak. He attended him once for a week, he could not sleep and rambled about at night. He had no doubt about him being insane.'

Andrew Lewis, a flax dresser who'd known him for six years said he 'had always thought him not right in the mind by his actions. He was once walking through Kirkham, about eight or nine at night, when he heard two persons speaking loudly behind him. When he turned around, there was Richard talking to himself.'

His brother Peter Bennet said, 'He often fell into fits of despondency, on the 2nd of August, he found him in the workshop talking to himself.'

The last defence witness to be called was Robert Ashcroft (the Bennet family's solicitor) who received five letters from Richard. He began to read out the contents to the court, much to everybody's amusement.

Letter one: I am going to put a bullet through my thick head, for a foolish thing I once did. I'd wish to know if you have any commands, to the shades below. The court erupted into laughter.

Letter two, six weeks later: Who steals my purse, steals trash, Shakespeare. The courtroom again laughed.

Letter three: If you had a friend who betrayed your confidence, how would you treat him. The court didn't find this funny.

Letter four, September: Othello, a poem in three cantos, a friend in need is a friend indeed. There was no response from the court.

Fifth and last letter:

> " Ohlll ponury repressed thclr nobio rage,
>   And frozo tho gonlal curront 'of tho soul,
> Slr, lf I mlstalco not, you aro a poscr, and cap all my acqualntanco, for
> It seems that wo havo unconsclously played a gamo tlint takes tho tasto
> of othors,   But If you tako any Intcrost In your brother's affalrs, tho
> sooner you look at tho abovo lines tho bettor; for without somo as-
> slstanco from somo quartor, the wholo must romaln undlgnlfiod, dcad,
> and Inort.   A spccuiation must bo glvon up In which thcro Is much
> to galn and nothing to loso; tho Polka must romaln Incomplcto, and
> that's poz.   Yours to command; Rara Avls."—(Grcat laughtor.)

Taken from the *Preston Chronicle*

Robert Ashcroft had no doubt about the prisoner's insanity.

Mr Justice Cresswell said to the jury, 'Throwing the pistol is out of the question, the prisoner is indicted for feloniously shooting, not assault. If at the time you think he was insane, acquit him.'

The jury, without hesitation, found him not guilty by reason of insanity. The prisoner was remanded at Her Majesty's pleasure, respecting him being ascertained. He was sent to Lancaster Asylum, where he stayed for 11 years.

Here he was assessed as being 'In general sullen, averse to enter into conversations, had delusions of loving character, chiefly those of suspicion'.

On 21 July 1856, he was admitted to Bethlem Hospital in London, from where he was discharged on 13 December 1856 aged 42.

The last two stories involve the murder of four girls, sad stories, which should have been remembered...

Betty Titterington 1857

On the evening of 12 May 1857, at seven o'clock, an argument involving children ended with the death of 14-year-old Betty Titterington.

Betty, the daughter of John and Ellan Titterington, was playing with seven friends in Little Lane, off Freckleton Street. Thomas Elliot, who was also aged fourteen, approached the girls, whilst carving a piece of wood into a guinea pig. When one of the girls, Elizabeth Rawstone, aged 12, told him mockingly, 'take care or you will cut yourself,' he threw a stone at her. The girls, instigated by Betty, then began to jeer him calling him 'tins', he then threw a stone at Betty. Betty picked up the stone and went over to him. Thomas kicked her and as she went to strike him with the stone, he struck her in the side of the neck, with the hand holding a knife. She screamed out and started to bleed from the neck. Thomas stood there for a few seconds and on seeing the blood, ran off down Back Lane (Marsden Street).

The event was witnessed by Mary Devannagh, whose husband placed his hand on the wound. She saw the blood come through his fingers and out of Betty's mouth and played no further role because she fainted. Betty's sister Ann, aged 12, had also witnessed the event, walking back from the water pump, carrying a bucket of water. Ellan Titterington, the girl's mother, ran out of the house after being told what had happened. Ellan saw the girl 'crozaling' down the road, covered in blood, bleeding from the neck. Betty collapsed and never spoke again.

Mr William Gradwell, a local surgeon, was called a little after seven. He found the poor girl lying on the floor. She had been dead for a few minutes. At the inquest, held in the Post Office Hotel, he reported that she had a one-and-a-half-inch wound, in the left side of the neck, two inches deep. The knife had severed the artery and jugular vein and part of the wind pipe. The cause of death was excessive loss of blood.

Thomas Elliot spent the night hiding in the fields. He was later found by Thomas Cowperthwaite, who handed him over to the police. When questioned by Superintendent John Francis Crane, Thomas claimed that she struck him first, the knife was closed, and that he caught her with his nail. When asked, he produced the knife out of his pocket. Blood was found on the blade.

Thomas was charged with manslaughter and committed to trial at Lancaster Assizes. On 8 August 1857 he was found guilty, with the recommendation of mercy, because of his age. The Judge said he 'did not think Thomas intended to injure the girl, but he could not go unpunished'. Thomas was jailed for one month.

The worst crime perpetrated in Kirkham was committed by a Policeman...

Pc Bligh 1886

Pc Alfred Bligh, aged 31, was a police officer in Kirkham. He was a well-respected officer, who had been awarded the badge of merit in 1885, whilst trying to arrest a man called Clancy. When arresting Clancy, he was attacked by a gang and kicked to the ground, but still manage to take him into custody. Clancy received two months' hard labour, his friends Mclean six weeks and Harvey three months' hard labour.

The following terrible events happened in Bligh's police house, behind the old police station.

On Saturday evening on 15 May 1886, Alfred Bligh murdered his three children, Leila Ada aged 6, Gertrude Marian aged 3, and Sarah Eleanor aged 1. He fractured their skulls with a wooden axe, and then choked them with pieces of bed sheets. Afterwards he cut his own throat with a razor, in an attempt to commit suicide.

Alfred Bligh came from Swaffham, Norfolk and left to take up a job as coachman at Arley Hall, near Wigan. Whilst at Arley he met his future wife, Elizabeth Turner, who was the cook there. They were married on 10 October 1878, at St John's Church. The couple moved around the north west for the next few years in different posts, during which time Leila Ada and Gertrude Marian were born. Alfred Bligh then joined the Lancashire Constabulary and after his probation was posted to Kirkham.

Elizabeth was pregnant with her third child Sarah Eleanor when she arrived in Kirkham. Sadly, Elizabeth died after giving birth on 7 December 1884, aged 35 years. Pc Bligh wrote to his sister-in-law, Annie Turner, three days after the funeral.

> **17, Freckleton-street, Kirkham, near Preston,**
> **10th December, 1884.**
>
> Dear Sister,—I write to know if you will come and take charge of my house and children, as you know how I am left, and I do not know anyone here that I can trust or ask to do it. I can trust you without any fear of anything. If you will come you shall have a good home, and I will pay you 5s a week, if that will suit you. I am doing well at present, and will be better off if I can get someone that will look after my house, and if I cannot I will have to leave here, and that will make my loss greater than ever, to take three little ones into a strange place, and amongst strangers. I hope you will consider this well over, if it is only for my children. Write and tell me if you will come. Sarah will come home on Friday night. She will wait until I get an answer.—From yours, &c., **ALFRED BLIGH.**
> P.S.—Write by return of post.

Annie took up the offer as a house keeper but left 11 months later, pregnant by Bligh. He then took on a new house keeper, Ann Pickford.

Annie Turner later raised a summons against Bligh, for the maintenance of her child, claiming him to be the father. Previous to this he was having money problems and was said to be in a depressed state. The court summons at Bolton would mean the end of his career, and he would lose his police house and job.

On the night in question, Ann Pickford's son, Frederick, was visiting from Manchester. Ann was getting Nelly (Sarah) ready to take her to visit Sangers Circus, which was showing in Kirkham. Bligh told her not to take her and go just with her son. Bligh had been to the circus in the day with the two elder children. She put the three children to bed, the two eldest in the front bedroom which they shared with their father, and Nelly in the back bedroom which she shared with Ann. Whilst doing this she noticed that Bligh was writing four letters.

One of the letters was addressed to Annie Turner, telling her she would receive no money, because she had caused him to be dismissed from the police. Another letter was to Alice Lea Turner, stating that she had got some good news coming. One letter was sent to his sister, with police insurance policies inside. He stated that there should be enough money in the policies to bury them all in one grave, with his wife Lizzie, and to pay Mrs Pickford the £3.00 he owed her, or that she could have the furniture. The last letter was addressed to Ann Pickford, asking her not to think the worse of him and that he was driven to it, he could stand it no longer.

> 17, Freckleton-street, Kirkham.
>
> Annie Turner,—You have brought me into a nice mess. You have been advised by other people, so you can go to them to keep you and the child. You have got me dismissed from the police force, so you will have to keep the child yourself. When you get this letter I shall be cold, and it is all through you summoning me.   ALFRED BLIGH.
>
> P.S.—I told you long ago if ever you did do it I would not pay anything, so I have made away with all of us.   A. B.

Earlier in the day, he had been to see his superintendent, and he had told Ann that he might have to resign. Ann said at the inquest the following Monday, that 'he seemed depressed and she felt uneasy, that he might hang himself.' Reluctantly, Ann went to the fair with her son, and on returning found the house locked. They returned half an hour later.

This time the house was unlocked, and after finding Bligh bleeding on the bedroom floor, they went back out to get help. When they returned with Superintendent Stafford and Pc Knott, Bligh was lying in the yard after jumping out of the window. They then found the girls, all dead, on one bed. Dr Thomas Shaw and his son Dr William Wright Shaw were called.

William Shaw attended to Bligh and Thomas Shaw to the girls. In his opinion, they had been hit first with the axe to render them insensible and then strangled with bed sheets. Bligh had a wound to his head, and a 6-inch cut in his neck. Four days after the event he was examined by Dr Wallace of Whittingham, who said he was recovering from a fit of insanity.

Bligh was taken from Kirkham to Preston Prison hospital, whilst there he requested an interview with Annie Turner which was granted, they shook hands and seemed on good terms. He was also visited by his brother and sister in Lancaster. Bligh was tried at Lancaster Assizes for murder. He was found guilty and sentenced to death on 13 July 1886. Mr Williamson MP and Mr Thomas Barrow of Lancaster appealed to the Home Secretary and Bligh was re-examined by two doctors, who backed up Dr Wallace's original report. He was granted a reprieve and on 7 September was sent to Broadmoor Asylum. Eleven years later, in February 1897, he was discharged into the care of his brother, who lived in Fitzroy St in Ashton under Lyne. It's thought that he changed his name and left for a new life in Canada.

After the murders, residents were allowed to view the girls in the bedroom, even though Bligh was in the other bedroom recovering, guarded by two policemen. So many people came to pay their respects, that the girls were moved downstairs. They were placed in small coffins, on a table, all three dressed in shrouds to hide any injuries. They were surrounded by wreaths and bouquets of flowers, sent by sympathising residents. One from their school friends at St Michael's, which read 'Gertie' 'Lillie' 'Nellie' with love from the scholars Kirkham Infant School.

The funeral left the police building on the following Tuesday at 4:25 p.m., the pine coffins carried on a bier along the crowd lined streets, by six men in the employ of funeral director Mr George Wood. Several hundred people lined the street down to the church, the procession showing the true scale of the tragedy. The church was full with over 1,000 people, including 150 fellow school children. The Rev. G. Powles of Weeton took the service, Rev. H. W. Mason being absent. After the church service, the girls were placed in the grave of their mother. It immediately began to rain, and the crowd dispersed, the girls fading into the mists of time.

Sometime after the funeral, a Miss Rogerson, whose father was a draper in Kirkham, organised a collection to erect a grave stone. She managed to collect £12 and the monument of Yorkshire stone, with a polished cross, was erected on 5 August 1886. Carved by Mr Wray of Church Street, it reads, 'In memory of Elizabeth, wife of Alfred Bligh, who died December 1st, 1884, aged 35 years; also, their children, Leila aged six years, Gertrude Maria, aged four years and Sarah Eleanor, aged 18 months, who fell asleep 15th May 1886.'

'It is well with the child, it is well.'

To not finish on a sad note, the following section covers the people of power, who helped develop Kirkham. This group took over from The Thirty Men and in 1895 handed all the institutions they had set up over to the council. The Gas Works, Fire Brigade, Water Board, Charities, Workhouse, in other words, nationalisation.

———◆◆◆———

The Birley family

The family with the greatest influence on Victorian Kirkham was the Birley family. They originally came from Ireland and first settled in Skippool, Poulton le Fylde, and then Kirkham. John Birley was the first to settle in Kirkham and lived in a small house next door to the Bowling Green Inn. He traded with the West Indies, through his firm Birley and Alker, West India Merchants.

In 1730, he married Ellen Harrison and they had four children, who all died early. John died in 1746 aged 15, Elias died in 1734, aged ten months old and Richard died in 1735, after two weeks. Ellen died whilst giving birth in 1737, and the baby, also christened Ellen, died a few days after her mother.

In 1741, John married Elizabeth Shepherd, whose father was a partner at Flaxfield Mill. He joined this firm and it began trading as Shepherd, Langton and Birley. This marriage produced ten children: Thomas, Richard, Janet, John, William, Mary, Cicely, Elizabeth, Martha and Margaret.

All the daughters died unmarried and without any children. The eldest son Thomas, who lived at The Corner House at the junction of Freckleton Street and Poulton Street, became a woollen draper. Richard moved to Blackburn. However, it was the third son John who continued with the flax manufacturing in Kirkham.

Old John Birley died on 12 May 1767 aged 68 and Elizabeth died on 27 January 1780, aged 61. After his father's death, John Birley bought out his partners at the Flaxfield Mill and started trading as John Birley and Sons.

This John Birley was born on 20 November 1747. He married Margaret Yate of Liverpool in 1776 and the marriage produced eight children, William, Thomas, Edward, Charles, Charles (both died after a few months), Yate, Hanna and Elizabeth. Margaret Birley died on 13 November 1830 and Mr Birley died on 31 May 1831, at his home, Croft House.

It was the two eldest sons who made the biggest impact on the local area, William and Thomas.

Their eldest son, William Birley, was born on 2 June 1779 and was a Magistrate for Lancashire. He married Mary Swainson of Preston, whose brother Charles went into partnership with William and Thomas Birley. The company, known as Swainson, Birley and Company, built Swainson Cotton Mills in Fishwick, Preston. Mary died on 6 February 1819. William later remarried Margaret Green of Liverpool.

William, who lived at Hillside House, died on 29 May 1850, whilst in London. William and his two wives were buried in the family crypt in St Michael's Graveyard. In 1853, a monument was erected in memory of William Birley. The monument was designed by architect, Mr E. T. Owens of Liverpool and sculptured in Preston. The monument itself sits on a base, fourteen feet by eleven feet and has four panels with inscriptions and a spire reaching nineteen feet high. All the Birleys' graves, are around, or to the left of this monument.

William Birley's, first marriage produced four children John Shepherd, William, Edmund and Mary; the second marriage being childless. This branch of the family drifted away from Kirkham, towards Preston.

Rev. John Shepherd Birley was born on 11 October 1805. He lived with his family on Church Street before being educated in Chester. He later went to Brazenose College, Oxford where he gained his BA in 1827 and his MA in 1830. Whilst in Oxford he was a member of the Oxford Eight rowing team and was friends with Mr Gladstone, Lord Cardwell, Lord Sherbrook and Cardinal Manning. He was ordained in 1830 by the Bishop of Chester and took Priest Orders the following year. His first curacy was at Brindle and the following ten years were at All Saints, Bolton. Whilst at Bolton he married Ann Hargreaves and had one daughter, Lucy Mary Shepherd. He resigned from All Saints due to ill health. In 1839, he became a Justice of the Peace and was a governor of Kirkham Grammar School. John Shepherd died on 1 July 1883 at his home Moss Lea, Sharples near Bolton. He's buried in St Cuthbert's Church Lytham.

The second son, William, was born in 1811 and lived at The Larches, Preston with his wife Elizabeth Hasting. He was a Magistrate for Lancashire and Mayor of Preston in 1858–59, a Conservative in politics. William was a partner at Swainson and Birleys, and died on 17 March 1894 aged 83 years.

The third son was Edmund, born in 1817. Edmund lived at Clifton Hall, with his wife Caroline Dorothy Moore. Dorothy was the daughter of Rev. Moore and sister of Kirkham Solicitor Richard Moore. Edmund was educated in Liverpool and later at Dr Arnold's School in Rugby. He started work in the counting house at Swainson's Mill working through every department until becoming the head of the firm. He was a Magistrate for Lancashire, Town Councillor for the Fishwick Ward, Mayor 1866–67 and Guild Mayor 1881–1882. Edmund died on 28 March 1895 aged 77, leaving £103,501 3*s*. 10*d*. which in today's money would equate to six and a half million pounds.

The second son of John Birley was called Thomas, and he married Ann Langton, the daughter of John Langton of Ash Tree House. They originally lived on Church Street until Thomas built Milbanke House. They had eight children Thomas Langton, Charles, James Webber, Francis Bradkirk, Edward, Arthur Leyland, Frederick and Gilmor (who died at birth). Thomas Birley died on 1 April 1847 and Ann Birley died in 1833.

Swainson and Birley Cotton Mills

Thomas Langton Birley was born on 18 June 1811, the eldest son of Thomas. In August 1836, he married Anne Birley, daughter of John Birley of Woodend, Egremont Cumbria. He went into management at Flaxfield Mill with his father and brothers, but a dispute about the direction of Flaxfield led to the separation of the family firm. In May 1841, his cousins William and Edmund withdrew from John Birley and Sons, and Thomas Langton and his father withdrew from Swainson and Birleys' Company. Thomas Langton and his brothers later established Hannover Mills in Preston, trading as Birley Brothers.

Thomas Langton later bought Carr Hill House, the church glebe land, and became Lord of the Manor. He was chairman of Liverpool, New York and Philadelphia Steamship Company and the North Lancashire Steam Navigation Company. He was also chairman of Fylde Water Company and trustee of Warton, Treales, Wrea Green and Kirkham Schools. Thomas Langton is best remembered as the man who improved Kirkham as chairman of the Local Board of Health. In 1872, he erected the gas lamp which still stands at the Fishstones. Thomas Langton died on 6 April 1874 aged 63; the brass lectern in St Michael's Church was presented in his memory.

The second son, Charles, was born in 1812. In 1843 he married Elizabeth Addison. He was a Justice of the Peace and Honorary Colonel of the 5th LAV Charles, and was the senior partner of the firm, Birley Brothers, Hannover Street Mills, Preston and Chief of the firm Stevenson and Co. engineers, Canal Foundry, Preston. Lord of the Manor of Woodplumpton; Charles owned 5,000 acres of land in the township, he died at his residence Bartle Hall aged 79 in 1891. He died a widower after Elizabeth died in 1867 and left one son Charles Addison Birley.

The third son, Rev. James Webber, was born in May 1814 and gained his MA at St John's College Cambridge. He was the Vicar of Littledale, Lancaster from 1848, a small parish of 120 souls. James died in February 1884 aged 69.

The fourth son, Rev. Francis Bradkirk, was born in October 1817 and lived in Canton, China. He married Melicina-Eleanor in Hong Kong in 1847, the daughter of Lieut. Col. Thornton. Francis died after a short illness, at his residence, Salwick Hall in August 1855 aged 38.

Edward Birley was born on 12 October 1818 and died on 22 November 1842, aged 22 years.

Arthur Leyland was born in 1820, at Milbanke, and was educated at Kirkham Grammar School. After his education, he joined his brothers Thomas and Charles at John Birley and Sons at Hannover Mills. He married Jane Addison in 1855 and they had two children, John Leyland and Edith Jane. Arthur took over Milbanke House from his father. In 1867, he withdrew from the family firms and from public life. He died on 31 December 1877. The five-light stained-glass window in St Michael's Church was donated by Arthur Leyland.

> The will of Mr. Arthur Leyland Birley, late of Millbanke, Kirkham, Lancashire, who died on Dec. 31 last, was proved on the 14th ult., at the Lancaster District Registry, by Hutton Birley and Charles Addison Birley, the nephews, the acting executors, the personal estate being sworn under £120,000. The testator bequeaths to his wife, Mrs. Jane Birley, all his wines, liquors, and consumable stores, horses, live and dead stock, and, for life or widowhood, his dwelling-house, Millbanke, with the furniture and effects, and the income of £35,000, in the event of her marrying again she is to have an annuity of £400; upon trust for his daughter, Miss Edith Jane Birley, £25,000, and a further sum of £15,000 on the death of her mother; the remainder of his property, real and personal, he gives to his son, John Leyland Birley.

The youngest son, Frederick, was born on 11 December 1822 and married the sister of his brother's wife Mary Addison. He died suddenly, at his residence, Ribby Villa, aged 31 on 26 September 1854.

By the turn of the century, there was only one descendent of William Birley alive, his granddaughter, Ada Birley. As for Thomas Birley, only three of his grandchildren still living on the Fylde: Henry Langton of Carr Hill, Hutton of Wrea Green and John Leyland of Milbanke.

The eldest, Henry Langton Birley of Carr Hill House, took over the house when his mother, Ann, died on 26 November 1893. Henry had taken over the running of Flaxfield Mill when his father Thomas Langton died in 1874. He was a director of the Fylde Water Works and guardian at the Fylde Union Workhouse. In his twenties, he was a Captain in the 10th LAV, resigning his commission to concentrate on running the family firm.

Like his parents, he opened the grounds of Carr Hill to the public on Club Day. Every Christmas he gave gifts to the inmates at the workhouse, tobacco, tea, sugar to the adults and an apple, orange and sweets for the children. He was an agriculturist and president of the Kirkham and District Chrysanthemum Society. Mr H. L. Birley, who was born in 1837, died a bachelor on 3 January 1920 aged 82. His closest surviving relation was his brother Hutton Birley.

The next was John Leyland Birley, who was born in 1857 and educated at Queen's College, Oxford. He took over Milbanke House after his mother died in 1889. John Leyland was a man of leisure and spent most of his time travelling the world with his camera, Japan being his favourite country. When at Milbanke, he spent most of his time in his large workshop engineering. He built a miniature railway in his grounds and built a steam yacht, in his workshop, which he sailed on the estate's boating lake. He had a yacht on Lake Windermere and two boats, *Lorna Dorne* and *Stephanie*, which he sailed off the Fylde Coast. He was a member of Lytham Orchestral Society and Lytham Tennis Club (he built five courts on his grounds). Locally, he was a guardian at the workhouse and a founder member of Wesham Parish Council. He opened his 20-acre estate each year to the children of Lytham Schools.

The last six years of his life were spent at his home, Hastings Place, Lytham, due to ill health after a serious operation, from which he never fully recovered. He went back to Milbanke House for the last few days of his life, where he died a bachelor on 11 March 1906.

The last Birley to live in Kirkham was Ada Birley of Hillside House. Ada Birley was the last surviving daughter of Edmund of Clifton Hall and moved to Kirkham when he died in 1895. She was born on 29 July 1856. Ada was famed for her charitable work and was known as the 'Fairy Godmother of the Fylde.' She was President of The Kirkham District Nursing Association, to whom she once donated a car. Ada was also the secretary of the local branch of the RSPCA and a staunch supporter of Kirkham Parish Church. When she advertised for staff, she made it clear that you had to be Church of England. A great supporter of the soldiers, both during and after the war, she was well known and liked. She became a Justice of the Peace in 1920 and was the first female councillor on Kirkham Urban District Council.

FUNERAL OF MR. J. LEYLAND BIRLEY

The funeral of the late Mr. J. Leyland Birley, of Mill Bank, Kirkham, took place yesterday at the Lytham Parish Churchyard. It was a quiet and simple interment.

A large number of deceased's Lytham friends and acquaintances joined the cortege at the church gates, and the chief mourners included Messrs. Philip and Eric Mellor (nephews), Horace Mellor, J.P. (brother-in-law), Hutton Birley, J.P., C. A. Birley, J.P., H. L. Birley, Rd. Birley, P. L. Birley, J.P., Alfred and Arthur Hassal (Cheshire). Amongst others present were the .;nant farmers on deceased's estate and other workpeople.

The service was conducted by the Rev. W. P. Mitton (vicar of Kirkham) and the Rev. Canon Hawkins (vicar of St. Cuthbert's), assisted by the Rev. F. Tike and the Rev. J. T. Thorpe.

A large number of floral tributes were sent.

Ada Birley died on 8 March 1934 aged 77 years and was buried in the family crypt with her grandfather, William Birley. Ada died nearly 200 years after her great, great grandfather John Birley had arrived in Kirkham. On that dark night, when his son John died in 1746 and he realised he'd lost his wife and four children and was now alone, he must have regretted moving to Kirkham. However, because he had the strength to carry on, he created one of the wealthiest and most influential families in Lancashire. A family once so important to the development of Kirkham, now remembered only by a side street, 'Birley Street'.

Hutton Birley, the younger brother of Henry Langton, lived at Ribby Villa. Hutton had taken over the running of the Birley Brothers, Hannover Street Mills in Preston. He was a J.P. for over 50 years, governor of the Grammar School and an officer in the Lancashire Artillery Volunteers. Hutton married Alice May Howard and they had three children. The eldest was the Rt Rev. Thomas Howard, Bishop of Zanzibar, the middle son was Percy Langton, who lived in Wrea Green, and the youngest William Arthur Hutton who emigrated to America. It was Percy Langton Birley who represented the family on the Fylde, but as far as Kirkham goes it ended with the 'Fairy Godmother of the Fylde.'

Langtons

Long before John Birley arrived on the Fylde, the Langtons had already established the foundations for the flax industry in Kirkham. The first Langton to arrive in Kirkham was Cornelius Langton, the great grandson of Roger Langton of Hougton Tower. Cornelius paid 30 shilling to gain the Freedom of the Borough and to trade as a woollen draper in Kirkham. He married Elizabeth, the daughter of Zachary Taylor, the headmaster of Kirkham Grammar School. This marriage produced five children:

Anne, born 14 May 1690 – died 1713 aged 23.

John, born 11 October 1691 – died 1762 aged 71.

Zachary born 1692 – died 1694. Aged 2.

Abigail born 24 September 1695 – died 1776 aged 81.

Zachary born 1698 – died 1786 aged 87.

Roger born 1 November 1700 – died 1727 aged 27.

Zachary Langton was 14 years old when his father died and in the will his father stated that he wanted Zachary to be a scholar and have a university education. He first went to Kirkham Grammar School, then Magdalen College, Oxford where he graduated with a BA on 18 December 1721. On 10 June 1724, he received his MA and entered the church. After a time in London he went to a remote part of Ireland with Bishop Clayton. He returned to Oxford in 1761, where he died on 1 February 1776.

Cornelius died in April 1712 aged 45, and his eldest son John became heir. John Langton married Elizabeth Browne and inherited Ash Tree House. In 1754, William Shepherd, John Langton and his son Thomas started to develop Flaxfield Mill on land known as the 'Barnfields or Wildings'.

After, John died in 1762, William and Thomas ran the company together, until John Birley joined. Thomas Langton died on 30 October 1794 and was succeeded by his son John.

John Langton is best known for setting up the Girls' Charity School along with Ann Hankinson. John married Betty Cuthbert; one of their children Anne was to marry Thomas Birley of Milbanke House. The eldest son Thomas was a Captain in the Kirkham Loyal Volunteers; he lived at Ash Tree House until his death on 2 November 1826. He died unmarried and was the last Langton to live in Kirkham. The name lived on when his sister Anne, named her eldest son, Thomas Langton Birley.

Hornby

Another family involved with the early development of the flax industry was the Hornby family of Newton. Hugh Hornby was the first member of this family to move to Kirkham in the early eighteenth century.

Hugh, born in 1719, married Margaret Hankinson of Kirkham and this marriage produced eight children. Joseph born in 1732, Robert born in 1750, but died aged 26 years. Thomas, born in 1759, married Cicely Langton, daughter of Thomas Langton of Ash Tree House. William, born in 1761, John, born in 1763, lived at Raikes Hall, Blackpool, Hugh, born in 1765, became the vicar of St Michael's on Wyre. Alice married Richard Birley of Blackburn (John Birley's son) and Elizabeth died in infancy.

Thomas Hornby's old house

Margaret Hankinson was the daughter of Joseph Hankinson, a dry salter of Kirkham. Margaret's brother Thomas went into the flax business with Hugh Hornby and when Thomas died in 1775, Margaret inherited his entire estate.

Hugh Hornby was a bailiff of Kirkham and a Thirty Man. The family set up three weaving sheds one on Freckleton Street, one at the bottom of Marsden Street and one on Moor Street. They also built a warehouse on Poulton Street; the town's weighbridge was outside this building. After Hugh died in 1781 the family business was taken over by his sons, Joseph, William and Thomas, trading as J. T. & W. Hornby.

The eldest son Joseph, the Deputy Lieutenant of Lancashire, built Ribby Hall. Thomas and William both died in 1824. Joseph died later in 1832, by which point the family had withdrawn from the flax industry. William Hornby's house, which stood on the corner of Poulton Street and The Square, was also demolished around this time.

Thomas Hornby's house stood empty for nearly 40 years, until it was also demolished in 1863. This is the house which was damaged when Thomas Parkinson's house was blown up by Richard Bennet.

FUNERAL OF THE LATE HUGH HORNBY, ESQ.— On Thursday, the remains of the late Hugh Hornby, Esq., of Ribby Hall, were interred in the family vault, in the Parish Church of Kirkham. The mournful procession left the railway station at half-past ten, in the following order:

MOURNING COACH, CONTAINING

Rev. G. L. Parsons;   Rev. — Williams;
Rev. — Wray;   Rev. R. Moore.
Tenantry.   THE HEARSE.   Tenantry.

MOURNING COACH, CONTAINING

Master Hornby;   Geo. Lloyd, Esq.;
T. L. Hilton, Esq.;   W. Langton, Esq.

MOURNING COACH, CONTAINING

Daniel Hornby, Esq.;   W. H. Hornby, Esq.;
Hugh Hornby, Esq.;   Rev. T. Hornby;
Rev. W. Hornby;   T. R. W. France, Esq.

MOURNING COACH, CONTAINING

Rev. R. Hornby;   Colonel Hilton Ford;
J. W. R. Wilson, Esq.;   J. Langton, Esq.

REV. W. HORNBY'S CARRIAGE, CONTAINING

Rev. L. C. Wood;   T. L. Birley, Esq.;
Joseph Hornby, Esq.

MR. W. H. HORNBY'S CARRIAGE, CONTAINING

Mr. Shaw.

MR. W. BIRLEY'S CARRIAGE, CONTAINING

Mr. Lambert;   Mr. Smith;
Mr. Carr;   Mr. Appleyard.

MR. WILSON FRANCE'S CARRIAGE;
MR. LANGTON BIRLEY'S CARRIAGE;
UNDERTAKERS' CARRIAGE.

Servants of the Family, on foot.

On the funeral *cortège* reaching the church, the service was read in an impressive manner by the Rev. G. L. Parsons, the vicar. The whole of the shops in Kirkham were closed, out of respect for the memory of the deceased, who was much respected and esteemed in the neighbourhood, for his great liberality and generosity, more especially to the poor. The funeral arrangements were under the superintendence of Messrs. Goudy and Garth, of this town.

Twelve homes were built on the site, two of which faced Poulton Street. A few years later, on the west side, a drill shed (where the community centre now stands) two warehouses, one for John Ward and one for John Rigby and the Water Board Offices, which faced Poulton Street, were built, all forming 'Birley Street'.

When Joseph Hornby died, most of the family had moved away from Kirkham to Liverpool. The family seat was now Ribby Hall, which was inherited by Thomas's only son Hugh Hornby. Hugh was born in 1799, and married Anne Hilton. They had three children, Hugh Hilton, Margaret Anne and Mary Alice. Hugh was born on 17 July 1799 and was more of a country squire than anything else. He re-established the Kirkham Harriers hunting pack and held steeple chases on his land. Most of his time was spent running the large family estate which consisted of 771 acres of land and six farms. Hugh died on 23 October 1849 aged 51 years at Heslington, York and his remains were brought back to Kirkham Station, from where his funeral procession started. After Hugh's death, his only son Hugh Hilton, took over the estate and he lived a similar life to his father as a country squire. Hugh Hilton was born on 10 September 1830, a former officer in The Duke of Lancaster's Own, a militia unit. He married Henrietta Hornby, the daughter of Rev. Robert Hornby of Shrewsbury, a family relation. Hugh Hilton collapsed after holding a party at his home and later died from a ruptured blood vessel, on 6 September 1877, aged 39.

Hugh and Henrietta's marriage was childless and when his two unmarried sisters died, (Margaret in 1899 and Mary in 1907), the family line at Ribby Hall came to an end.

In Kirkham during the mid-nineteenth century, there was a high society of wealthy young men and women. This group was dominated by the Birleys, but also included the Hornbys of Ribby Hall and the Westbys of Mowbreck. When they weren't holding parties at each others' country homes or hunting with the Kirkham Harriers, they were involved in the day to day life of an average Kirkham family.

These people were the officers in the volunteer service, the employers, the landlords, the organisers of children's education, the influencers in the church and the judge if a person did something wrong. Whether they were responsible for the working class's life of long hours of work, low pay and poverty, or whether they did much to try and improve their lives, with education, law and order, better health, etc., is difficult to say, but Kirkham would have been a different town without them.

In Kirkham there was an upper-middle-class group, often involved with the development of Kirkham, starting with Dr Shaw.

Dr Thomas Shaw

The stalwart of Victorian Kirkham was Dr Thomas Shaw, the last person to be elected to the Thirty Men and at the time of his death the oldest practising surgeon in the country. He was born at Treales, on 17 March 1815 and was the eldest of six children. As a young man, he was apprenticed to Dr Brown of Preston. He gained his diploma at the Old St Thomas' Hospital London in 1836 and returned to Kirkham. He held surgery with Dr Knipe in Kirkham and eventually took over the practice.

A typical Victorian sportsman, he was an original member of Kirkham Cricket Club. He was a fan of cockfighting, but hare coursing was his main passion. In 1855 at the Ridgway November Meeting, he won the North Lancashire Stakes, South Lancashire Stakes and was the runner up for the Clifton Cup. In the February meeting, he again won the North Lancashire Stakes and was beaten in the final course for the Clifton Cup.

Mrs Shaw outside
Shepherd House with
her children

In 1860, he became Medical Officer for the Kirkham Artillery Volunteer and was also one of their best marksmen. His other roles included Director of Fylde Waterworks, Chairman of Kirkham Gas Company, Medical Officer of Fylde Union Workhouse, Governor of Kirkham Grammar School and Treales School. In 1891, he became a J.P. and sat on the Kirkham Bench.

He rented William Shepherd's old house on Preston Street, until he built his own house on the opposite side of the road. Harvey House was a large residence with three entertaining rooms, seven bedrooms on the first floor and three bedrooms on the second floor. The building also had a large garden, stables and garage. After Mrs Shaw died, the house was still used as a surgery but this time for a vet called Joseph Woods; it's now split into three separate buildings.

Two years before his death he suffered an attack of apoplexy (a stroke). He suffered a second attack, after being on duty at Kirkham Court, from which he never recovered. He died on Saturday 28 January 1893. At the time of his death he was in the care of his son Dr William Wright Shaw and Dr Brown of Preston. He left a widow, three sons and four daughters. Thomas was buried in the family vault in St Michael's; a wake was held in the Black Horse Hotel.

William Segar Hodgson

William Segar Hodgson was the son of Thomas and Ann who were ironmongers in Kirkham. William himself ended up as a successful farmer owning farms in Thistleton and Greenhalgh. He was born in 1833 and lived at Freckleton Cottage, Freckleton. As well as farming, he was a J.P., shareholder and chairman at The Fylde Mill on Orders Lane. William was on the board of guardians at the Kirkham workhouse for nearly 50 years and chairman for 28 years. In that time, he never missed a meeting and was only late once; resigning from the board in April 1901. He died on 18 April 1910.

William died a bachelor and had no heirs, leaving £100 to his servant Elizabeth Porter, £50 to his servant Alice Prescott and £50 to John Thomas

Rigby, Freckleton Town Clerk. The rest of his estate, £15,000, he left in trust to erect a swimming pool for the inhabitants of Kirkham. The remaining money was to be spent on projects that would be of benefit to the people of Kirkham. By 1941, the cost of running the baths was too expensive for the trust and the council was unable to contribute because of legal reasons. In July that year, the baths and 3,244 acres of land were donated to the council by the trustees. In August 1956, the trustees offered the council a further 8 acres of land on Coronation Road to be used as a playing fields and to be named after William Hodgson. The William Segar Hodgson Trust is still in existence today.

———◆◆◆———

R. C. Richards

Roger Charnock Richards, who was always known as R. C. Richards, was born in Walker-Fold in Chaigely near Clitheroe in 1810. He was the third son of Rev. John Richards, Congressional Minister of Walker-Fold Chapel for 40 years. R. C. Richards served his apprenticeship in Clitheroe, specialising in the Chemical and Medical aspects of veterinary, before moving to Preston.

At the age of 21, he moved to Kirkham and in 1847, he bought Hornby's old mill on Freckleton Street and converted it to cotton production. In 1852, he built Phoenix Mill in Wesham, with W. H. Bowlder, and joined a company which built Wesham Mills. By 1860 he had retired from these firms and in 1862 bought his home, Clifton Lodge and the associated farm to follow his interest of agriculture.

He was a founding member of the Kirkham Agricultural Society in 1856 and bred heavy horses and kept short horn cattle. He was the chairman of the board of guardians at the workhouse for 11 years, and a member of the Kirkham Local board of Health. In 1862, he qualified as a Magistrate and sat on the bench at Kirkham Court.

In politics, he was a Liberal and in religion he was a Congressionalist. Roger worshipped at the Zion Chapel in Kirkham and donated land to build a chapel in Wesham. He also took an interest in the Elswick Independent

Chapel, where he built a tower in memory of his sister. This chapel is also his final resting place.

He married his cousin Ann Poole of Treales in 1834, but she died a year later leaving one daughter. His daughter died from scarlet fever six years later. After his older brother John died, Roger adopted his children, and his sister moved in as his housekeeper. Two of his nephews took over Freckleton Street Mill.

Mr Richards once had a conversation with the proprietor of the *Manchester Guardian*, Mr Evans, about the need for a good supply of milk for Manchester. Roger said that, 'He could supply the milk if Evans would create an Evening Paper to report the markets.' Mr Evans agreed and set up the half penny *Manchester Evening News* and Mr Richards kept his promise and the Fylde Dairy was formed.

After being ill for two years he died on Tuesday 20 February 1877 aged 66, at his home Clifton Lodge. The cause was a serious internal haemorrhage caused by a rupture of the artery, whilst in the care of Dr Walker of Kirkham and Dr Fearnside of Preston.

William Henry Bowdler

Another Victorian industrialist was W. H. Bowdler who often worked in partnership with R. C. Richards. They were coal merchants together and jointly established Phoenix Mill. When Richards left Selby Mill, William took over his partnership there. He became a J.P. in 1877 and sat at Kirkham Court. He was a governor at KGS, superintendent at the Independent School Kirkham, a Liberal in politics and a member of the British Temperance League. He lived on the Market Square Kirkham, where he died on 22 February 1890 aged 52 years. He was buried in the Zion Chapel graveyard. William had seven children, one Audley Bowdler became a Liberal MP in the 1920s for The Holderness Division, North Yorkshire.

Richard Moore

There were two Richard Moores associated with Kirkham; Reverend Richard Moore and his son Richard Moore, the solicitor.

The Reverend Richard Moore was born on 19 August 1782 in Halsall, Ormskirk, where his father was the vicar. He and his twin brother Edward both went into the clergy. Richard was ordained deacon in 1815 and priest in 1817. He was curate at St Michael's Church for three years under vicar Webber until he left to take up the curacy of Whittington, Carnforth. When the vicar of St John's Lund, Reverend Thomas Stephenson died in 1820, Richard Moore became the next incumbent.

Reverend Moore was on the board of guardians at the Union workhouse, a Thirty Man, and a trustee at K.G.S. Grimbaldston's Charity at Treales and Kirkham and Newton Blue Coats School. He became a Justice of the Peace on 17 August 1823 and was still on the bench 63 years later. He was a man who could look after himself, as Richard Bennet found out, when he attacked him in Preston. He was physically fit, famed for often walking from Salwick to Longridge, taking two services and walking back the same day.

He married Marianne Hedgson on 13 January 1816. They had four children, Richard, born 1820, Edward Cornelius, born 1824, Caroline Dorothy, born 1826, who married Edmund Birley of Clifton Hall and Mary Ann, born 1830 who married Thomas Charles Thompson, the former MP for Durham.

When Richard Moore died at the age of 93 he was the oldest magistrate in the country and the second oldest clergyman in the Church of England.

Marianne Moore died on 28 September 1872 and the Reverend Moore died on 19 April 1886. He was buried with his first wife in St Michael's Graveyard.

Reverend Moore's eldest son was also called Richard Moore and was born on 30 December 1820. He was a solicitor and insurance officer for Guardian Insurance. He was heavily involved with the local board of health, and solicitor for the Fylde Water Works. Richard was clerk to Kirkham Court for

25 years and clerk to the visiting justices at Marsden Hall Asylum, Burnley. Richard married Dorothy Myers of Finsbury, Kent and they moved into Ash Tree House. When Richard died he was working at parliament, on the Railway Acts required to expand the railway infrastructure on the Fylde. He died on 2 January 1870, aged 49 years, and was buried in Finsbury's Churchyard. A brass tablet was placed in St Michael's Church by his widow in July that year.

Robert Catterall

Robert Catterall was another self-made man who moved to Wesham from Inskip with his family when his father, Cuthbert Catterall, bought Mill Farm. He was born on 18 April 1830 and after arriving in Wesham started selling seeds from bags. By 1860 he was a successful seed merchant with premises in Kirkham and Ormskirk.

> **IMPORTANT TO FARMERS.**
> SEEDS and SACKS, prime in quality and at the lowest price.—ROBERT CATTERALL, Wesham, near Kirkham, having bought a large lot of SEEDS in the best markets, is prepared to offer them at such a price as must command a ready sale, and of such a quality as will ensure a good crop. All kinds of clover and rye grass, turnip and mangold seeds, &c.
> BAGS AND SACKS OF THE BEST DESCRIPTION.

Like a lot of self-made men of the time, he was a Liberal and a congregational, worshipping at the Zion Chapel. Interested in farming, he was on the council of the Royal Lancashire Agriculture Society. Robert and his Father Cuthbert were both at the centre of the church rate contests. In March 1893, Robert was made a county magistrate.

The night before his death he attended a parish meeting in Wesham, falling ill the following morning. His son Walter was reading to him when his condition became worse. Dr Shaw was called, and he thought he was suffering from kidney problems. By teatime Robert was dead. He left a widow, four sons and five daughters. He is buried at the Baptist Chapel at Inskip. His father, Cuthbert Catterall, died at the age of 81 years, on 12 October 1866, the year of the church rate contest.

Robert Catterall lived in John Birley's old home, Croft House. Like Harvey House, it was divided into three by Arthur Ward in 1921. Arthur Ward was an international referee, and secretary of the West Lancashire League.

Mrs Edward Birley put the house up for sale in September 1831. Along with its 2,296 square yards of garden, the house consisted of:

> The House is in a perfect state of repair, and comprises Dining-room, 25 feet by 18½,—Drawing-room, 19 feet by 19.—Breakfast-room,—Ten Bed-rooms, — Dressing-rooms, —Closets, —large and well-arranged Kitchens.— Butler's Pantry,—Cook's Pantry,—Store-room,—Laundry,—extensive Wine and Beer Cellars, and every requisite convenience.
>
> The detached offices consist of a Coach-house, Harness and Boot-houses, and an excellent Three Stalled Stable.

Three priests oversaw the move from the catholic chapel and school at Mowbreck Hall, to the building of new schools and churches in Kirkham, Wesham and Westby.

❖

Irving Brothers

Prior to 1809, Mowbreck Hall was the centre of the catholic faith, with its school and chapel. This changed in 1809, when the Willows was developed under the guidance of two brothers, William and Thomas Irving. Their father was Joseph Irving, a woollen draper, their mother Alice née Sherbourne.

The eldest son William was born on 15 May 1776 and went to the Mowbreck school until 1792, when at the age of nine, he left for the English school in Valladolid, Spain. He was ordained in 1800. William returned to England in 1802 and took over from Father Bannister at Mowbreck. Money left by William Cotton enabled him to build the first Willows chapel and presbytery. In 1813, William went back to Valladolid, which had been badly damaged in the Napoleonic wars. He borrowed money from the English Secular Clergy Fund, and from his brother Thomas, and started restoring the English School. He died in 1822, aged 46, and was buried in the school chapel.

Thomas Irving was born in 1779, and like his brother went to the Mowbreck Chapel, then to Valladolid. He was ordained in 1803, taking his mother's maiden name. From now on he was known as Thomas Sherbourne. When he returned to England he was sent by Bishop Gibson to Claughton under Father Barrow. After a short period, he was appointed to the charge of the Blackburn mission. At this point in his life he met William Heatley esq of Brindle Lodge, who was to become an extremely rich man, famed for his 'munificent donations' to the Catholic church.

In 1813, Thomas replaced his brother at the Willows, who'd been offered the rectorship at the English college at Valladolid. In 1814 the old graveyard was opened by Father Sherbourne, behind the old presbytery. He replaced his brother in Spain, between 1822 and 1825. After his return from Spain in 1825 he started work on the new school. In 1845, he erected the present church and started the custom of having two priests at the Willows. In 1854 Father Hines came to the Willows and became Father Sherbourne's assistant. Thomas Sherbourne died aged 75 years on Sunday, 17 December 1854. He'd been in poor health for four years and collapsed on his way home after being in Kirkham. He was helped home and seemed fine, until Saturday, when his conditioned deteriorated. He passed away at 8 o'clock on Sunday night.

Father Frederick Hines

Father Frederick Hines was born in Durham in 1824. He went to Stoneyhurst College, then to the English College in Rome where he was ordained in 1853. He replaced Reverend Charles Teebay as Thomas Sherborne's assistant in 1854. He became assistant to Reverend James Swarbrick, until replacing him as the head priest in 1857. In 1860 Father Hines provided a new church, school and presbytery at Westby. In 1871 he extended the Kirkham school, and in 1880 opened the new graveyard opposite the Willows church. In 1883 he had the old chapel demolished and extended the Presbytery. His biggest project was the building of St Joseph's Church in Wesham in 1886. He retired from active service in 1895, after serving 41 years at the Willows, and moved to Skerton in Lancaster. In 1902, he went to live in Beechwood, Ashton on Ribble, where he died on 10 December 1906.

———◆◆◆———

The last things purchased by the Local Board in 1894 were a steam roller for £330, a stone breaker for £110 and a water cart for £30. The town could now replace the 'Petrified Kidneys' as they called the stones used to make the roads with tar macadam. Queen Victoria had seven more years on the throne. The previous people mentioned were dead or old men and women from a different world, before long they too would drift into the mists of time.